The Naked Anthropologist

The Wadsworth Modern Anthropology Library

The Naked Anthropologist
Tales from Around the World

Edited by
Philip R. DeVita
State University of New York, Plattsburgh

Wadsworth Publishing Company
Belmont, California
A Division of Wadsworth, Inc.

Anthropology Editor: *Peggy Adams*
Editorial Assistant: *Tammy Goldfeld*
Production Editor: *Deborah Cogan*
Managing Designer: *Cindy Schultz*
Print Buyer: *Martha Branch*
Permissions Editor: *Jeanne Bosschart*
Designer: *Donna Davis*
Copy Editor: *Margaret Moore*
Compositor: *Bookends Typesetting*
Maps: *Sherwood Keyser*
Cover: *Adriann Dinihanian*
Printing: *The Maple-Vail Book Manufacturing Group*

*This book is printed on acid-free paper that meets
Environmental Protection Agency standards for
recycled paper.*

1 2 3 4 5 6 7 8 9 10—95 94 93 92 91

Library of Congress Cataloging-in-Publication Data

The Naked anthropologist: tales from around the world / edited by
   Philip R. DeVita.
      p.   cm. — (The Wadsworth anthropology library)
   Includes bibliographical references.
   ISBN 0-534-16266-5
   1. Ethnology—Field work.   2. Ethnologists—United States—
Biography.   3. Cook, Edwin A.   I. DeVita, Philip R., 1932– .
II. Series.
   GN346.N35   1991
   301′.092′2—dc20   91-9896

For Kelley:
This will never make up for all the years I was away.

This volume, as well as the first, begun by both of us years ago, is dedicated to the memory of Edwin Aubrey Cook (1932–1984), friend and mentor, committed anthropologist, the wearer of so many hats and that rare, occasionally irascible human who most often knew what was best for those for whom he cared, but not necessarily for himself.

> *I see you now*
> *(even in this present sunlight)*
> *Clay feet and all*
> *Whistling and dancing finally*

EXCERPT FROM A POEM BY
KEN HOECK, ONE OF ED'S
STUDENTS AT FLORIDA STATE

 # Contents

As anthropologists, we search for satisfying and rational truths and structured explanations based primarily on Western scientific models. In our efforts to put the cultural puzzle together, we eventually discover that the cultural others we encounter either don't use the same pieces or are satisfied to solve their puzzles with some of the pieces missing. While we're looking for the four corners of a rectangle, we lose sight of the fact that their puzzles might be circular or without a logic with which we are familiar. Furthermore, they often hide some of the pieces from us.

There's no magic formula for getting to the cultural puzzle box or for finding the logic behind the way the pieces fit. The writers of the essays in this section describe their attempts to make sense of another culture and the surprises they found in the process. Douglas Raybeck's entry into fieldwork began with his being escorted through the village by the local half-wit. Linda Kent, in her sensitive and honest introspection, admittedly failed through no fault of her own, but rather through a series of misadventures that never permitted her to see any of the puzzle pieces. Ellen Holmes expected the pieces to nicely lock together; everything looked familiar, but appearances were, in her case, deceptive. James Clifton, after several warnings from those who knew better, found himself dealing with a sorcerer, a bottle of beer in his hand and the claws of a screaming eagle in his face. Michael Kearney became innocently involved in village matters where, after the fact, he was warned to leave and, for all his scientific expertise, became seemingly bewitched. Kearney, by accident, and Clifton, through pig-headed persistence, both ended up with puzzle pieces that neither had in their wildest dreams envisioned. Phyllis Morrow learned well of differing logical systems and was eventually able to put significant segments of the puzzle together.

This section is made up of tales of anthropological fieldwork, but none will be found within the pages of the traditional dissertation. These are non-traditional essays, containing personalized reflections and critical discoveries that transcend the general prescriptions of the ethnographic literature—discoveries that, however, address in a humanistic fashion the persistent anthropological issues of ethics, values, the supernatural, ethno-centricity, role relationships, kinship and marriage, politics and economics, and much more, from a cross-cultural perspective. The common threads throughout these uncommon essays involve the conflicts between the ethnographer as scientist and humanist, between differing values, realities, and actions of cultural appropriateness, and between what we know from our own culture and what we've learned by living in other cultures.

The lessons to be found here are valuable even though, in most cases, experienced in a fashion totally unexpected. In the end, we've all come to a conclusion quite similar to that of Roger Keesing: We each ended up as "an outsider who knows something of what it is to be an insider." We learn of the seeming strangenesses, but their appearances are only less strange to the professional stranger who has, in unanticipated ways, learned to look below the surface in uncommon, unprogrammed ways. We may laugh at Goodenough, cry with Richardson, feel sorry for the dolphins, get angry at Neni Bai's useless death, and empathize with all the other fieldworkers, but in the end we have, as have they, only begun to learn.

🎏 Foreword to the Series

Modern cultural anthropology encompasses the full diversity of all humankind with a mix of methods, styles, ideas, and approaches. No longer is the subject matter of this field confined to exotic cultures, the "primitive," or small rural folk communities. Today, students are as likely to find an anthropologist at work in an urban school setting or a corporate boardroom as among a band of African hunters and gatherers. To a large degree, the currents in modern anthropology reflect changes in the world over the past century. Today there are no isolated archaic societies available for study. All the world's peoples have become enveloped in widespread regional social, political, and economic systems. The daughters and sons of yesterday's yam gardeners and reindeer hunters are operating computers, organizing marketing cooperatives, serving as delegates to parliaments, and watching television news. The lesson of cultural anthropology, and this series, is that such peoples, when transformed, are no less interesting and no less culturally different because of such dramatic changes.

Cultural anthropology's scope has grown to encompass more than simply the changes in the primitive or peasant world, its original subject matter. The methods and ideas developed for the study of small-scale societies are now creatively applied to the most complex of social and cultural systems, giving us a new and stronger understanding of the full diversity of human living. Increasingly, cultural anthropologists also work toward solving practical problems of the cultures they study, in addition to pursuing more traditional basic research endeavors.

Yet cultural anthropology's enlarged agenda has not meant abandonment of its own heritage. The ethnographic case study remains the bedrock of the cultural anthropologist's methods for gathering knowledge of the peoples of the world, although today's case study may focus on a British urban neighborhood or a new American cult as often as on efforts of a formerly isolated Pacific island people to cope with bureaucracy. Similarly, systematic comparison of the experiences and adaptations of different societies is an old approach that is increasingly applied to new issues.

The books in the Wadsworth Modern Anthropology Library reflect cultural anthropology's greater breadth of interests. They include introductory texts and supporting anthologies of readings, as well as advanced texts dealing with more specialized fields and methods of cultural anthropology.

However, the hub of the series consists of topical studies that concentrate on either a single community or a number of communities. Each of these topical studies is strongly issue-focused. As anthropology has always done, these topical studies raise far-reaching questions about the problems people confront and the variety of human experience. They do so through close face-to-face study of people in many places and settings. In these studies, the core idiom of cultural anthropology lies exposed. Cultural anthropologists still, as always, go forth among the cultures of the world and return to inform. Only where they go and what they report has changed.

James A. Clifton
Series Editor

🌀 Preface

One of my professors, when asked what to do in the field, responded that I should go find myself. If this was to be the goal, pity the poor community of my choice.

George N. Appell (1989:48)

In August of 1983, Ed Cook and I sat talking on a porch overlooking Lake Champlain. There I proposed the ideas for a collection of articles by Pacific anthropologists which was originally to be edited by both of us. For the remaining three days of his visit, we retreated to my farmhouse in the Adirondacks, where we formulated strategies and developed scenarios for the completion of what we believed was to be a unique set of essays by anthropologists—essays which focused on unexpected encounters in Oceanic fieldwork, written in a style comprehensible to a general audience and, hopefully, of some interest to the specialist.

I had developed the idea for a single Oceanic volume. Ed enthusiastically argued that we develop two volumes, one on the Pacific Islands, a second to similarly focus on ethnographic problems throughout the world. That was vintage Ed Cook. For him, there was always something reachable beyond what was the readily imagined. He was a kid in an intellectual candy shop who wouldn't settle for the jelly beans. His sights were set on the jars beyond ordinary vision . . . those undiscovered, extraordinary goodies on the topmost shelves. The first volume was published in 1990 (*The Humbled Anthropologist: Tales from the Pacific*). This, also published in Ed Cook's memory, is the second volume—his original idea.

The ideas for the collection germinated over my fourteen years of friendship with Ed Cook. They derived from four essential issues which had coalesced during that junction of Ed's pilgrimage to visit old friends—a pilgrimage which Ivan Brady and I suspected was, more honestly, a farewell journey. First, Ed's great success in the classroom, especially at the undergraduate level, was due to his genuine concern for his students as participants in the anthropological experience. As a graduate student, I sat in on many of his undergraduate classes. Whether teaching an introductory cultural course, a course on the Pacific, on kinship, or on language and culture, he had a rare, engaging habit of emphasizing a critical intellectual issue by referring to a particular personal event wherein he, a most rigorous and dedicated social scientist, had either misunderstood the situation or had screwed up in his fieldwork. Unknowingly, I stole this practice from him and soon thereafter employed similar practices in my own teaching. I have found this method of accenting an issue by displaying oneself with "egg on the face" to be most successful—not as a strategy for amusement, but as a means of providing a personalized account to complement, and often confound, a particular anthropological point.

Second, from attending national anthropological meetings for the primary purpose of spending time with Ed, I discovered another fact. During our extended social hours many of *his* friends, colleagues, and former students would join us, and I listened to humorous tales of how they had also screwed up in their fieldwork. However, as with Ed's classroom stories, these anthropologists were telling more than humorous stories. There were, in most cases, important lessons embedded in the content of their experiences. If one listened closely and paid attention to not only what was said, but also what was left unsaid, there were lessons to be learned—lessons about the anthropologist, about the people being studied, and about human experiences in a cross-cultural context. I stole these stories also and, where applicable, used them with success in my lectures.

Third, especially in teaching the introductory course in anthropology, I earlier decided not to make the mistake that I'd found evident during my undergraduate training in engineering, mathematics, and philosophy. Whether valid or not, I remain convinced that the problem which most educators have is with their approaches to teaching the particular subjects in their particular discipline. I've publicly argued in guest lectures, especially to students and professors of mathematics and computer science, that they might seriously reconsider their pedagogical approaches to the general classroom audience. If they are, as seems the case, teaching to train students to become mathematicians, or computer scientists—to become *like them*—they might be severely missing the boat. A more pragmatic and successful approach might be to teach students—who, at the undergraduate level, are more generally enrolled in these classes simply to fulfill some college-wide requirement—"what" mathematics or philosophy can teach them about such issues as problem solving, decision making, or universal social issues, and how the subject matter might further contribute to the excitement of logical thinking and a sensitivity to the vast complexities of the human situation.

Whether or not this approach has been as successful as I intend, it is how I approach my lower-division classes. I do not teach to convert students to the discipline of anthropology. I make every deliberate effort to introduce the introductory audience to "what" anthropology can teach us about others and ourselves—to help us to better understand the complex nature of the human condition, ours and others', especially

in this rapidly shrinking world. In the introductory course, the less traditional, more personal, literate, and humanistic writings of Bohannan
(1966), Chagnon (1983), Hayano (1990), Lee (1969), Turnbull (1962), Ward
(1989), and a few others have measurably tendered more productive
seeds to the inititates to this discipline. These writings have been the
honey that makes the vinegar more palatable, the humanistic interlude
that breathes life into the otherwise sterile, theoretical, and methodological concepts in anthropology. Where, in anthropology, beyond the
classroom, do our students discover the social scientists to be the
humanists that they are—*someone* so much more than a reference in
a text or an author in a collection of readings?

The fourth feature behind the form and substance of this project has
a direct relationship to the enterprise of ethnographic fieldwork. I had
spent approximately fifteen years living outside the United States—not
as an anthropologist, but in various capacities on sailing and motor
vessels. I'd prefer to forget many of the personally embarrassing encounters in foreign places but cannot. Too many times, especially when
younger, I found myself screwing up on someone else's turf—doing
something that I believed proper in my own country, but later learning
that the behavior was quite inappropriate in the host's arena. As the years
passed and as I grew (hopefully) wiser, I developed a strategy whenever
finding myself in new places: Keep my big mouth shut and drink a lot
of water!

I had to learn to not impose my behavioral rules and expectations
on others. I had to learn *how to learn* about others instead of innocently-
but-inconsiderately operating within a set of preconceptions based on
my own Western value orientations. I was, after all, a guest in someone
else's home.

Once I began to open my eyes, to develop a sensitivity to the contrasting worlds of my new friends in South American jungles or South
Pacific islands, I, in turn, began to learn another important fact. From
all the traveling, from these wondrous experiences, I was indeed learning about others but, more importantly, I was also learning about myself,
about my own society's values, and about my place in a world of differing realities.

The focus of this and the first volume is not on the significant "others"
that are so important in the ethnographic enterprise. The focus is
foremost on ourselves as anthropologists and the lessons we've learned
in living with and trying to understand others.

The projects did not turn out entirely as Ed Cook and I had envisioned. First of all, Ed died five months after we began the project. In
working to complete a memorial to a special friend, I discovered that
many of his colleagues did not wish to commit to writing those precious
stories they had shared in a private forum. Second, in the seven years
it has taken to complete these two editorial projects, I've discovered
that, unlike Ed in his fieldwork and me in my sailing adventures, most

anthropologists haven't really screwed up as much as we thought, or else they have chosen not to write about these experiences.

However, as will become evident from the readings in both collections, we learn that much of what anthropologists have learned about themselves and others was totally unanticipated. These lessons, none for which their academic training had prepared them, remain, perhaps, the most memorable and critical lessons of ethnographic fieldwork. They are lessons about *us,* which we learned from *them.*

The longer I labored with the tasks of editing both volumes, the more manifest became the sense of underlying structures. These were not stories about screwing up in the field. These were tales of human experiences where, in most instances, the ethnographic stranger stumbled into a situation where he or she learned something for which he or she had not been trained or prepared. And, in the enterprise, important lessons were learned: lessons about the contact culture, about the ethnographer, about the ethnographic process. Moreover, in nearly all cases, there were significant contrastive lessons learned about issues of cross-cultural humanity and humanness, derived more often than not from serendipity than from the deliberate practice of social science.

For the reader expecting Indiana Jones sans clothing, the title is most seriously meant, with a margin of tongue-in-cheek, to imply a different type of nakedness. Mac Marshall, or more accurately, Margery Wolf, finally hit on the perfect title for the first volume. It is from Mac's poignant introduction to *The Humbled Anthropologist* (1990:xix–xxiv) that the title for this volume derives justification. Mac compared the anthropologist to the fabled emperor who, in the fieldwork experience, may in so many instances have no clothes. We often go so very naked and childlike as strangers into unfamiliar settings, having first to learn to crawl before we can walk. And in these new worlds of bewilderment, we stumble, and fall, and sometimes cry.

It has been argued that American cultural anthropology, at least, lacks the rigorously defined methodological principles that are both traditionally and contemporarily part of archaeology, linguistics, and physical anthropology. We may be practitioners of a subdiscipline still in search of a methodology.

These collections of fieldwork experiences represent new exercises in learning, in the epistemology of fieldwork. These exercises, to reflect on Gregory Bateson's (1942) concepts of deutero-learning, apply to the ethnographic processes. We may have to learn to learn about how we learn as cultural anthropologists. Richard Feynman, in speaking of his own discipline, physics, advises, "In summary, the idea is to try to give *all* of the information to help others to judge the value of your contributions; not just the information that leads to judgment in one particular direction or another" (1985:312–313). Further, he argues:

But this long history of learning how not to fool ourselves—of having utter scientific integrity—is, I'm sorry to say, something that we haven't specifically included in any particular course that I know of. We just hope you've caught on by osmosis.

The first principle is that you must not fool yourself—and you are the easiest person to fool. So you have to be very careful about that. After you've not fooled yourself, it's easy not to fool other scientists. You just have to be honest in a conventional way after that.

The late Nobel scientist could have been directly talking to the form and substance of these ethnographic reflections: "I would like to add something that's not essential to the science, but something I kind of believe, which is that you should not fool the layman when you're talking as a scientist." Cultural anthropology may be further advised by Feynman's critique: "If you've made up your mind to test a theory, or you want to explain some idea, you should always decide to publish it, whichever way it comes out. If we only publish results of a certain kind, we can make the argument look good. We must publish *both* kinds of results" (314).

There are many people responsible for the completion of these memorials to Edwin Aubrey Cook. The earlier, unwavering enthusiasm of Mac Marshall, Jim Watson, and Dorothy and David Counts was especially instrumental at a time when I was ready to scrap the projects in favor of a more traditional collection of ethnographic readings. Sue Pflanz-Cook, a friend since graduate school, remained close at the annual meetings of the Association for Social Anthropology in Oceania, knowing full well, especially without Ed, that I am not at all comfortable at public gatherings. My respected friend of many years, Dr. H. Z. Liu, Dean of Arts and Sciences, must be thanked for his unending confidence in me and these nontraditional projects by digging for funding to support my attendance at the annual Oceanic meetings. Jim Clifton's early commitment and editorial efforts were the cornerstones on which all of us were able to build. I'd like to thank James Funaro, Cabrillo College; Alice Pomponio, St. Lawrence University; and Miles Richardson, Louisiana State University, for their reviews of the manuscript.

Most especially, profound gratitude must be tendered to Sheryl Fullerton and Peg Adams for their willingness to gamble on publishing the Oceanic volume at a time when other publishers were interested only in this one. Debbie Cogan, Wadsworth Publishing's professional and understanding production editor, has been more help than she will ever comprehend. And, again, I owe thanks to Sherwood Keyser for his splendid work on the maps for this volume.

Finally, I'd like to thank each of those anthropologists for their patience and willingness to share their personal experiences in ethnographic fieldwork.

Phil DeVita
Plattsburgh, N.Y.

REFERENCES

APPELL, GEORGE N.
1989   British- vs American-Trained Ethnographers. Anthropology Newsletter. American Anthropological Association 30(9):48.

BATESON, GREGORY
1942   Social Planning and the Concept of "Deutero-learning." Conference on Science, Philosophy and Religion, Second Symposium. New York: Harper & Row.

BOHANNAN, LAURA
1966   Shakespeare in the Bush. Natural History 75(7):28–33.

CHAGNON, NAPOLEON A.
1983   Yanomamo: The Fierce People. New York: Holt, Rinehart, & Winston.

DeVITA, PHILIP R., ED.
1990   The Humbled Anthropologist: Tales from the Pacific. Belmont, CA: Wadsworth.

FEYNMAN, RICHARD P.
1985   "Surely You're Joking, Mr. Feynman!" Adventures of a Curious Character. New York: Norton.

HAYANO, DAVID M.
1990   Road Through the Rain Forest: Living Anthropology in Highland Papua New Guinea. Prospect Heights, IL: Waveland Press.

LEE, RICHARD BORSHAY
1969   Eating Christmas in the Kalahari. Natural History 78(10):14–27.

TURNBULL, COLIN
1962   The Forest People. New York: American Museum of Natural History.

WARD, MARTHA C.
1989   Nest in the Wind: Adventures in Anthropology on a Tropical Island. Prospect Heights, IL: Waveland Press.

Goy in the Promised Land;
or, Murphy's Law and the
Outcome of Fieldwork

JAMES ARMSTRONG

Most sociocultural anthropologists, modeling the writing of those by whom we have been trained, hide who we are and the roles we play in our research when writing for our professional colleagues. Although increasingly there are exceptions, we are often invisible, uninvolved narrators who supposedly offer objective portrayals of the cultures we study. In other settings we share the problems we encounter in the field with each other and use these adventures to spice up our lectures to students. Recently, however, we have begun to more frequently reveal the personal experiences, mistakes, and self-discovery that are the inevitable meat and potatoes of field research. *The Naked Anthropologist* belongs to this genre. It brings together a variety of articles that explore the personal side of fieldwork.

I was excited when Phil DeVita described the original project he and Ed Cook were about to begin in 1983 (DeVita 1990). I thought that accounts which focused on learning from the mistakes of fieldwork would begin to tilt the balance toward honesty in our professional presentation of self. I was sure that it would make us appear more human, while making the cultures we work in and the way we work more accessible to our students and other readers, including our colleagues. I was a bit disappointed, I must admit, by the fact that the original project was going to focus only on Pacific Ocean cultures because I would have a difficult time using it in any of my classes. Thus, when Phil told me that he was planning a second volume of articles of the same kind with no geographic limitations, I was pleased. This would be a book I could use in my classes, I thought to myself. Students would read it without much prodding or protest. They would learn about doing cultural anthropology as it really happens, full of mistakes, false starts, and accidental insights. As a result, their own beginning attempts at fieldwork wouldn't be burdened by the false ideal that there is a secret formula for successful research in anthropology.

Although many of the articles deviate from the "mistake-then-insight" scenario of the original plan for the book, this collection hangs together with its anthropologist as human being, field research as adventure, and method as accident theme. It presents anthropologists as people who don't have all of the answers and, by doing so, provides students with the message that there isn't just one right answer. And, perhaps most importantly, we can all see more clearly that the fieldwork process, doing cultural anthropology, isn't strictly formatted but rather stems from human beings interacting with other human beings.

Included in this volume are a variety of articles illustrating the ways we try to understand others along with the problems this creates. Still, the one thing that struck me most when reading this collection for the first time, was how much I had in common with the authors. It occurred to me how significant going to the field is as part of the anthropological identity.

This rite of passage is perhaps the main trial that gives us something in common, that creates a community out of a diverse group of people. We can come together, swap "tales of the field," to use Van Maanen's (1988) term, and immediately feel affinity for one another, even if we share little else. At the same time, the articles in this book build community among us, because they remind us that we do have much in common.

As I mentioned above, these articles reminded me of the ritual, coming-of-age aspects of fieldwork. In the past, not much training was given to those about to undertake the ethnographic enterprise. The prevailing attitude through the 1960s was that fieldworkers are born not trained, or that learning can take place only in the field itself. That is not to say that anthropologists went to the field unprepared; on the contrary, during this era most cultural anthropologists did everything they could to prepare themselves through reading the history and ethnography of the region to which they were going. Relevant languages were also learned when possible. But cultural anthropologists weren't prepared to do field research, except through the idealized descriptions of it in the ethnographies they read.

My training was different. During graduate school I took a year-long sequence of methodology courses designed to prepare me for fieldwork. I learned interviewing techniques, collecting genealogies, mapping, sampling, constructing questionnaires, not to mention statistical analysis, photography, field-note management, description and inference. In addition, I spoke the language and had spent a substantial amount of time in Israel with the people I hoped to study. I really can't imagine anyone better prepared to enter this rite of passage.

Thus, in the fall of 1977 I arrived in Israel full of optimism. My wife and two-year-old daughter were with me, anxious to discover why I was so enthralled with this relatively new society with ancient roots. My original plan had been to return to a kibbutz where I had worked several years before. I had made close friends with a number of people there, and although earlier communications had indicated that housing might be a problem, I remained certain that my connections would ultimately secure me a place to stay. Even if this fell through, my research could be accommodated without living on a kibbutz since I was primarily interested in understanding why young people decided to abandon their home kibbutzim. In the interim I had a place to stay in Tel Aviv with a close friend and his family. As you all know, "Fish and guests smell after three days," and we had been staying with Moshe for about two weeks while I made arrangements. To make a long story short, let me remind you of Murphy's law. "If anything can go wrong it will." Like me, however, Murphy was an optimist.

The first thing I had to do was find somewhere for me and my family to stay while I finished making arrangements to do ethnography on "my" kibbutz. But finding a place to stay is no easy task in a country with a permanent housing shortage. Thus, I snapped up the first affordable apartment I could find. Another friend of mine, Shlomo, found this two-room flat in an old building along the Yarkon River on the north edge of the city. Actually, he was interested in renting this place himself but took pity on me. This of course created a lifelong obligation that plagued me on and off over the next twelve months, but that is another story. In order to rent this apartment, I had to sign a twelve-month lease and pay three months rent in advance. The decision to rent this place was influenced strongly by the deteriorating relationship between our hosts (Moshe and Nurit) and ourselves (James and Rachelle). I knew committing myself to a long-term address might have serious implications for my ability to do ethnography elsewhere, and furthermore it tied up a considerable amount of my assets. Even solutions are sometimes mistakes, to paraphrase one of the corollaries to Murphy's law, but we have to live with the choices we make. As time passed and we became ensconced in our Tel Aviv home, it became increasingly clear that I wasn't going to be able to do ethnography on a kibbutz, at least in the usual anthropological manner of direct participant observation. That left me with the options of commuting to and from the kibbutz or studying the kibbutzniks living in the environs of Tel Aviv, those who had opted out of utopia.

The second option seemed the more realistic, and I began finding informants wherever I could. Although the interviews were productive and my informants were cooperative, this kind of fieldwork fell short of my expectations of becoming part of a community and sharing their day-to-day existence. I wasn't part of the lives of my informants. I was some "goy" nuisance who, at best, helped some people rationalize their decision to leave and at worst asked perplexing questions that reminded them of home. After much soul searching, I decided to abandon this line of research.

In the meantime, my wife was adjusting to her first time east of the Mississippi with some difficulty. I wasn't much help, I must admit. After all, I had places to go, people to see, and a social network that offered me emotional support. Rachelle, in contrast, had only our daughter and me, and I was gone much of the time.

I had been in the field for only a month by this time and had already alienated my best friend, Moshe, sacrificed my carefully planned and long awaited study of a kibbutz, undermined my marital stability (not irreparably), abandoned an alternative study, and rented an apartment overlooking a smoke-spewing power plant in a city in which I had little interest. Obviously, things worked out for the better or I wouldn't be writing this introduction.

I ended up studying the relationships and social networks that structured the day-to-day life of the people I knew. This line of research came about by accident. After my first two false starts, I had decided to investigate the connections among Israelis' conceptions of success, socioeconomic background, and career decisions. Although this research bears little surface resemblance to the subject of my kibbutz research, it depended largely on the same methodology. After spending so much time in graduate school learning methodology, I'd be damned if I wasn't going to use some of it. In this new line of research, I could use any number of cognitively oriented techniques to get at the underlying structure of success conceptualization and collect life histories in much the same way I would have with kibbutzniks. Unfortunately, many of my informants (I was relying on people I knew or had come to know in Tel Aviv) weren't very interested in talking about succeeding although they loved to talk to me about almost anything else. We would spend hours chatting in coffee shops, in their places of work, or in their living rooms eating sunflower seeds, drinking coffee, and smoking the communal package of cigarettes, but whenever the subject of success arose, the subject changed or their enthusiasm waned. I still don't know why this happened. Many of these people were successful by anyone's definition, and those who hadn't achieved monetary success were clearly interested in improving their socioeconomic status.

As time went by, I found myself increasingly caught in the middle of minor conflicts between the people I knew best. These were often uncomfortable situations for me that involved hearing a good deal of gossip, backbiting, and carping. Occasionally the conflicts would factionalize large segments of the network, and usually the patterns were predictable. It became clear to me that I was providing a useful service to my friends as a kind of mediator among several small sets of friends with overlapping ties to each other, as well as some long-term animosities. At the same time, the significance of the social relationships that constituted this group became clear as did the ways these relationships changed through time. Furthermore, I became increasingly aware of the significance that such groups, called *chevre* by Israelis, played for so many of the people I encountered in Tel Aviv. At this point, I began to formalize my questioning about relationships without any objections from those I was studying. I had discovered a topic of communal interest. Thus, quite by chance, I became an urban anthropologist studying social structural responses to urbanism and interpersonal relationships. I barely realized what I was studying while I was in the field and had absolutely no inkling that this is what I would be doing before I got there.

By now you are probably wondering what this protracted discussion of my field research has to do with introducing this collection of essays. First, in reading this collection I was reminded of many personal experiences that structured my research, and I couldn't resist swapping a tale or two. Second, I simply wanted to show how important mistakes and serendipity are in determining the process and outcome of our enterprise. Finally, I wanted to emphasize, as do all of these essays, the significance of the social context in doing research, especially as the researcher relates to this context. To a large extent, the social context of research along with accidental encounters, misperceptions, mistakes, and personal realizations are the themes that run through all of the essays in this collection. I would bet they play a role in virtually all fieldwork.

The first time I read through these essays I spent a good deal of mental energy recollecting what went wrong and what went right in my Israeli research. The second time through the essays I began to focus on how I would use them in classes. Each of these essays will serve multiple purposes. The collection, as a whole, is especially appropriate for a methods course. It covers a variety of kinds of research in a variety of contexts. It presents research issues ranging from gaining entry (Raybeck and Kent) to the ethics of research (Heggenhoughen, Richardson, Geertz). Many of the articles deal with developing rapport and with both appropriate and problematical role relations with informants (Raybeck, Kent, Kearney, Hull, Picchi, DeVita, Gmelch, Melnick, Messenger, and Dwyer-Shick). All of the essays teach lessons about doing research, about the relationship between objectivity and subjectivity, about science and humanism, and about self and other.

This last set of lessons, about self and other, makes this collection especially appropriate for an introductory course in cultural anthropology. These essays cover virtually all of the questions, issues, and subjects that I entertain in my freshman-level course. Clearly, most of the essays can be used to introduce participant observation and to humanize fieldwork. In this regard, I was especially enthralled with Kent's essay concerning failed research, with which many students should identify.

I often use the articles and ethnographies I assign to force students into reflecting on their own culture. I hope they can at least begin to step outside their own experience (predominantly white, middle-class, eastern United States), look back critically at their assumptions about the world, and learn that there is value in the alternatives that other cultures present. Since all of the essays in this volume are personal and self-aware, they provide students with models for self-assessment and reflection. Many of the essays consciously compare the cultures being studied to the culture of the researcher and will be especially valuable in stimulating discussion about the values and behavior of the students most anthropologists teach (see especially Goodenough, Keesing, Farrer, Morrow, Winther, Nanda, Holmes, Kaprow, and Dwyer-Shick). Similarly, most of the esssays deal with ethnocentrism and cultural relativism, with the expectations of the observers and the observed (see especially Kearney, Picchi, Raybeck, Murphy, Grindal, and Eames).

For courses structured around subjects, this collection has excellent coverage of social organization including status and role, gender, friendship, marriage, kinship, and the family (see Raybeck, Farrer, Hull, Nanda, Picchi, DeVita, Melnick, Kaprow, and Dwyer-Shick). A number of essays focus on religion and the supernatural (see Clifton, Kearney, Winther, Picchi, Grindal, and Messenger). Several essays deal with political, economic, and development issues (Holmes, Gmelch, Murphy, Anonymous, and Colfer). Issues surrounding poverty and colonialism are poignantly raised by Richardson, Melnick, and Heggenhoughen. This volume also provides wide ethnographic exposure with essays from North and Central America (Kent, Clifton, Kearney, Morrow, Farrer, Richardson, Hull, DeVita, Gmelch, Geertz, Heggenhoughen), South America (Picchi), Africa (Grindal, Eames, Melnick), Asia (Raybeck, Colfer, Winther, Nanda, Anonymous [maybe]), the Middle East (Dwyer-Shick), the Pacific (Holmes, Keesing, Goodenough), and Europe (Murphy, Messenger, Kaprow).

To conclude, I want to add that the major feature of this collection is its readability. These articles are engaging reading, and most importantly, they will appeal to students of all levels. When Phil DeVita explained his plan for this book to me, I was excited. Now that I have read it, I am thrilled.

REFERENCES

DEVITA, PHILIP R.
1990   The Humbled Anthropologist: Tales from the Pacific. Belmont, CA: Wadsworth.

VAN MAANEN, JOHN
1988   Tales of the Field: On Writing Ethnography. Chicago: University of Chicago Press.

PART ONE

Learning from Mistakes

🦋 Getting Below the Surface

D O U G L A S R A Y B E C K
Hamilton College

INTRODUCTION[1]

Beginning fieldwork in a foreign culture is a bit like diving into an unfamiliar pond in which you suspect there may be underwater hazards.
You may examine the surface of the pond at length (and breadth and
width for that matter); you may even review the observations of others
who have swum in the pond, yet when you leap in yourself, you still
have an excellent chance of landing headfirst on a submerged boulder.
This essay describes a few such accidents as well as the understanding,
humility, and of course, bruises that such experiences leave behind.
Ultimately, it also relates a process of becoming familiar with the uneven
cultural terrain that lies below the seeming placidity of the surface. As
fieldwork is a very personal experience, so will this be a personal tale
of misperception and insight, of innocence and guile, culminating in
a bit of personal growth and some painfully acquired self-knowledge.

Interested in Southeast Asia, I did my graduate work in anthropology
in the mid-60s at Cornell University, a school noted for its excellent
Southeast Asia Program. While there, various members of the anthropology faculty impressed me, and other graduate students, with the
mystique of fieldwork. We were informed that it was a singularly important and necessary part of becoming an anthropologist (library theses
were discouraged). We were given the impression that this rite de passage
transformed one from a pedestrian scholar to a sensitive and perceptive observer of the human condition, possessed of increased wisdom
and maturity.[2]

Despite the centrality of fieldwork to our chosen profession, I and
other graduate students received no instruction in what it was or how
to do it. Indeed, when I, attempting to improve my grasp of this impalp-
able method, enrolled in a seminar titled "Methods in Anthropology,"
I found that it involved reading most of the writings of Malinowski.
While such works as *The Sexual Life of Savages* were interesting and
even edifying, they did little to reduce the mysteries surrounding
fieldwork. Even reading the then recently published (and expurgated)
field diary of Malinowski provided few pointers beyond the obvious:

Fieldwork was a difficult, lonely experience that could exacerbate personal problems.

I had decided to carry out my fieldwork in the state of Kelantan on the east coast of the Malay Peninsula. It met all of the requirements that I understood were necessary for a successful fieldwork experience. It was exotic, little studied, and reasonably accessible. Also, the Malay language is one of the easiest to master in Southeast Asia, although Kelantanese were reputed to speak a somewhat difficult dialect of Malay. Furthermore, compared to the states on the west coast, Kelantan was comparatively undeveloped and possessed of a traditional Malay culture that elsewhere had been adulterated by modernization and exposure to other cultural influences.[3]

In preparation for my field experience, I spent two years studying Malay (actually Indonesian, which is essentially the same language). I also read virtually all of the anthropology and much other literature written about Kelantan (a relatively modest task in the mid-60s), and I obtained a field research grant from the National Institute of Mental Health. I even managed to arrange a semester in London prior to entering the field. There I had the good fortune to study some of the Kelantanese dialect at the School of Oriental and African Studies with Amin Sweeney, at that time a graduate student about to undertake his dissertation research. Amin was and is a singular person who figured prominently in my fieldwork experiences. Finally, I contacted Raymond Firth who, together with his wife Rosemary, had worked in Kelantan. I have a very high regard for Firth's unassuming brilliance and for his kind and gentle manner toward the most fumbling of graduate students. He generously provided me with assistance and my first real advice about the fieldwork process.

Suitably armored against ignorance and error, I arrived with my wife at Kota Bharu, the capital of Kelantan, on January 9, 1968. We took up temporary residence in the Hotel Rex, a cubical-stucco compromise between comfort and going native, while I set about trying to familiarize myself with the city, buy a secondhand motorcycle, locate a suitable field site and, coincidentally, understand what was being said to me. It seems that people could understand my halting standard Malay, but insisted on answering in machine-gun bursts of plosives, fricatives, and sibilants that bore little relation to the language I had learned at Cornell, and that was both much more rapid and much less intelligible than the kindly paced and carefully articulated phrases Amin had exposed me to only months earlier.

Amidst considerable frustration, persistent dysentery, occasional heat prostration (we were approximately six degrees north of the equator), and continuing bewilderment, there was one precious asset, an experienced pilot to assist in navigating these unfamiliar waters—Amin Sweeney—who had arrived in Kelantan a month before us and who

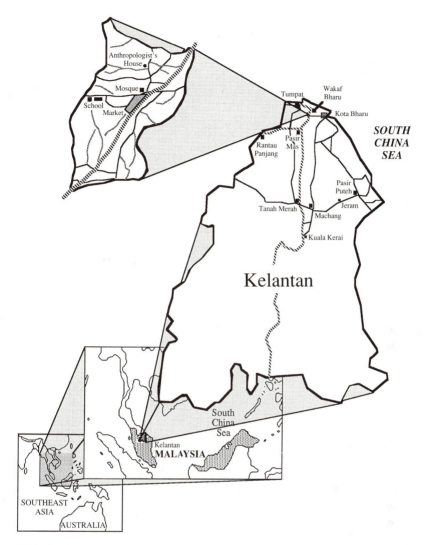

Wakaf Bharu, Kelantan, Malaysia.

charitably provided his time, assistance, and friendship throughout the fieldwork period. Born in England, Amin had lived for years in Kelantan, married a local woman, learned both the native language and the customs, and was exceptionally well suited to assist wandering would-be anthropologists in search of truth and beauty.

The problem with fieldwork is not that *things* are different; one expects *things* to be different. The difficulty is that nearly all *things* are or can be different, and the neophyte has no means of anticipating which *things* require special attention. It is not the big questions that exhaust you; those have been planned for and are, at least in part, anticipated. It is the little, commonplace experiences that would ordinarily be taken for granted that are the source of unending concern. People smile. Why did they smile? Are they simply being friendly, or did I do something foolish? Should I smile back? How long? How broadly? Am I too concerned about this? I cannot detail here the myriad ways in which Amin and his wife, Zainab, eased the initial shock of fieldwork and provided a psychological haven from the storms of insecurity that attend such endeavors, but the debt is both significant and enduring.

The choice of a field site is among the most important decisions made in the initial stages of fieldwork. It takes months even to start becoming familiar with a community, to build rapport, and to develop a sense of mutual trust between participant-observer and observed. Choose an inappropriate setting and those months are largely wasted.

Since my research was to focus principally upon traditional values and deviance, I knew that I would have to invest a good deal of time gaining the acceptance and trust of those with whom I would be living for a year and a half. I also knew the qualities of the community I was seeking: It should be a reasonably typical, traditional peasant village subsisting on wet rice agriculture; it should possess a standard market and thus serve as a locus of activity for surrounding communities; and it should have a fair-sized Chinese population as interethnic relations was one of the topics in which I was interested. All of these were good, objective, professional considerations, but in addition, my wife and I were hoping to be near the state capital where we could buy such necessary provisions as film, canned food, pocket books, and ice cream, and where we could see the occasional movie.

On my well-used and underpowered Yamaha, I began to explore roads, paths, and trails in search of an appropriate village (*kampong*). The strategy was both simple and ineffective. When I came across a promising village, I would stop at a local coffee shop, which both my reading and Amin assured me was a center for local gossip and information. I would make inquiries concerning the nature of the village and whether or not there was a house to rent. This slapdash approach led to numerous conversations with assorted villagers of a semi-intelligible nature. They could generally understand me; I seldom understood them. Finally, in a fit of humility, I asked Amin for suggestions and he recommended Wakaf Bharu, a village that met the criteria above and was situated on Kelantan's lone railway just across the Kelantan River only eight miles from Kota Bharu, the state capital.

One of the few fieldwork recommendations with which I was familiar was to contact a local person of high status prior to entering a fieldwork setting. Thus, with the assistance of Amin I met with the local *Imam,* the Islamic priest, and learned that, in addition to the characteristics enumerated above, Wakaf Bharu also possessed a mosque, a grade school, and a small police post that kept local demographic records (more or less, as I was to discover later). The population was just over 2,000, a bit large but not unmanageable, since my research did not require detailed household registries and the like, and there was a nice, new house that could be rented for a reasonable sum. In short, the village appeared very appropriate for my research needs.

JUMPING IN

With practically no acquaintance with the village, my wife and I moved in on a Thursday afternoon on February first, three weeks after arriving in the country. Our initial discovery was easily made: The villagers of Wakaf Bharu were as interested in us as we were in them. We are both Caucasian and my wife at five-feet-five was taller than most Malay males, while I at six-feet-four was an extreme oddity. People surrounded the house to watch us unpack. Little children ran through the house checking our belongings and reporting back to their better-mannered parents. We had not quite finished unpacking when I had to attend to my first social obligation in the village. Prior to our arrival, I had made an arrangement with the man whose house we had rented that proved to be very valuable.

For complex current and historical reasons, Kelantanese villagers distrust outsiders, especially representatives of authority, and prefer to address their own problems independently. During a nine-month period preceding our arrival, Wakaf Bharu villagers had suffered a number of break-ins and thefts, but unlike a U.S. community, which would have summoned the police, they determined to deal with the problem themselves. The village mounted a guard (*jaga*) consisting of male volunteers, mostly younger married men, who would give one or two evenings a week to safeguard the village. Thus, each night several Malay males armed with clubs would patrol village pathways from ten in the evening to four in the morning seeking evildoers. Since the man from whom I was renting the house was scheduled to do guard duty on Tuesday and Thursday evenings, I had (rather cleverly) arranged to take on his obligation, thereby making a statement to the village that I was not simply an interloper but was willing to assume some responsibilities for the privilege of residence there.

Thus, at approximately ten o'clock on my first evening in the village four Malay males arrived at my front door and announced in a quiet fashion that it was time to patrol the village. Two of the four were to become close friends and valuable, if not always subtle, sources of information. Yusof, a stolid, strongly built man in his early twenties with an open and (for a Kelantanese) somewhat assertive style, had been known for youthful misbehavior but, recently married, seemed to have settled down to a degree. Mat, a clever, wiry young man possessing a quick sense of humor and an occasionally mischievous manner, was a frequent companion of Yusof, and the two, as I was to discover, were still capable of the sporadic solecism.

The four young men introduced themselves, waited while I located a suitable pick-axe handle, and then set off to escort me through the twisting maze of arteries and capillaries linking the houses and neighborhoods of the village organism. Thoroughly lost and bemused by the barrage of questions I was continually encountering, I was delighted to discover that the formidable *jaga* was, at least for the first two hours of its operation, largely a social affair. As we passed by houses, we were frequently invited to stop in for coffee and conversation. I don't doubt my presence increased the frequency of the invitations, but I found that this was customary even in my absence. Thus, I was presented to villagers, not simply as a nosey busybody (it became clear later that such was my true calling) but as a visitor willing to share in the social life and responsibilities of the village. Further, the continuing association with the young men of the *jaga* was to lead to my first real success in delving below the surface calm of Kelantanese village culture.

Arising early the next morning, I found my first hazard waiting outside our front door wearing a broad grin and a dirty sarong. His manner was expansive and his language incomprehensible. Gradually he made it apparent that he wished to offer me a tour of the village and that his name was Ché Din. Quite reasonably, I attributed our communication difficulties to my unfamiliarity with the Kelantanese dialect and with local customs. Pleased at the friendly offer and the prospect of beginning to become familiar with the tortuous network that comprised the village pathways, I told my wife that I would skip breakfast and headed off after Ché Din.

Thoroughly lost and bemused by the barrage of comments (does this sound familiar?) that Ché Din kept up concerning people and houses we were passing, I nodded and smiled at everyone we passed or chanced across. Villagers returned my smile with broad grins and quizzical looks probably, I thought, occasioned by my odd appearance. As we wound our way among the maze of trails, we came to a remarkably dilapidated house that had buckling sides and only part of its thatch roof. Ché Din indicated with some pride that this was his home and I nodded, confirming my initial and professionally sensitive judgment that he was not a wealthy man.

After more than an hour, with the sun suggesting that we were traveling back toward our point of departure, we came across three children playing in their yard near the path. The oldest boy looked up, pointed directly at my companion, laughed, and shouted, quite clearly "*orang nakal!*" Now, my reading had informed me that Malay parents took great pains to train their children to be very polite toward adults. Nonetheless, a Kelantanese youth had just called my guide a "naughty person," raising the not inappropriate question: Just who the hell was I walking around with, anyhow?

Despite my increasing unease, nothing untoward transpired and we arrived back at my house shortly after having encountered the children. With my thanks and to my relief, Ché Din soon took his leave, whereupon Hussein, my next-door neighbor, walked over with a smile and the inquiry "Why were you going about the village with *tiga-suku?*" *Tiga-suku* translates as three-quarters and is a colloquial Kelantanese term for someone who is intellectually impaired. I had just been squired about the community by the village half-wit.

What makes this occurrence particularly poignant, and perhaps even educational, is that I genuinely thought Ché Din was simply a poor Kelantanese. I had studied the language for two years, read all of the anthropology written on the area, worked in a profession that sensitizes one to interpersonal behaviors, and I still couldn't perceive the difference between a typical Kelantanese and one who was mentally disabled. Lacking a sound basis for comparison, I assumed that Ché Din was simply poor and perhaps a bit odd, but maybe many Kelantanese appeared a bit odd to outsiders.

LEARNING TO SWIM

My difficulties in making such simple discriminations as the difference between normal and abnormal villagers should provide some sense of the bewilderment that often accompanies fieldwork. In many respects, it involves a return to childhood when little is known and less is understood. Happily, the villagers of Wakaf Bharu proved to be tolerant and helpful parents who undertook my education with enthusiasm and good humor.

Their good humor was usually occasioned by one of my gaffes, which tended to be of two sorts: those which could be attributed to absolute ignorance often coupled with a tendency to transpose assumptions from U.S. to Kelantanese culture, and those which arose from well-meaning, but imperfectly executed, efforts to adapt to village society. Two examples will illustrate the differing ways in which I learned humility, though I would entreat the reader not to view these as typical of my fieldwork.

Very early in my fieldwork I was invited to attend a traditional Kelantanese wedding. Following the wedding, I was seated cross-legged on a woven pandanus mat in a circle of five males preparing to enjoy the postwedding feast. There was shallow bowl before me and a glass of clear, cool water by my right hand. I was the only one in the circle so equipped, but I assumed that my companions were simply making life easy for me as they had done several times already. As it was a hot after-noon (it seemed they all were), I picked up the glass and took a long drink, noticing gradually the somewhat curious looks my associates were giving me. Finally, one of my companions leaned toward me and whispered some useful information. It seems Malyas eat with their right hands and prior to meals (why wasn't this in any of the ethnographies I had read?) they wash the right hand by pouring water over it into a shal-low bowl. I had just drunk the wash water, an act akin to sipping from a finger bowl.

The second class of gaffe is illustrated by a series of events that occurred after two months in Wakaf Bharu, when some of my village friends suggested I might be more comfortable wearing a local sarong (*kain pelékat*) rather than the hotter and more confining trousers I had worn to that point. Attracted by an invitation that seemed to suggest increasing acceptance of mc (it did), I went with a friend to purchase several *kain* at the local market.

Most *kain* are imported, preferably from India but increasingly from Japan, and are a standard length of approximately four feet. They are sewn longitudinally forming a tube which is donned over the head, snugged with two center tucks, and then folded down until a roll of fabric forms a natural belt. Kelantanese males pull their *kain* up just under their armpits and then roll the fabric down to their waists where it supplies stability and insurance against embarrassment. This leaves them with the bottom of the *kain* just brushing the top of the feet; only a crude and uneducated hick (*orang darat*) would wear his *kain* halfway up his ankles.

Now the average Kelantanese male is about five-feet-four and I am a foot taller. This simple fact created a simple dilemma. Being tall, I could not begin to roll my *kain* under my armpits and still have the bottom anywhere in the vicinity of my feet. I could either wear my *kain* accord-ing to the dictates of fashion or wear it securely, but not both. I opted for social acceptance and wore my *kain* as low as possible, allowing myself only two fragile rolls of the material to secure my modesty. In the process of accustoming myself to wearing a *kain*, I made some im-portant and expensive discoveries: Sarongs are remarkably poorly suited for motorcycle riding and, as most women already know, when climb-ing stairs, the hem of a long garment should be lifted. My "discoveries" were invariably accompanied by a good deal of amusement on the part of villagers, but they seemed to appreciate that I was making a genuine, if frequently inept, attempt to adapt to their mores. Adding fuel to a well-tended fire, I further agreed to wear a *baju Melayu*, a Malay-style overshirt of light cotton that is cut full with a belled waist and belled sleeves. Kelantanese, being of modest stature, look quite attractive in such garb. However, I am long and lanky and when attired in sarong and *baju Melayu* my mirror informed me that, despite the compliments

I received from villagers, I most closely resembled a becalmed sailing ship.

Fortunately for me and my few tatters of remaining dignity, some villagers actively, albeit indirectly, instructed me in the niceties of social behavior.

Malays in general and Kelantanese in particular are very sensitive to interpersonal relations, and they are quite concerned with maintaining interpersonal harmony within the village context. To facilitate harmonious relations, all villagers are schooled in a well-developed courtesy code (*budi bahasa*). This involves not only a set of rules for proper behavior but also the cultivation of a proper demeanor characterized by humility and indirection.

Hussein was my next-door neighbor, a particularly small and swarthy man possessing a quick intelligence and an excellent familiarity with *budi bahasa*. He was also one of few villagers willing to give me advice concerning social matters, a mission that he carried out with great sensitivity and tact. Rather than provide direct advice, a behavior that risks embarrassing both the giver and the receiver, Hussein would use personal references of transparent relevance. On one occasion when he wished to suggest that my behavior was not as tactful as it might have been he made the following observation:

> I was not born here and I do not have my relatives here. I have to be careful of my behavior. When you go to live in a place where you weren't born, you behave like a hen, not like a rooster. This is proper. In my own kampong I can behave more importantly, but here I must be careful not to give offense.

I got the idea.

Such solicitous assistance saved me numerous blunders during the first months of fieldwork. Villagers had responded positively to my explanation that I was a student of their culture who would return to the United States to teach others about the customs of the Kelantanese. Kelantanese are aware and proud that they maintain a rich, traditional Malay culture that elsewhere on the peninsula has largely succumbed to other cultural influences and to modernization.[4] Things seemed to be going well. My note cards multiplied at an appropriate rate, and people were quite helpful concerning many of my questions. I quickly discovered, however, that there were distinct limits on the kinds of questions with which I could expect assistance.

Those questions which concerned factual minutiae pertaining to such mundane activities as planting, family life, common rituals, and the like, were answered readily and fully. However, since my major interests dealt with values and deviant behavior, I also somewhat naively asked about the existence of misbehaviors such as gambling, drinking, premarital sex, and so forth. My friends and acquaintances gave me to believe that

Kelantanese were among the most law-abiding and proper individuals on the planet. No one drank, gambled, fooled around or, it seemed, even spoke ill of others.

My suspicions that people were being less than candid with me were exacerbated one day when I attempted to ascertain the reasons behind a heated and loud quarrel between a man and a woman that I had heard the preceding evening. I inquired of a variety of villagers, whom I knew to be closer to the disturbance than I had been, what the argument concerned and who the principals were. I received a notably uniform reply: "What argument? Sorry, but I didn't hear any argument." I realized that I was still not sufficiently trusted to be made privy to the sensitive and sometimes less than ideal social life of the village. Access to such information would give me a means to harm village interests, and as I was still seen largely as an outsider, villagers could not be certain I wouldn't use such means against their interests.

Presented with an image of a deceptive exterior calm, I needed a means to delve below the surface boundaries of village life where I might encounter the muddiness and unevenness that constitutes a portion of all human relationships. As in most aspects of fieldwork, the solution to my problem came in an unforeseen manner, from an unexpected source, and owed little to the anthropologist's intelligence.

GETTING BELOW THE SURFACE

Gaining the trust of those with whom you work is a slow process generally characterized by numerous small exchanges that gradually add to mutual understanding and acceptance. Seldom are there break-throughs in trust of the sort to which one can point. Nonetheless, I can date exactly when I was enabled to dive below the surface calm of village society: March 18, 1968, a Monday.

Throughout the early months of fieldwork, I continued to participate in the evening guard (*jaga*) twice a week. This regularly placed me in the company of married males a few years younger than myself with whom I shared several interests. As time progressed and they, especially Mat and Yusof, grew more comfortable with me, they asked questions about that preeminent concern of young males—sex. They wished to know about the sexual mores of contemporary U.S. society, which in the 60s had rather a lurid reputation. I answered their questions candidly and responded with queries of my own. They began giving me my first evidence that Kelantanese were as frailly human as the rest of us.

Eventually we even exchanged swearwords, an extremely important aspect of language, curiously absent from language classes. They traded Kelantanese curses for English profanities and seemed pleased with the secret power the words conferred. Mat, the more playful of the two, delighted in approaching young women, smiling and saying "Fook!" (his pronunciation lacked total accuracy) before cackling and running away.

After months of this sort of banter, we had become quite comfortable with each other and were developing close friendships. One Thursday evening as we were ending our *jaga*, Yusof asked me if it would be possible for three people to travel on my motorcycle. I remarked that it probably was feasible and asked why he wished to know. His response was both opaque and promising: He asked me to meet Mat and him Monday evening on the main road at the edge of the village and commented that there was something he wanted to show me.

That Monday night I met Mat and Yusof at the designated location and the three of us set off on my motorcycle under Yusof's direction. Questions concerning our destination were greeted with smiles, and directions were confined to immediate turns. I was guided into the capital, Kota Bharu, down a side street, through a maze of paths, and into a dark, dead-end alley where we dismounted. Yusof beckoned me to follow him, which I did with only a slight frisson of apprehension.

We approached the side a of darkened building where Yusof opened a door and ushered me into a noisy, dingy, low-ceilinged room occupied by both men and women. Within three minutes, Yusof had purchased beers for all of us and had a "waitress" sitting on my lap. With both he and Mat watching me closely, I realized the significance of the risk they were taking and the importance of my response. I drank the beer, joked with the waitress and thanked them for both opportunities. After I declined their kind invitation to retire with my waitress to a loft over the room, we settled in for some pleasant drinking and conversation.

It seems that there were numerous "bars" of the same sort throughout Kota Bharu. People from a given village tended to patronize a single location, thus ensuring a degree of confidentiality. Villagers engaged in similar deviance at a shared locale were unlikely to inform on one another, partly due to bonds of solidarity and partly because doing so would raise questions regarding how one knew of the behavior. Indeed, I learned later that Yusof and Mat were very interested in compromising me as soon as possible and were somewhat disappointed that I hadn't taken the waitress upstairs. Had I done so, they would have had even greater insurance that I would not mention our recent activities upon returning to the village.

That evening perceptibly changed my relationship with Yusof and Mat. I now had two friends who had taken me below the surface and who counted on me to be circumspect about the experience. They had invested their trust in me and we had shared solecisms. Each possessed information that could be detrimental to the others, were it to enter the ever-active village gossip network. That evening also represented a major breakthrough in my fieldwork. Soon I could approach Yusof and Mat with questions concerning subsurface elements of village behavior, and they would delight in telling me whatever relevant gossip they knew. As gossiping is a favored pastime, they usually had useful information concerning any event about which I might ask.

Information garnered from Yusof and Mat allowed me to ask very different and far more successful questions of other villagers. Instead of asking open-ended questions betraying my near total ignorance of a situation, I could now inquire about events in a manner suggesting I was already privy to the main issues and only wished clarification of details. Instead of asking "What was that argument last night and who took part in it?" I could now inquire, "Were Minah and Dir arguing about her sister's inheritance again?"

This approach immediately placed me below the surface, for I could not be familiar with such information unless other villagers already trusted me. In this fashion, I rapidly increased my access to information that hitherto had been denied me, and as it became increasingly apparent that I neither disclosed nor abused this knowledge, other villagers began to accord me a trust similar, but not identical, to that which Yusof and Mat had displayed.

From this point forward, my work progressed nicely. The more time spent delving below the boundary between surface ideals and subsurface reality, the more familiar the terrain became and the easier it was to navigate among half-hidden forms.

CONCLUSION

I suggested at the beginning of this essay that fieldwork changes the anthropologist in ways that can be only imperfectly understood. For a period of time, the investigator knows what it is to be a member of a minority denied full access to the surrounding society. One is forced to acknowledge weaknesses and encouraged to discover strengths in ways that are more often mundane than exotic. Similarly, the anthropologist comes face-to-face with the limitations of both science and one's ability to determine the outcome of events.

Certainly, an increasing sensitivity to others is one of the benefits of the fieldwork experience. Equally likely gains are improved self-knowledge and a finer sense of humility (though I confess the writings of some anthropologists belie this assertion). A major result of my fieldwork, as my teachers had suggested, was to transform me into a more sensitive and perceptive observer of the human condition, possessed of increased wisdom and maturity. (Note I didn't say how greatly increased.) At the very least, I learned that the evolution of trust involves mutual vulnerability. I can never forget that I owe much of my fieldwork success less to my own professional acumen than to a night out on the town in the company of good friends.

NOTES

1. The information on which this essay is based was gathered during eighteen months of fieldwork beginning January, 1968, in Kelantan, Malaysia. I am grateful for the National Institute of Mental Health Grant (NH 11486) that supported this research. I also want to thank the Southeast Asia Program, and especially Tom Kirsch and the Department of Anthropology of Cornell University for providing me with a quiet and comfortable place to complete this and other writings. Finally, I want to express my deep appreciation for the efforts of my wife, Karen, who not only steadfastly endured an experience she found less than enthralling but who also had the good sense to maintain a daily journal in which she noted many details that escaped my field notes.

2. So that you will be apprised of my biases, I should inform you that I have come to share this assessment in large degree, though I would not argue, as would some, that it is necessary to carry out fieldwork in a foreign and preferably exotic land in order to enjoy such benefits.

3. This essay is clearly not an ethnographic study of the Kelantanese, and the interested reader might wish to examine works by Raymond Firth (1966), Rosemary Firth (1966), Clive Kessler (1978), and William Roff (1974) among others.

4. An excellent example of traditional culture preserved in Kelantan and not elsewhere is a curing ceremony, *main puteri*, which combines both traditional healing and spirit beliefs (see Firth 1967, 1974, Kessler 1977, Raybeck 1974).

REFERENCES

FIRTH, RAYMOND W.
1966   Malay Fishermen: Their Peasant Economy. London: Routledge & Kegan Paul Ltd. (first publ. 1946).
1967   Ritual and Drama in Malay Spirit Mediumship. Comparative Studies in Society and History 9:190–207.
1974   Faith and Scepticism in Kelantan Village Magic. *In* Kelantan: Religion, Society and Politics in a Malay State. W. R. Roff, ed. Kuala Lumpur: Oxford University Press.

FIRTH, ROSEMARY
1966   Housekeeping Among Malay Peasants. 2d ed. London: Athalone Press (first publ. 1943).

KESSLER, CLIVE
1977   Conflict and Sovereignty in Kelantanese Malay Spirit Seances. *In* Case Studies in Spirit Possession. V. Crapanzano and V. Garrison, eds. New York: John Wiley & Sons.
1978   Islam and Politics in a Malay State: Kelantan 1838–1969. Ithaca, NY: Cornell University Press.

RAYBECK, DOUGLAS
1974   Social Stress and Social Structure in Kelantan Village Life. *In* Kelantan: Religion, Society and Politics in a Malay State. W. R. Roff, ed. Kuala Lumpur: Oxford University Press.

ROFF, WILLIAM
1974   Kelantan: Religion, Society and Politics in a Malay State. Kuala Lumpur: Oxford University Press.

SUGGESTED READINGS

CHAN SU MING
1965   Kelantan and Trengganu, 1909–1939. Journal of the Malaysian Branch of the Royal Asiatic Society 38:159–198.

DOWNS, RICHARD
1967   A Kelantanese Village of Malaysia. *In* Contemporary Change in Traditional Societies. Asian Rural Societies, Vol. 2. Julian Steward, ed. Urbana: University of Illinois Press.

RAYBECK, DOUGLAS
1975   The Semantic Differential and Kelantanese Malay Values: A Methodological Innovation in the Study of Social and Cultural Values. Doctoral dissertation, Cornell University, Ithaca, NY.
1980   Ethnicity and Accommodation: Malay-Chinese Relations in Kelantan, Malaysia. Ethnic Groups 2:241–268.
1980– The Ideal and the Real: The Status of Women in Kelantan Malay Society.
 1981 Women and Politics 1:7–21.
1986   The Elastic Rule: Conformity and Deviance in Kelantan Village Life. *In* Cultural Identity in Northern Peninsular Malaysia. S. Carstens, ed. Athens, OH: Ohio University Press.

WILSON, PETER
1967   A Malay Village and Malaysia. New Haven: HRAF Press.

🌀 Fieldwork That Failed

LINDA L. KENT
State University of New York, Plattsburgh

Fieldwork is the hallmark of cultural anthropology. It is the way we explore and learn about the vast detailed intricacy of human culture and individual behavior and it is, importantly, the way in which most cultural anthropologists earn and maintain their professional standing.

Some of the early personal accounts of anthropologists in the field make fieldwork sound exciting, adventuresome, certainly exotic, sometimes easy. Margaret Mead, in a preface to *Coming of Age in Samoa* (1949), related her despair of ever learning the native language, only to find herself one day thinking those same thoughts *in* the native language. From there on it was, apparently, all downhill. Malinowski, the classic anthropological fieldworker, describes the early stages of fieldwork as "a strange, sometimes unpleasant, sometimes intensely interesting adventure [which] soon adopts quite a natural course" (1961:7). He goes on to describe his daily routine of strolling through the village observing the intimate details of family life, and as he tells it, such observations seem possible and accessible. The trick is in the stroll.

In more recent years there have been numerous realistic accounts of fieldwork (e.g., Cesara 1982, Golde 1986, Spindler 1970, Whitehead and Conaway 1986) which portray the difficult, dirty, depressing, discouraging conditions of fieldwork as well as the thrill of insight and discovery, and the challenge presented to the ethnographer's self-esteem and confidence. In a wonderful article in the *American Ethnologist*, Miles Richardson (1975:525) writes about the realities of his own fieldwork:

> Later that morning, I thought I would be like Malinowski and walk through the village, etc., so I got Tex and went out. The men had left for their work, the women were cleaning house behind closed doors and windows, and the kids were in school. But at least Tex enjoyed it. Being a Labrador, he couldn't resist jumping into a large spring boxed in with concrete. As I called him out, a man walking by muttered, "Gringos! Washing their dogs in water that people bathe in."

Hortense Powdermaker (1966:53) describes her reaction to being all alone at last in Lesu:

> A day or two later, my anthrolopogist friends left me to return to their own work. As I waved goodbye, I felt like Robinson Crusoe, but without a man Friday. That evening as I ate my dinner, I felt very low. I took a quinine pill to ward off malaria. Suddenly I saw myself at the edge of the world, and *alone*. I was scared and close to panic.

Despite both the glossing over and the gnashing of teeth, these accounts have in common the fact that the fieldwork, however romantic or scary, was, in some sense, successful. The anthropologist stuck it out, gained entry, established rapport, collected data, wrapped up, returned home, and published.

Less well documented are the fieldwork attempts that fizzled. These attempts may be instructive, both because they outline some of the pitfalls and because they show that there are some endeavors that just aren't going to be successful, and no fault to anyone. Discussion of fieldwork that failed, although there may not be the need to dwell on it, can also make the whole enterprise of ethnography a bit more human and accessible to new or aspiring anthropologists.

I have two stories to offer in the context of fieldwork that fizzled. The first took place when I was a student interested in studying Gypsies for my master's thesis. I was interested in how Gypsies use caricature as cultural camouflage, how they deliberately exaggerate *our* notions, or images, of them and thereby reinforce the stereotype and protect their "real" identity at the same time. It was of course their "real" identity I was after. Having identified the cleverness with which they fooled others, I never considered my own stereotypical notions about Gypsies. I certainly never thought I would be putty in their hands.

In 1974, toward the end of my first year of graduate study at Louisiana State University in Baton Rouge, I had decided to begin fieldwork for my thesis during the summer in New Orleans. From my reading, I knew that there was a strong possibility that New Orleans would have a sizeable Gypsy population, since Gypsies abound both in large cities and in the South. I also wanted to experience living in New Orleans, an exciting, romantic city, if only to enjoy the contrast with Baton Rouge. I was awarded a small research grant from the Student Government Association and I set upon my new adventure with a curious blend of confidence and fear.

It was odd that I had gone to Louisiana in the first place. A Massachusetts Yankee descended from generations of Massachusetts Yankees, I could certainly have found reason to stay in the northeast. But I had always found fascination in other peoples and places, a fascination that drew me to anthropology and ultimately to the study of traveling peoples, Gypsies and Tinkers. How I happened to find myself in Louisiana was the result of a comedy of circumstances, as much due to youthful confusion and lack of planning as to anything else.

In my first semester of graduate work, I experienced incredible isolation, loneliness, and an overwhelming lack of confidence. I had majored in history as an undergraduate and had very little preparation for the seminars and advanced courses I was taking. I struggled to understand new words like *nomothetic*, *emic*, and *etic*, and pushed my way through Marvin Harris's redoubtable tome, *The Rise of Anthropological Theory* (1968). Where were the people and places I had come to learn about?

Second semester I took a course in ethnographic methodology and a little cool breeze began to pierce the steamy humidity of Louisiana. I loved the course, I loved interviewing, I loved having constant feedback, support, and advice as I handed in my "fieldnotes." And I loved most of all the idea of myself as a fieldworker. With visions of Margaret Mead in my head, I set out for New Orleans that summer to find Gypsies, discover their secrets, and do great things. I had all the confidence of the unborn. But in my glow of optimism there was a small constant tick of dread. My major professor would be out of the country for the summer, and my small circle of new friends in Baton Rouge was likewise dispersing. I would be completely on my own.

Looking back across the years at this first adventure, I now see much more clearly the impact of personal circumstances on the choices and responses I made at that time. At that point in my mid-twenties, I was alienated from my family of origin, seriously introverted and self-isolating, and had great difficulty forming close relationships or initiating interaction with others. I don't know how I ever thought I could do fieldwork. I did not take any of these factors into account when I left for the field. I didn't consider how that may have influenced my selection of topic for study or my ability to carry out such a study. I never thought I was running away from anything nor did I imagine that my interest in Gypsies, or in anthropology, had anything to do with disenchantment with my own society and myself in it.

In New Orleans, I sublet a cockroach-riddled student apartment on the second floor of a house on a quiet street not far from Tulane University. I began what I thought was a systematic search for my study population. I interviewed people in organizations I thought might have contact with Gypsies: the New Orleans Police Department, state and city welfare, Board of Education, Salvation Army, Travelers' Aid. I read through news archives and history books. Through these efforts I did in fact compile a list of Gypsy addresses in the New Orleans area, but my efforts to contact these "elusive laughing vagabonds" (my own unquestioned stereotype) were futile.

I spent endless days walking or riding buses to places where Gypsies had just been, or used to be, but no longer were. Sometimes it seemed, from the material things left behind, that they had indeed "just left," and perhaps in a hurry. In other cases I found vacant lots, abandoned mobile homes, rundown apartment buildings. More than once I found myself in neighborhoods that felt decidedly unsafe. I frequently returned home through the incredible summer heat with a feeling of resignation and despair—how could I be a famous anthropologist if I couldn't even *find* my informants? But I also had very private, unacknowledged feelings of relief: If I couldn't find Gypsies I wouldn't have to talk to them, I wouldn't have to justify my inquiring presence, beg their acceptance of me. If I dutifully covered all of the bases, searched diligently, and genuinely couldn't contact them, then who could blame me if my fieldwork failed?

For weeks I wrestled between being a victim of, or taking charge of, my research. I eventually reached a point, the low point, where I dreaded actually meeting a Gypsy. It was then, of course, that I found Madame Ruby.

Madame Ruby and her family lived in a small house on a rural highway leading into New Orleans. A large sign outside the house showed the palm of a hand, with the lines of fortune emphasized. Almost resentfully, I went up and knocked on the door. A dark-haired woman in a headscarf and a long colorful dress invited me in and asked what I wanted. My memory obscures my exact words, but I stumbled through some sort of introduction, saying I was interested in Gypsies and that I was a student. She responded by telling me her fortune telling rates (three different prices depending on how much detail I wanted) and then said she wasn't a Gypsy so she couldn't tell me anything about them.

I looked at her in disbelief. Not a Gypsy? Of course she was a Gypsy—she fit everything I had read about them. Her occupation, her dress, her features, her accent, everything seemed "Gypsy." And as sure as I was about it, I was equally sure from her direct, slightly amused denial that I had come to an ethnographic dead-end. I told her, a bit insistently, that I thought she was a Gypsy. She denied it again (yes you are, no I'm not) and wouldn't entertain any more discussion about it. Did I want my fortune told or not? Numbed, I took the five-dollar version. "You will have good luck in the future." Sure I would.

No one had ever told me, nor had it occurred to me, that I would run into such an impasse. (I never doubted then, and do not now, that she was a Gypsy.) I see now how naive I was to try to "gain entry" into a group whose existence depends on camouflage and who had every reason to suspect my motives. Without someone to serve as an intermediary, someone trusted by the Gypsies, to introduce me and explain what I wanted to do, my efforts were doomed from the start. In all of my reading about how Gypsies exaggerate some of their stereotypical characteristics in order to protect their identity, I never realized that they also rely on denying their identity to achieve the same purpose. Madame Ruby told me she was Mexican; Gypsies frequently claim a nationality rather than an ethnicity when it seems advantageous to do so.

After six weeks of heat, complete isolation, and cockroaches, this was the last straw. I gave up and went to Boston. There, in the company of friends and with the pain of this first lesson in fieldwork fresh in my mind, I set about studying Gypsies again. And the "good luck" foretold by Madame Ruby came to pass, resulting in a master's thesis on the life history of a Gypsy headman (Kent 1975).

There are many "lessons" to be learned from this experience: Some of them I am still learning, others probably have yet to be realized. The lesson I stress here is that the fieldworker is a person as well as a scholar, with attitudes, emotions, habits, fears, and experiences that trot right along beside the scholar and indeed inform the scholarship. A second lesson is that "good" fieldwork is not, as Rosalie Wax (1986) points out, the result of any one person alone. The fieldworker, even if deliberately alone in the field, must have someone with whom to communicate and consult about the work. In my often self-imposed isolation and my efforts to do it all myself, yet disregarding myself in the process, I lost both my focus and my spirit.

In the course of my research on Gypsies, I came across the sparse but fascinating literature on the Traveling People, or Tinkers, of Ireland. I also learned that there were Irish Travelers living in the United States (see, for example, Harper 1971). Although my first choice was to do my doctoral fieldwork in Ireland, I determined in the fall of 1977 to carry out a preliminary study in Mississippi. Earlier that year I had been admitted to candidacy for the Ph.D. at the University of Oregon and had spent the spring semester teaching at Idaho State University. I approached my new adventure with optimism and confidence.

My first step was to contact the anthropology department at Memphis State University. I explained what I wanted to do and asked about sharing an apartment with graduate students. The response was reassuringly warm. The faculty offered suggestions, ideas, and interest in my project, and I received an offer from a young graduate student couple who were willing to let me stay in a spare room. I moved to Memphis, found my way around, talked to faculty and other people who knew about the Travelers, gave a student lecture on Gypsies, and became a volunteer at the Southern Folklore Center. Within a few days I had identified a mobile home park, just across the border in Mississippi, which was home to several Traveler families.

Again, without the critical trusted intermediary person to introduce me, my entry into the Traveler encampment would be virtually impossible. The only person who really knew and was respected by these Travelers was a priest named Father Mike. Father Mike agreed to host a meeting with some of the Traveler elders whose approval I would need before I could go further. The meeting was arranged but was continuously called off, first due to the death and funeral of a respected Traveler, then canceled or postponed for a variety of reasons. I sensed that Father

Mike was reluctant to share "his" Travelers with me. When I finally suggested that I would try to make contact on my own, he agreed to let me use his name. I began visiting the park cautiously, respectfully, talking to women as they worked outside in their yards, hanging laundry or looking after their children and gardens. I felt uncomfortable walking through the park, doing the Malinowski stroll, observing the intimate details of family life. I hung around the edges of the park, trying my best to be innocuous, hoping for some sign of welcome. I "succeeded" to the point where I was invited inside one of the mobile homes and was introduced by a woman to her family and neighbors. A small, precious, precarious beginning.

Then an odd thing happened. Some Gypsies passed through Memphis and were accused of petty theft and vandalism. The local television station decided to do a human-interest news feature on Gypsies and called the anthropology department at the university to inquire whether anyone there knew about them. I had just given my Gypsy lecture to an undergraduate class and my name was mentioned to reporters. Without thinking about the Travelers, I said yes to the request for an interview, parts of which were aired on the five o'clock news. To my great surprise I was introduced as an "expert who had come to Memphis to devote her life to the study of Gypsies"!

Two days later Father Mike called to inform me that the Travelers had met to discuss the news interview and had decided not to meet with me anymore. Didn't I know, Father Mike added parenthetically, that Gypsies and Travelers are archenemies? The one is always being blamed for what the other does and vice versa. And they compete for some of the same economic territory, such as paving driveways and selling used cars. If I had indeed come to the area to study Gypsies, then why was I hanging around the Travelers? The Travelers were suspicious, and I was no longer welcome.

In panic I drove to the mobile home park and tried to talk with one of the elders. I explained the inaccuracy of the news reporter's statements about me. I swore (truthfully) that I hadn't seen or spoken to any Gypsies in the area at all, that I was interested in the Travelers. I found myself trying to convince him not only that I was sincere but also that I was a good person, as if *that* were somehow the issue at stake.

During this encounter, the Traveler elder's statements and questions revealed to me in short order the enormity of the task I had set upon myself in trying to gain entry into this community. What was my religion? (The Travelers are virtually all Roman Catholic; I have a Protestant background.) Why did I come down here from the north? Why was I, a single female, traveling around alone? Why did I want to study the Travelers? He said he had seen me on television and that he didn't think the Travelers would do me any good and that I certainly wouldn't do them any good. He asked me to leave and, as his parting shot, told me to "be sweet."

I crept away, humiliated and angry. I was angry at the injustice of this Traveler, judging me in terms of my religion, marital status, gender, and geography. (Yet certainly some of those same categories were of significance to my interest in the Travelers.) I was angry at Father Mike for not helping me, at the news reporter for making inaccurate statements. I was angry because I had invested considerable time, travel, money, and energy in this project and because I really believed I was ready, professionally, to do it (something I hadn't felt in New Orleans). I left Memphis feeling frustrated and sorry for myself.

What I only began to learn from this experience at the time was how important it was to me to be seen as a "good person," how much I was seeking approval from my informants or potential informants. I realized that I had wanted the same approval from the Gypsies and, in the course of my master's fieldwork in Boston, felt I had indeed attained a measure of it. This need continued even after the debacle in Mississippi and played itself out again in my more successful doctoral fieldwork in Ireland the following year (Kent 1980).

The need for approval at least partly results from the reality that the fieldworker comes uninvited and, no matter how skilled, is bound to be intrusive. She offers little or nothing in return for the privilege of entry into her informants' lives and may receive rewards and recognition back home, even financial profit, which her informants do not share. Somehow, if the people she studies can at least like her—that is, find her pleasant, amusing, interesting—then perhaps these qualities will constitute a form of repayment for all she takes and learns from them. For me, wanting to be seen as a good person was also a need for acceptance and wanting to belong, obviously something I didn't feel among my own people. I suspect this may be an unspoken motive for many anthropologists, especially those who have not yet found professional acceptance within the discipline. I know it was true for me. The paradox is that my fieldwork failed in part *because* I needly so badly for it to succeed. The importance of being accepted clouded my ability to look at and plan the most advantageous course of action. In both cases, among Gypsies and Travelers, I presented myself as a puppy in the rain, pleading to be taken in, hoping I would be seen as pitiable and harmless enough to be accepted. It has been a long, hard lesson to realize that this is not the road to acceptance, either in the field or at home.

Richardson's "myth teller" (1975) is still an inspirational piece. It speaks eloquently of the magic, wonder, and mystery of this most human of enterprises: the challenge of understanding other humans. In recent years, with the emergence of interpretive and then reflexive anthropology (Wilson 1988), the challenge of understanding oneself in the process of understanding others has earned our attention. It is through failures as well as successes, both our own and those of others, that we learn about being human.

REFERENCES

CESARA, MANDA
1982   Reflections of a Woman Anthropologist: No Hiding Place. New York: Academic Press.

GOLDE, PEGGY, ED.
1986   Women in the Field: Anthropological Experiences. 2d ed. Berkeley: University of California Press.

HARPER, JARED
1971   "Gypsy" Research in the South. *In* The Not So Solid South. J. Kenneth Morland, ed. Pp. 16–24. Southern Anthropological Society Proceedings No. 4.

HARRIS, MARVIN
1968   The Rise of Anthropological Theory. New York: Thomas Y. Crowell.

KENT, LINDA
1975   The End of the Road: The Life History of the Gypsy Headman in Boston, Massachusetts. Master's thesis, Department of Geography and Anthrolopogy, Louisiana State University, Baton Rouge.
1980   "In the Houses of Strangers": The Impact of Government Policy on the Irish Travellers. Doctoral dissertation, Department of Anthropology, University of Oregon, Eugene.

MALINOWSKI, BRONISLAW
1961   Argonauts of the Western Pacific. New York: E. P. Dutton (first publ. 1922).

MEAD, MARGARET
1949   Coming of Age in Samoa. New York: Mentor Books (first publ. 1928).

POWDERMAKER, HORTENSE
1966   Stranger and Friend: The Way of an Anthropologist. New York: W. W. Norton.

RICHARDSON, MILES
1975   Anthropologist—The Myth Teller. American Ethnologist 2(3):517–533.

SPINDLER, GEORGE
1970   Being an Anthropologist: Fieldwork in Eleven Cultures. New York: Holt, Rinehart & Winston.

WAX, ROSALIE
1986   Gender and Age in Fieldwork and Fieldwork Education: "Not Any Good Thing Is Done by One Man Alone." *In* Self, Sex, and Gender in Cross-Cultural Fieldwork. Tony Larry Whitehead and Mary Ellen Conaway, eds. Urbana: University of Illinois Press.

WHITEHEAD, TONY LARRY, AND MARY ELLEN CONAWAY, EDS.
1986   Self, Sex, and Gender in Cross-Cultural Fieldwork. Urbana: University of Illinois Press.

WILSON, LYNN
1988   Epistemology and Power: Rethinking Ethnography at Greenham. *In* Anthropology for the Nineties: Introductory Readings. Johnnetta Cole, ed. Pp. 42–48. New York: Free Press.

THREE

Culture Shock in Paradise

ELLEN HOLMES
Wichita State University

Anthropology has fascinated me since I first heard an anthropologist speak to a group of students' wives many years ago. Sitting in that small audience I resolved that if or when I resumed my college education, an anthropology course would be at the top of my list of subjects to explore. Little did I know that within a few years I would be a widow (at age twenty-eight) faced with caring for two young daughters and making unexpected new decisions. One of those decisions was to complete my undergraduate degree, so when my girls went off to first and third grades, I went to the local university and enrolled in introductory anthropology as one of my first courses.

Once I took that first anthropology course I was hooked, but I gave minimal thought to becoming a "real" anthropologist. And fieldwork was something I knew about only through reading and from hearing about the experiences of my professors: Personal participation in such an adventure seemed an unlikely possibility. Once I completed the baccalaureate degree some of my professors encouraged me to continue my education, and I made the decision to enter graduate school to work toward a Master of Arts degree. By the time I accomplished this goal, I was clearly committed to anthropology as the only possible profession. And so at the age of thirty-six I entered a Ph.D. program, regularly commuting 350 miles round-trip in pursuit of this goal.

I negotiated the coursework easily enough, but there remained the question of fieldwork. My interests were in Polynesia, but my children had now turned into teenagers and the prospect of venturing to the South Seas seemed complex, if not impossible. A job opportunity presented itself in the newly established gerontology program at the university in my community, and I seized upon it. It was not anthropology, but at least it put me in the academic sphere, which is where I preferred to be. While I worked (and waited), the teenagers grew older and somewhat more responsible. And then a colleague/friend, who was later to become my husband, received a grant to return to the Samoan Islands to assess the impact of modernization on the aged in that society, and there was money to take a research associate along—me.

By this time my children were old enough to be left at home and this did not make them unhappy. Since I had a faculty position in a program devoted to the study of aging, the research topic pleased the director, thus facilitating my taking a leave of absence, and the fieldwork opportunity would allow me to complete my degree and thereby improve my job security. So here I was, going to American Samoa, which had been a territory of the United States for many years, where most people speak English, where the total culture has been well documented, where health risks are few and the climate pleasant, and most important, in the company of a seasoned fieldworker, well acquainted with Samoans and their culture. What could be more ideal?

In retrospect, it really was ideal. I, however, did not respond ideally. Culture shock set in soon and continued or recurred throughout much of the research period. It was not that I did not expect culture shock: Like all students of anthropology I had read and heard much about this phenomenon. Perhaps it is a bit like having a first child: The impending arrival is known well in advance and occupies much of the prospective parents' thoughts, but they may not think about what their life will be like after the birth of the child. Anticipating culture shock may not include the realistic consideration of a long-term adjustment process.

I was aware that anthropologists often encounter a variety of "primitive" field conditions, but my field setting was hardly in that category. Upon arrival I found the islands of American Samoa in the process of modernizing American-style, and this included electricity, paved roads (at least on the main island), telephones, an air-conditioned hotel, restaurants, a bank, supermarkets, buses for local travel, regular air service to nearby islands and major South Sea ports, and a hospital staffed by U.S. public-health doctors. How much adjustment could be required in such a place? This was my naive view upon entering the field, and therein lay a major problem.

The tropical paradise I expected was in many ways just that—spectacular scenery, lush vegetation, colorful flowers and houses. On the other hand, in Fagatogo, the port town in Pago Pago Bay, once one moved inland from the main road there was a dense jumble of houses, some quite dilapidated, rocky streets and paths, water pipes running above ground, perennial mud puddles—in all, a depressing site in comparison with the outlying villages. I learned quickly that "paradise," like other less romantically viewed settings, has more than one face.

My more traumatic experiences began at the bank. As we had arrived at the beginning of a holiday weekend, it was several days before we could establish accounts at the bank, hoping thereby to simplify our monetary transactions during the research period. I was encouraged by the fact that the bank was a branch of the Bank of Hawaii, which suggested a stateside banking system and therefore something familiar. It was a very modern-looking facility with personnel who appeared to be pleasant and competent. For any purpose, however, the bank was a place of perpetual long lines. After a lengthy wait, someone helped us with the necessary paperwork. We needed cash immediately, but it was bank policy to allow no withdrawals until checks deposited into the account initially had cleared, a process that would take about two weeks since we were 6,000 miles from home. Our persistent efforts to acquire operating funds for the interim included being led through a maze of desks to explain our problem again and again to a series of Samoan and American bank officials. We finally succeeded, and as we walked out of the bank two hours after entering, we resolved that on future research trips to this country, we would use a cashier's check to establish an account.

An even more disconcerting event for me occurred the day we picked up our personalized checks. Imprinted on the checks with the lovely South Sea background design was my name with the wrong middle initial. When I expressed concern about the inaccuracy to the young Samoan bank employee, she simply responded, "You can just sign them that way!" "I can't do that. That's not me!" I protested. It now seems very funny to me, but at the time I was overwhelmed. What kind of system was this? Were errors acceptable routinely? I had visions of myself being charged with fraud or forgery or who knows what sort of illegal activity if I used these checks. My solution was to make the correction to the imprinted name on each check, sign them correctly, and to use the checks only for withdrawing cash from my own bank.

This incident was soon followed by a surprise of a different sort. Because our research plan involved moving to several different locales within the islands, we lived in the hotel while on the main island (Tutuila). It proved to be a very nice facility, consisting of several large two-story structures and some small two-unit buildings, designed like traditional Samoan *fale* (houses) and located along the waterfront. We considered ourselves fortunate to be able to rent one of these at a reasonable monthly rate. It was out on a point overlooking the bay and at some distance from most hotel traffic. From the little porch with its patio furniture we also had a spectacular view, much better than most hotel guests did. With air conditioning, a boon in this climate, and a telephone to aid in making appointments, our housing was ideal. That was the case until the middle of the night when I went into the bathroom and confronted a rat peeking from behind the toilet. Neither the rat nor I knew which way to go, but I screamed and the rat ran out of the bathroom, across the bedroom, up the drapes, and then disappeared. I wondered how it had gained entry and, more importantly at the moment, whether or not it would return. I slept very little the rest of that night.

Within a day or so, as I continued to be apprehensive about rodents, I had an encounter with a gecko. These little lizards are benevolent residents of Polynesian houses (and sometimes hotel rooms), where they cling to rafters, ceilings, or upper walls making little chirping noises as they help diminish the mosquito populations. They are certainly not to be feared but are not so attractive that I wanted to share my bed with one either. It was a bit startling to have a less than surefooted gecko fall onto my pillow as I lay reading one evening. Things were definitely closing in on me, and an entry in my notebook reflected my feelings:

> There is this problem that might seem ridiculous to those who have done fieldwork under real primitive (in the sense of undeveloped) conditions. One would expect things to be easy—even soft—in a somewhat Americanized society, living in a hotel, and with access to a number of modern conveniences. What is true is that while there is all this stuff, nothing works very well. The phone book is two years old and half the pages are missing and the phone system itself is incredible. It is rare to make contact with the person you wish to reach by phone. The hotel is o.k. if you don't mind rats and lizards that persist in coming inside. The ground transportation is o.k. considering there's no place we need to go. You try to send a cable thinking it will be easier than calling overseas and the message is mis-typed. Perhaps it's easier to adjust to a field situation where there is no expectation of real modernization as we understand it. Then anything you find is a bonus. When you know the conveniences are there, there's a tendency to expect things to work. And when they don't it is doubly frustrating—especially when the humidity is about 90%.

It was about this time that my co-worker remarked that just possibly I was too old to be doing fieldwork in a foreign setting for the first time. Was he right? Was this my midlife crisis? I was forty-one at the time, and perhaps I was less flexible than a younger person might have been. Perhaps I felt that it was more important to be successful—to prove that I could succeed as well as a younger student. In any case, it was obvious that I was suffering from culture shock complete with depression, anger, and periodic tears. In an attempt to ease some of the tension, we moved into the newest wing of the hotel at the end of the first month in the field. It did not look as traditional as the *fale*, but we escaped rats and geckos. As it turned out, that was to be true only for the Tutuila work. Later I was to have other adventures on Ta'u and in Western Samoa with centipedes and even a snake.

Interisland transportation was another source of trauma. The local airline provided service to the Manu'an island group, sixty miles east of Tutuila, and also to Western Samoa. Service to Western Samoa was much more predictable since it was classified as international travel; it also involved travel between airports with relatively modern communication and weather facilities and concrete runways suitable even for large jet aircraft. Within the American territory, however, flying was a bit more haphazard and there seemed to be no requirement for adherence to a strict schedule. There were landing strips of variable quality and safety on the islands of Ofu and Ta'u, but no aircraft control or repair facilities and no weather information available. These were essentially fair-weather destinations. Ofu had the edge with its gravel landing strip; on Ta'u planes landed on top of a hill above Ta'u village where men had cleared the area with machetes. There were coconut trees at one end of the field and a cliff dropping to the sea at the other. Regardless of wind direction, planes had to land toward the trees. No sensible pilot (or passenger) could be happy with this arrangement. Ta'u was our next destination, and being ignorant of most of these details we had chosen to fly rather than travel by interisland boat.

The day of our planned departure for Ta'u the flight was canceled because of bad weather, and the next day the weather was equally dismal—rainy and completely overcast. Since there was no weather station on Ta'u, the pilot had to guess about actual conditions. In midafternoon the decision was made to make the flight. He would land if possible and, if not, return to Tutuila. The plane was a twin-engine, fixed-landing-gear craft, and the plane's size and the landing strips made weight a critical issue. Passengers and baggage were weighed and adjustments made in either passenger load or baggage as needed. The prevalence of obesity in Samoan adults and many children complicated the airline employees' job, and passengers did not always understand the nature of the problem. Such confusion is evident in an example we learned of from a colleague: A mother offered to hold her 75-pound child on her lap as a solution to excessive weight in the passenger load. On this flight my associate was given the co-pilot's seat, while I, as the skinniest passenger, was directed to the seat in the tail section of the plane, behind several obese Samoan women and their children. In the cargo compartment, the most important shipment was a large quantity of melting ice cream, destined for the upcoming White Sunday celebration a few days later.

I was uneasy about this flight, more honestly I was terrified. Flying over water was new and generally unsettling for me, the trip from California to the islands having been my first such experience. Landing planes on a dot of mountainous land in the ocean seemed incompatible with feelings of security. And from my vantage point in the rear of this plane, I had a clear view of all the rusting rivets on the wings, which along with the weather was not reassuring. Another factor was no doubt contributing to my fear as well. My husband had been a test pilot/aeronautical engineer and had been killed in a light-plane crash. I thought I had adjusted reasonably well since I had subsequently traveled routinely by air. However, all of my flying experience in small aircraft had occurred years earlier with him as pilot. Having lived with a pilot, I probably knew more than the average air traveler about flight safety issues and had heard too many stories of actual or near disasters. Flying over sixty miles of ocean in a rusting plane clearly seemed to be a foolish move. But we were about to do it, and if an award had been given for stoicism I might have won.

The flight was not a long one, although it seemed interminable to me. We were able to make the scheduled stop on the Manu'an island of Ofu, and the remainder of the flight to Ta'u took only a few minutes. After a pass over the grass landing strip, the pilot decided to land. I could hardly believe my reaction as we approached the ground: I had found the trip so unnerving that the prospect of being back on land again outweighed any other consideration and I found myself thinking, "So we hit the trees, how bad can that be?"

Several weeks later, as we watched the plane land on the day we planned to return to Tutuila, it really did lose brake power and had run into the bush. No one was injured, but the damage to the plane effectively canceled air service between Manu'a and Tutuila. For us this meant remaining a few days longer and returning by boat, giving me the opportunity to experience yet another form of transportation available to the people of American Samoa.

There was no dock on Ta'u, so passengers had to be ferried out through the reef in a surf boat to the vessel that would transport us to Tutuila. This process required that one wade out into the water to a depth of two feet carrying shoes and other belongings and somehow hoist oneself into the surf boat. Fortunately I was unceremoniously but securely carried and and lifted into the boat with little effort by a very husky Samoan man. The islander rowed us out to the ship, where the wave action and lack of a long boarding ladder presented another real challenge.

Once on board the vessel most of the Samoan passengers laid on the after deck (where there was protection from the tropical sun) and slept. We found a wooden box on the forward deck where we could sit and thereby see where we were going. One of our traveling companions was an American biologist who had also been conducting research on the fauna of American Samoa, most recently on Ta'u. With him was a very large live snake he had found a few days earlier; it was in a cloth bag, which he placed on deck. Quite literally the very thought of snakes has always given me a creepy feeling; even when watching movies I would lift my feet off the floor when a snake appeared in a scene. Since snakes are not that common in American Samoa, it had not been determined what kind this one was. Yet here I was sitting on a box with a snake about a foot away from me for the entire six-hour trip. I knew I had reached a new phase of adjustment to fieldwork.

A critical event had occurred during our work in Ta'u, which probably served in some sense as a turning point in my experiences with culture shock. We were living next door to the dispensary, a nice-looking, relatively new building. It was normally staffed by a local Samoan licensed practical nurse, but a doctor from the hospital on Tutuila came over once a month to see patients. A young doctor completing a residency in Samoa accompanied the regular doctor on his trip to Ta'u during our stay there, and we had an opportunity to visit with him at length. We had already learned from the *palagi* (white) schoolteachers that medical care was very limited on Ta'u, and the doctor further confirmed that. He told us that the radio at the dispensary did not work—this was the means by which they would normally contact Ofu if the inter-island boat needed to be recalled after leaving Ta'u. He also indicated that the lab equipment was insufficient for any diagnostic tests—there was a microscope, covered with cobwebs, but there were no slides. Some of the instruments appeared never to have been unwrapped. Our friends residing on the island had told us that although a doctor is supposed to be there part of each month, that had not been the case during the past year. Seriously ill people are also supposed to be flown to the hospital on Tutuila at government expense, but this assumes that the plane is operational and the weather is good. I was quite distressed about this situation and got very angry.

After writing my reactions in my notebook, I discussed them (complete with tearful outbursts) with my colleague. He suggested that perhaps it was not as bad in the local people's view as it appeared to me. He also expressed a feeling that I was fighting the system—that I was coming face-to-face with the force of culture and that the sooner I could come to terms with the variance in my view and theirs, the sooner I would be on my way. He reminded me of the fatalistic world view of Samoans, of which I had already seen some evidence.

I thought about this and began to see that my reaction was based on an assumption that, because the American government had been in control of these islands for so long (seventy-six years) and had deliberately introduced most of the changes that had occurred, the people had obviously been misled about the quality of services available to them. Presumably the changes were to improve the conditions in the country, and yet nothing worked quite as it should, if at all. I was upset and I thought the Samoan people had every reason to be equally upset. Quite clearly I also assumed that the Samoan people had the same expectations of the system that I did. And somewhere in the back of my mind was a conflict about thinking, "These people just don't care," which suggested to me that I was being ethnocentric.

I had to admit that I had never seen people for whom "God's will" was a prevailing explanation for almost any occurrence. It was certainly borne out in some of their actions. A woman who had an eye infection but would not walk the short distance to the dispensary to see the doctor lost the sight in her eye. There was the young man who stepped on a nail and was told he should go to the hospital in Tutuila for further treatment, but who refused to board the plane when it arrived. When he did decide to go, it was too late and he died in the hospital shortly thereafter. Such occurrences may well attest to lack of faith in a foreign medical system and, in the young man's case, may seem to provide evidence that it does not work anyway. I was having a profound struggle with being relativistic, and yet that was what was required.

As for the banking system, lots of Samoans patronized the bank, but many used it primarily for cashing paychecks or remittance checks from overseas relatives. Savings accounts have not traditionally been popular in that society because the support patterns of the Samoan extended family almost guarantee that anyone with a nest egg will be expected to share it with relatives. This monetary institution probably did not play the part in their lives that it normally did in mine.

It would not be fair to suggest that Samoans had no positive expectations of foreign technological developments in their country; rather, they no doubt had very different expectations than I did. Once I began to accept unpredictability in certain situations as a given, I suffered less anguish about life in the islands and consequently became happier for the remainder of our fieldwork.

Most of the last six weeks of the research project were spent in Western Samoa, an independent country that was culturally similar to American Samoa. In spite of its larger population and greater land mass, this country is much poorer economically than the American territory and, in the late 1970s, remained much more traditional in many respects. There were adjustments to be made in moving there, but I found it easier making the transition. Very soon such events as driving along a narrow road in a remote area and finding our way blocked by a huge fallen tree or having to rescue our field notes from wind and rain in the dark during an unanticipated hurricane represented annoyances rather than traumas.

I approached Western Samoa more as a foreign country and had fewer preconceived ideas—I was more open-minded, so to speak—than when I arrived in American Samoa. Whether it was the open-minded stance or the fact that I had finally overcome my culture shock that explained the difference, I do not know. And I still do not know if, or how much, my being an older novice at fieldwork affected my response. But I have two conclusions about my own experience with culture shock. First, I doubt that any one of us can convey adequately to an inexperienced fieldworker *the* formula for preventing culture shock; and secondly, at least in my case, the remedy for this malady was learning to "go with the flow" of the culture, and perhaps, after all, that's one of the purposes of fieldwork.

By the time I returned home I was convinced that my field experiences had taught me so much about adaptation to change and about differences in what is considered important or trivial that nothing would perturb me in the future. But of course, one gets over that and has to readjust to one's own culture again, a process that not infrequently involves reverse culture shock!

In the summer of 1988, we returned to American Samoa for five weeks after an absence of twelve years. We were astounded by the changes that had occurred—some for the better and others clearly problematic. I must have learned my lesson well previously, however, because none of the anguish I experienced on the first field trip recurred. The bank had even longer lines than before, the hotel had significantly deteriorated accommodations (complete with cockroaches), and there were now three local airlines trying to stay in business with questionable success. Plane crashes had become more commonplace, leading me to conclude that it was quite rational to be skeptical of one's safety under the circumstances. There were still some difficulties in conducting fieldwork, but nothing that seemed to be unreasonable. I had acquired a flexibility that is essential to the fieldwork process. I was comfortable with this culture, and after a week's visit to the kingdom of Tonga, the return to Samoa seemed like a trip home. Maybe I am a "real" anthropologist at last.

SUGGESTED READINGS

AGAR, MICHAEL
1980   The Professional Stranger. New York: Academic Press.

GEORGES, ROBERT A., AND MICHAEL O. JONES
1980   People Studying People: The Human Element in Fieldwork. Berkeley: University of California Press.

POWDERMAKER, HORTENSE
1966   Stranger and Friend: The Way of an Anthropologist. New York: W. W. Norton.

SPINDLER, GEORGE
1970   Being an Anthropologist. New York: Holt, Rinehart & Winston.

WARD, MARTHA C.
1989   Nest in the Wind. Prospect Heights, IL: Waveland Press.

WHYTE, W. F.
1984   Learning from the Field: A Guide from Experience. Beverly Hills, CA: Sage.

Don't Mess with Eagle Power!

JAMES CLIFTON
Western Michigan University

Afterwards I asked myself, "Why the devil did I let myself fall into the clutches of that old bird?" My defense was always the same. Anthropologists must double-check data and interpretations, diligently searching for evidence that might require changing strong first impressions, even the firmest conclusions. We have to track down fresh leads, more so to open-mindedly cross-check the contrary findings of other scholars. Nothing other than scientific responsibility pushed me into old *Menisi*'s grasp.[1] That and some simple curiosity: what did an apparently much feared, allegedly self-confessed, reputedly all-too-successful Potawatomi Indian wizard really look like?

Two compelling questions nudged me toward an interview—and a confrontation—with the aged, illusive *Menisi* (Swoops Down). For more than a year I had studied the Kansas Potawatomi "Dream Dance" rites. These I knew centered on six large, richly decorated, much venerated sacred drums, each in its liturgical turn addressed as *Mishomonon* (Our Grandfather). Then I heard allusions to a seventh important drum, one never seen in public. This was the "oldest great drum," I was told, "maybe the original Potawatomi drum." "What is its name?" I asked. "The old flat drum," was a standard reply. "What does it look like?" I persisted. "You'll have to see for yourself," came the response.

The Young Dawn Man tried to advise me fully and to warn me off, I realized too late. "you could call that old flat drum the 'Vanilla' drum, maybe the 'Joker,'" Young Dawn Man told me, saying everything in a few words that were, to my later misfortune, utterly beyond my understanding. I never did pay close enough attention to Young Dawn Man's austere metaphors or his cautions. "Who is the Old Flat Drum's 'owner'?" I asked. "There's no 'owner.' That drum belongs to the *Neshnabek* [The People].[2] Swoops Down's got it at his place but won't give it up." These were the replies.

There was a seventh important drum, I concluded, tentatively. It might be the Potawatomi's first Dream Dance drum, perhaps. Or it could have some other significance. So, to solve the "Mystery of the Old Flat Drum," I went hunting for the secretive *Menisi*. I would do my Columbo routine. That ancient recluse, suitably coaxed, would play show and tell,

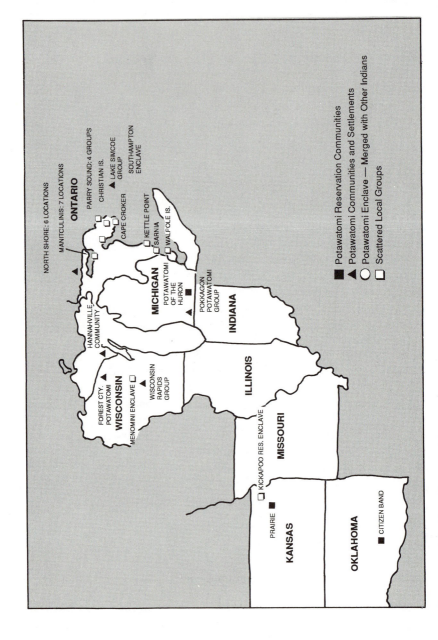

Potawatomi Indian Communities

unlocking his mysteries. Such was my plan. As events developed, I had more confidence than good sense.

Solving the mystery of the old flat drum was the lesser of two sound reasons for seeking out *Menisi*. The second was far more important. After a year's productive research, I thought I had the fundamentals of Prairie Potawatomi culture and society pretty well pegged. Then I learned an esteemed predecessor, the renowned Ruth Landes, had studied these *Neshnabek* during the mid-1930s. Because her work was still unpublished, I did not locate it in my library search. Nonetheless, a brief exchange of correspondence brought back in the mail two twenty-year-old manuscripts, one for her monograph *Potawatomi Medicine,* the second for her *Prairie Potawatomi.*[3]

The first of these instantly threw me off balance. *Potawatomi Medicine* opened with the line "Not often can even a simple culture be understood from the clue of one powerful bent." Landes followed this lead with a full description of a community menaced, oppressed, and abused by a class of sorcerers. The sorcerers she met and described were private practitioners who regularly bullied, intimidated, and magically assaulted their victims, then boasted publicly of their evil exploits. Magical "hooliganism," "terrorism," Landes called this openly avowed diabolic wizardry, and her key informants (themselves self-proclaimed perpetrators) gleefully applauded her assessment.[4]

More than a year of close observation and in-depth interviewing by myself, my wife, and several keen-eyed apprentice anthropologists had detected no hint of any such occult oppressors. We had closely studied the Dream Dance religion's seasonal rites, funeral and naming rituals, peyote religion sessions, and assorted other religious ceremonies and beliefs, even interviewing the only three remaining adherents (an elderly Ojibwa married to a Prairie Potawatomi woman and his two adult sons) of the classic *Midewiwin* (the Grand Medicine Lodge). I knew the Prairie Band community was perennially embroiled in a noxious internal conflict; however, this was a secular affair fought out in the political arena, covertly as well as publicly. But not the slightest glimmer of anything like the terror tactics of a gang of arrogant sorcerers had come to me, not between 1962 and the summer of 1963.

I was faced with the classic ethnographer's dilemma: Anthropologist Masterful studies Community Hermetic and discovers cultural patterns X; then Anthropologist Proficient studies the same Community Hermetic but describes a dramatically different ethos Y. I was not personally disposed to prosecuting a *Derek Freeman* v. *Margaret Mead* style indictment before the court of Anthropological Loyalties.[5] At any rate, had I been so inclined, Ruth Landes was alive, vigorous, and would have clobbered me had I been so presumptuous. Plus, in my own training I was taught to expect just such contradictions. Hadn't my teacher, Robert Redfield, responded civilly and intelligently to the contrary findings of Oscar Lewis in their separate studies of Tepoztlán with the suggestion that he had asked, "What made these people happy?" whereas Lewis was asking, "What made them miserable?" Even more sensibly and recently, when Jack Fischer and Ward Goodenough discovered they had produced opposite conclusions about Trukese social structure, they put their heads together cooperatively to find out why so, pushing anthropological methods and theory forward a notch in the process, not dishonoring themselves by academic foul play.[6]

How could I explain the differences between what Ruth Landes found among the Kansas Potawatomi in 1935–36 and what I had learned about this same society in 1962–63? In part, I surmised, we started from different conceptual premises and asked unmatched questions in our separate ways. Her opening line in the *Potawatomi Medicine* monograph was a theoretical giveaway, I recognized. The comment about a "single powerful bent" characterizing Potawatomi culture, I knew, reflected classic Benedictine configurationalism in its heyday. Landes was viewing Potawatomi culture through the evil eyes of this community's sorcerers, much as Ruth Benedict had greatly simplified the Zuni "Apollonian" ethos by overemphasis on the ideals of that Pueblo's priests.[7]

By itself this assessment was not enough. It left me still at square one. For with much detail Landes had described the attitudes, behaviors, styles, and tactics of a good many *named* Potawatomi sorcerers, and I had encountered and heard of none. How had I missed them? Or, where had they gone? Knowing that in 1935–36 Landes's mystic hooligans were mainly elderly men, most long dead by my time, was no help. They should have had successors. So, substantial social and cultural change in the intervening decades was another possible explanation. Nonetheless, if Landes witnessed these mighty terrorists, however much she might have exaggerated their significance, there were some nasty sorcerers—in her time. Where stood Potawatomi sorcery in the 1960s?

And so that summer, on the stifling prairie lands making up the Potawatomi reservation, I went on a witch hunt. Now, finding a sorcerer when an anthropologist wants one is easier said than done. Flat out questions directed to respected informants—"Show me a sorcerer," or "Identify a witch for me, please," or "Tell me all you know of witchcraft"— bring only flat denials, disclaimers, or declarations of ignorance. A standard evasion was, "Well, there may have been somebody with power like that in the old, old, days, but not in my time." Part of my problem was that I had been concentrating on the sunny side of the Potawatomi ethos, I came to understand. So the people I knew best were letting me see only the good stuff. My new task was to penetrate into what anthropologists sometimes call the "back regions" of this culture. To do this I had to shift my research gears. The subject of sorcery, especially when dealing with reluctant (maybe intimidated?) true believers, had to be approached like an annoyed wolverine: obliquely, cautiously.

Since sorcery involves cultural commitment to a theory of intolerable, otherwise inexplicable calamity, that was the indirect trail I had to take with my prodding.[8] Among these *Neshnabek* were people with chronic illnesses cured or alleviated by neither American nor Potawatomi therapists. And there were many curious accidents, mysterious sudden deaths, and other baffling afflictions. Persistently asking about the "real causes" of such hardships eventually paid off. Soon I had collected many hesitant, fragmentary admissions (possibly . . . maybe . . . I'm not sure, but . . . people say . . . some still think, not me) that there was still around "somebody owning" the old malevolent powers like those bad actors Landes had known and described.[9]

But specific accusations there were none. No Potawatomi would point a blaming finger. Named wrongdoers? Not one. When I insisted on asking for an identification, people looked the other way or changed the subject, nervously so. I realized I was treading on a source of high anxiety, for no one scoffed or played the skeptic. The consternation, even fear, provoked by my inquiries itself was clear evidence of at least some continuing belief in the power of sorcery as described by Landes, no matter how few or submerged the actual practitioners might now be. Uncertainty and unpredictability were what plagued these *Neshnabek* most. And insecurity was precisely that mood which Potawatomi sorcerers played on for their own malicious purposes. No one was willing to risk their own welfare by being first to speak an accusatory name. Retaliation, I understood from Landes's pages, was what vengeance-minded Potawatomi conjurers most relished. In the end, Whirlpool Woman and Downward Lightning set me straight. "You'll have to figure it out for yourself," I was admonished—flatly, with finality.

Figuring it out for myself required some disciplined thinking, the sorting of information, and contextualizing. The power and reputation of sorcerers accumulates with age. So, because the Potawatomi cherish great age, almost putting their well-scrubbed old folks on outright display, which elder males still living on the reservation were rarely seen in public? Of those, *Menisi* was one of a scant few. Of these, which had no kin willing to show him off or to speak proudly and lovingly of him? Here, *Menisi* was nearly alone. Who closely held and would not share some object of general ritual significance much valued by the Potawatomi? Once more Swoops Down—he had the Old Flat Drum and kept it to and for himself. There were no other suspects I could identify. All circumstantial evidence pointed straight to *Menisi*. Asocial he surely was. Was he also supremely antisocial?

My deducting done, I sought confirmation: obliquely, cautiously. "I've found out where Swoops Down lives," I mentioned to Watching Over, hinting I might drop by for a pleasant chat. "I wouldn't if I were you," he retorted emphatically, adding, "He's got a *bad* reputation." "What kind of a reputation?" I probed. "Well, you know, the old people used to say he maybe could steal a man's tongue." (*Aha! A Potawatomi sorcerer's favorite trophy was his victim's tongue.*) "How about driving out with me and introducing me to Swoops Down?" I asked Half

Day Sky. "Not me!" he responded. "Next week I'm going out to talk to *Menisi* about the Old Flat Drum," I told North Wind Woman, committing myself firmly. "Don't go out there alone! Don't let him look you in the eye! Don't go there after dark! Don't go in that shack of his with him!" she worriedly counseled. Oh that I might have had sense enough to follow all of North Wind Woman's grandmotherly advice!

Now better equipped to identify and chase my prey, I turned to trusty Young Dawn Man. If anyone around had supernatural power equal to some time-worn witch, it was he. "I hear Swoops Down is a shape-changer, that he claims he can hurt people," I suggested.[10] "Yup. Maybe so. Some people say that," he responded noncommittally. "I'm going out to his place tomorrow to see the Old Flat Drum, talk to him about things," I said, suggestively. Abruptly, Young Dawn Man sat up straight and leaned forward, sighed with resignation and cautioned me. "Clifton," he said, "he's got the power. He's killed thirteen people we know of, two just last year, and sickened plenty more. And he *brags* on it." The implication was *Menisi* had power enough to flaunt his triumphs, but Young Dawn Man, proper Potawatomi, was not about to tell me flatly not to go. A man will do what he's gotta do, was his philosophy. I was on my own. He concluded his admonitions: "Clifton, *we* don't mess with Eagle power!"

Forewarned, if not forearmed, the next afternoon I set out to corner *Menisi*. No flicker of vigilant doubt troubled my mind as I drove west along the gravel section line road. "Technique was everything," I advised myself. I drew near the turnoff. "Approach him gently," I rehearsed, "politely, indirectly, respectfully, firmly." I cut right, down a disused dirt road, doing my inventory while watching the ruts and humps: "Got everything I need—questions, note cards, ball-points, some Prince Albert and roll-your-own papers if that's his smoke, two packs of Luckies if he prefers tailor-mades." In the back of the dusty Chevy wagon was my ace in the hole: a cooler with a six-pack of Miller's High Life on ice, complete with church key. "I'm prepared for anything"—optimistic, poised, experienced. "Shoot, one sharp rational Ph.D. can handle one shabby braggart of a 'witch' any day. This old buzzard will soon be wagging his tongue for me."

The "road" soon narrowed into an overgrown footpath. Parking, I knelt to put my tracker's eye on the trail, searching for spoor. "Hmm. No sign. Not used for a couple of weeks, anyway. Not since the last rain. Is this turkey home?" Starting down the path afoot, every so often I called out: "*Menisi. Menisi!*" No answer came in the midafternoon heat. After a hundred or so paces I walked into a clearing, centered on a long unpainted, ramshackle cottage—Bureau of Indian Affairs modern, vintage 1905, never repaired since, sagging porch, holed roof, cracked windows, and all. I called out again, hearkening to a welcoming human voice or the unfriendly baying of hounds. Not a whimper.[11]

On my second circuit around *Menisi's* spread at last I noticed something promising. There a dozen yards west of the house lay a rusty iron bedspring. On the bedspring, face skyward, arms outstretched, was a form dressed in much bleached singlet and jeans, bare of foot and head covering. *"Menisi?"* I called. Not a murmur in return. "Has this old fart died on me?" I reflected. Stepping near, looking down at him, I could see the answer was no: wide open unblinking eyes staring upward but not seeing me, parched lips slightly parted though wordless—there *was* the faintest hint of respiration, but no response to my (unexpected?) coming.

Was he in a coma? In trance state? Meditating? Communing with his guardian spirit? Sunbathing? I was at the right place. He was old—*old* old. I had never seen him before. This had to be my quarry. None other. There lay Swoops Down himself in the sun-bronzed flesh like a Hindu fakir on his bed of nails, pondering some Potawatomi nothingness.

Polite, imperturbable, unswervable anthropologist, I presented myself. *"Bozhu, Bozhu,"* I said in greeting. "I'm Jim Clifton." Not a wink. "I'm Professor James Clifton from the university." Not a blink. "I'm the anthropologist who's been studying the *Neshnabek* the last couple of years." Not a twitch in response. "I hear you've got the Old Flat Drum . . . the one some folks call the 'Joker' or 'Vanilla.' . . . I'd sure like to learn more about that drum." Not the least breath of a comeback. None of my overtures produced a perceptible response. "Remember," I reflected with self-discipline, "there's nothing that unhinges an American more than a guy who won't chatter back in a two-person set. You're talking too much. You'll have to sit this sun-dried cow chip out." I cast around for something to perch on, spied a weathered milk bottle box, up-ended it a few feet from my uninformative informant, squatted, settled down, prepared to wait him out. The sun was now well past its meridian, falling toward the western horizon and into my eyes. I *had* forgotten something, my sunglasses.

Minutes passed. I grew restless. Another half-hour then three-quarters was gone. I was uncomfortable in the Kansas heat and humidity, half-blinded by the sun. Hauling out pipe and pouch I fired up, blowing a seductive cloud of smoke toward *Menisi*. Not a sniff in response. I waited a time, then displayed my presents: "Smoke? I've got some Prince Albert and papers." Not a whisker of movement from Swoops Down. I bided my time, puffing away, then tried again: "I've got some Luckies if you prefer them." Utter, total silence in return. An unsociable fellow, this one.

After another half-hour or so I grew restive. "Time's wasting," I reflected, "Now play your hole-card." "Pretty hot day," I observed coyly, adding, considerately, "You must be sweltering there. Happens I've got a six-pack of iced Miller's in the car. I think I'll have one. Care to join me?" There! Did I detect the least inclination of chin toward breastbone? A nonverbal affirmative? Surely it had to be. The old bugger was thirsty. I'd won the round. Gotcha!

Standing and stretching, I ambled around the house back to the car and broke out a pair of cold ones. When I returned, Swoops Down was still laid out, sizzling on his grill. I walked over, popped a cap, set the bottle down within *Menisi's* reach, turned, sat down again, opened my own Miller's, downed half the bottle, then resumed my vigil, refreshed and expectant. There lay Swoops Down, eyes still skyward, moist lips slightly parted—but where was his bottle? Nowhere in sight. Had he eaten it?

I swallowed the last of my beer, then glanced up. Swoops Down was standing outlined against the red flare of the setting sun. I stood and faced him. He stepped forward. I stood my ground. "Over six feet," I observed, "maybe one seventy-five pounds, not an ounce of flab on him . . . striking, aquiline features. A handsome devil." He stared straight at me, flat-faced, expressionless, eyeball-to-eyeball. Not to be put down, I held his gaze. *Menisi* now was up on tiptoes stretching sideways with both arms, flexing and rippling his muscles like some overage Charles Atlas. "Jesus H. Christ!" I thought, "Look at those pecs and lats. He must have been one powerful bastard when he was younger." Swoops Down then rotated his wrists, spreading then curling his fingers into hooked . . .

Suddenly this huge snarling Eagle dove out of the sun at me, sharp open beak thrusting at my face, talons slashing at my eyes! I was hit by a massive adrenalin rush. Heart pounding I leaped back, fell ass-over-teakettle on top of the milk box, hit the dirt, hard.

Flee! My old combat training asserted itself reflexively. I did a clumsy double combat roll sideways, out of the line of fire, searching for a hole, a hump, any cover to protect me from this shocking attack.

Fight! Quickly I scanned around, looking for a weapon—a club, a rock—anything to defend myself against that damned eagle.

What eagle? Heart still thumping I looked up half fearfully, protecting my face with one arm. There was no eagle. That miserable sorcerer was standing there perfectly relaxed, arms at his side, the hint of a sneer on pursed lips, glancing at me contemptuously with a glint of a satisfied malice in his eyes.

I stood, stepped to one side to get the sun out of my eyes, peered sideways at *Menisi*, and started dusting off my dignity. We both stood there for minutes more. Then Swoops Down stepped around me toward the door to his coop. After a few seconds hesitation, I followed—a respectful distance behind.

Once on his ramshackle porch *Menisi* turned and spoke for the first time. Like some suave maître d'hôtel he gestured gracefully—one-handed, palm upward—toward the murky interior of his lair. "You wanna see my drum? Come along, it's inside." Then, gesturing, "You first." Momentarily, as dusk gathered around us, I pondered this proposition. I had already ignored Young Dawn Man's sound advice, much to my embarrassment. And to my chagrin I had violated three of North Wind Woman's four commandments for dealing with *Menisi*. Should I hazard ignoring the fourth?

Clifton. Be sensible! Walk through that door and see the Old Flat Drum! What's to be afraid of?

Clifton. You're tired. It's been a long day. It's time for home and a hot meal.

"No thank you," I replied, "not just now. I'll take a rain check on that. *Mgwetch*—Thanks. Nice meeting ya." I turned and left, keeping an eye out behind me as I retreated toward the sanctuary of my car.

On the drive homeward I sorted out the day's experience. What had I learned? Although easily the best performance I had seen so far, old *Menisi*'s attacking eagle stunt was part of a larger pattern of Potawatomi expressive culture. These people were once masters of the fine art of animal mimicry, in public gatherings usually delivered as ritual dancing.[12] Twice, for example, at the end of an all night funeral ritual, near dawn, I had "seen" four Thunderbirds swoop in from the east, gather up the corpse, and carry it off to the west. That is, much fatigued and half-mesmerized by hours of thudding drum beats and monotonous chanting in a confined space, I had seen four highly skilled dancers impersonate the Thunders. Old Swoops Down was a master of this art form, obviously.

Oh! He had plenty more witch's tricks in his kit bag. For weeks I had been muddling around asking about and looking for a sorcerer. The moccasin telegraph surely delivered this news to him. He was waiting for me, waiting and ready. When Clifton the Gullible arrived, he'd out-silenced me, stalled until I was nervous, dehydrated, suggestible, half-broiled, and more than half-blinded by the sun. Then Swoops Down pounced on his prey. A man of impressive deeds but few words, he delivered up a vivid, terrifying sampling of his repertoire. I had come looking for a witch. *Menisi* had shown me one in action.

Rationally, I could understand—now the front end of my brain was working again—that his tricks included a bit of prestidigitation, more than a little skilled playing with my own autosuggestability, maybe even some ventriloquism with that screaming eagle bit, and above all that marvelous—ghastly—plunging-eagle body language. Later, using my forebrain, I could reason this out. But face-to-face Swoops Down by-passed his victims' logical faculties and struck directly at their deepest, irrational emotions. Landes had been entirely right. There be Potawatomi wizards here—at least one of them.

But there was a then and now historical difference between Landes's observations and my own. Then, in 1935–36, these Potawatomi were generations closer to the time when many shamans—good or evil as the mood suited them—walked the earth. Swoops Down was born at a time when they were numerous, presenting him with many mentors. 1935–36 was also the height of the Great Depression, when Kansas was the heart of the Plains Dust Bowl, its topsoil and riches blown away. Then the Potawatomi were experiencing stress and poverty almost unparalleled in their history. In that historical context there was an outburst of great frustration and hostility turned inward, encouraged and facilitated by Potawatomi men-of-power working against their own. Such circumstances were fertile ground for the remaining Potawatomi wizards, all older men acting out their anger and their ambitions for power amidst a community containing many much deprived ardent believers.

Now, in 1962–64, was different. In the meantime there had been major efforts at political and social reform from within this reservation community. The Potawatomi had never exactly rejoiced in the terrors the old-time sorcerers dumped on then. Over the years they had worked at suppressing such fearsome disorder, striving for a greater sense of well-being, more supernatural and secular peace and quiet. By my time, except for the solitary *Menisi*, the sorcerers were pretty much gone, although the beliefs that supported such roles were still present, at least latently. Without much commotion, the Potawatomi had effectively stifled the evil influence of those flamboyant men and their grandiose claims to supernatural power. Anger, hostility, frustration, competitiveness, and rivalries there were still aplenty, but these were acted out in secular contexts, more often than not directed at outsiders, not themselves.[13]

A year or so later my nemesis Swoops Down died (under suspicious circumstances, others hinted). He had no apprentices and left no trained successors. After his death, the drum he had hidden surfaced again, but it was not thereafter given much ritual significance.

As for this "Mystery of the Old Flat Drum," I might better have stayed home. There was no great enigma to it. Its chief significance was that *Menisi* had it and would not share. When it passed into other hands and onto the public scene, it no longer possessed much import. It *was* an old drum I learned later, though not a Dream Dance drum, nothing like it. What it was was a simple, undecorated, one-sided tambourine drum, of the sort that Potawatomi shamans has used in earlier decades during curing rites or divining rituals. It was an heirloom. At last, when the moment was opportune, I asked Young Dawn Man the questions I should have asked in the beginning.

"When you told me you might call that flat drum the 'Joker' or the 'Vanilla' drum, what did you mean?" "Just what I said," he replied. "You could call it the 'Vanilla' drum cause it ain't got no rules on it, nothing special about it. And you can call it the 'Joker' like in a deck of cards, 'cause you can use it instead of any of the regular dream drums."

Young Dawn Man's interest in the Old Flat Drum, like that of other Potawatomi ritualists, reflected their efforts to cope with some serious problems. Mainly these had to do with the staffing and performance of their Dream Dance rituals. Each of the six sacred drums was supported by a set of "offices" (ritual roles), which totaled 282. There were far too few suitably disposed adult Potawatomi in 1964 for each of these offices to be taken and played by a separate individual, hence there was much doubling and tripling up. Young Dawn Man himself sometimes acted as Staffman for one drum, then North Pole Drummer for a second, Speaker for a third, and Waiter for another, as each drum took its turn in the ritual rounds.

Even with some ritualists doubling in brass, assembling enough skilled, knowledgeable performers to act out the required roles for a major seasonal rite was difficult. Bringing together the needed ceremonial crew on short notice, such as for a fast funeral in midsummer, was often near impossible. This was so because each "officer" had to be fully versed in the entire myriad of complex prescriptions and taboos, the hundreds of songs, the many courtesies and special ritual acts "belonging" to each of the drums. The Potawatomi's problem with the Dream Dance religion in 1964, simply put, was too few ritualists, too many ritual roles and rules.

In the Old Flat Drum, some like Young Dawn Man saw a possible solution. It was a drum with no rules whatever and no established offices "belonging" to it. If they could bring it into the public domain, the leading ritualists might be able to convert that venerable shaman's drum into a suitable liturgical instrument, one that could be used for a quickie funeral or an ad hoc naming ceremony, perhaps even a poorly atttended midwinter seasonal rite, whereupon there would be no worry about "not getting it done right." All of the talk about the Old Flat Drum I had noted represented an ongoing process of creative innovation. The Potawatomi were busy trying to invent a new religious tradition, one better fitting their circumstances in the mid-1960s.

The demise of active sorcerers and the rise of the Dream Dance rites as the Kansas Potawatomi's central religious institution were connected, I realized at last. The former represented successful efforts to suppress the influence of those who threaten with disruptive evil doing, the latter efforts to promote consensus and community well-being. Whether this good versus evil dialectic represented a durable ritual substitution, a recurrent, cyclic ebb and flow, or neither, I cannot say. A quarter century later, this is for someone else, double-checking Landes 1935 and Clifton 1964, to discover. But I do have some prudent, personally tested advice for any such venturesome, maybe overconfident young anthropologist: Why take unnecessary chances? *Don't mess with Eagle power!*

NOTES

1. The traditionalist Potawatomi I knew in Kansas resented (or feared) having their names used in publications, and I promised never to do so. All personal names used in this essay are pseudonyms. They are authentic clan names borrowed from pretwentieth-century historic figures. However, the Potawatomi for centuries have regularly bestowed the names of the dead on newborn children, so there may be living individuals with these same names. If so, they are not the people I write about here.

2. The ethnonym, or self name, of the people commonly called Potawatomi is *Neshnabek* (pl.).

3. Landes's studies were later published as "Potawatomi Medicine," *Transactions of the Kansas Academy of Science* 66 (1963): 553–599, and *The Prairie Potawatomi: Tradition and Ritual in the Twentieth Century* (Madison: University of Wisconsin Press, 1970). For more on Potawatomi sorcery, also see Alanson Skinner's *The Mascoutens or Prairie Potawatomi Indians,* Bulletin of the Public Museum of the City of Milwaukee, vol. 6, no. 1, p. 1 (1924): 204–209.

4. The public boasting about their exploits of self-proclaimed sorcerers characteristic of the traditional Potawatomi and related Algonquian peoples is rare elsewhere in the world. Witchcraft (or sorcery) is ordinarily a theory of misfortune. Those accused of being witches are thus scapegoats, ill-fated innocents for some reason suspected or accused by people who feel themselves mysteriously aggrieved for suffering a calamity. Potawatomi witches were different: They were the self-confessed *enemies* of society.

5. For a discussion of this travesty of academic justice, see Lowell D. Holmes's *Quest for the Real Samoa: The Mead-Freeman Controversy and Beyond* (Westport, CT: Bergin & Garvey, 1988).

6. See Jack L. Fischer, "The Classification of Residence in Censuses," *American Anthropologist* 60 (1958): 508–517.

7. Ruth Benedict, *Patterns of Culture* (Boston: Houghton-Mifflin) and John J. Honigman, *The Development of Anthropological Ideas* (Homewood, IL: Dorsey), pp. 169–179, 203–208.

8. For an excellent overview of the subject, see Lucy Mair, *Witchcraft* (New York: McGraw-Hill, World University Library, 1975).

9. Traditional Potawatomi believed that the power of sorcerers derived from ownership of a special, evil "medicine bundle," a decorated animal skin containing powerful charms and fetishes.

10. Traditional *Neshnabek* were convinced sorcerers would assume the shapes of various animals, mostly at night, to work their evil deeds.

11. Potawatomi witches/sorcerers were thought to own particularly ferocious dogs. So far as the author is concerned, all dogs are vicious and never to be trusted however harmless their owners. In any event, in *Menisi's* case, one should beware of the master, not the dog.

12. The film *Neshnabek* contains some brief black-and-white scenes of Potawatomi animal mimicry in brief clips of clan feasts. If viewers watch closely, they can see Potawatomi men shambling like bears and stalking like wolves. This film is an edited montage of footage shot about 1936–37, and is available from the Department of Anthropology, University of Kansas.

13. A full scale ethnohistorical treatment of the background of these events and developments is in the author's *The Prairie People: Continuity and Change in Potawatomi Indian Culture, 1665–1965* (Lawrence, KS: Regents Press of Kansas, 1977).

FIVE

🌀 A Very Bad Disease of the Arms

MICHAEL KEARNEY
University of California, Riverside

As a graduate student in the Anthropology Department at Berkeley in the mid-1960s I decided to go to southern Mexico to do my doctoral research. I had spent a previous summer in the Sierra Juarez of Oaxaca, and it was to this general area that I decided to return. After reconnoitering for several weeks, I chose the town of Santa Catarina Ixtepeji and took up residence there. Ixtepeji is splashed on the northern side of a rugged ridge high in the mountains east of the valley of Oaxaca. Winter days and nights are crisp and clear, but weeks can pass in the summer months without a ray of sun penetrating the dense fog and mists that shroud these high retreats.

At that time I was interested in relationships between the world view of the people of Ixtepeji and their social structure and environment. My primary ethnographic task was to discover the basic structure and content of the Ixtepejanos' world view. My theoretical perspective then, as now, was that the contents of a world view are largely a reflection of the lived in social and material environment (Kearney 1972, 1984). I also assumed that a dialectic relationship exists between world view and the social and geographic environment in that, insofar as human behavior is shaped by world view, it alters, it creates to a great extent, that very environment which is reflected in the world view. I thought of my own world view as scientific and materialist and quite consciously accepted that my perspective was the lens through which I was refracting the very different world view of the people of Ixtepeji.

What most fascinated me was that I and the Ixtepejanos could walk the same streets, abide in the same houses, eat the same foods, and yet live in such different cognitive universes. With my comfortable background and my financial and cultural capital resources, I faced each day with a sense of security and control over most conditions affecting me. I attributed my fortunes in life compared with the poverty of my hosts to the fact that our respective ancestors had been born into and swept along by very different currents of history which had been further textured by accidents of biography. They for their part attributed their lot in life to "fate," "the will of God," the intrusion into human affairs of spirits, and to the malevolence of witches and other "bad people."

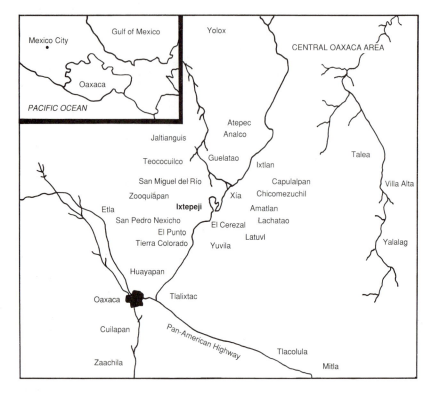

Ixtepeji, Oaxaca, Mexico

I came to realize that they perceived their world as virtually saturated with harmful, even lethal immaterial forces. The most potent of these were "bad airs" that could be sent into one's body by witches. Witches themselves personify evil and malevolence. They rely on deception and stealth to penetrate their victims' defenses. Some are thought to transform themselves into seemingly harmless animals and in this form do their evil. The most insidious of all may even take on the form of a person trusted by the victim and, so deceiving him or her, do that person great harm. Others can use black magic to send airs across town to harm or kill.

This then was the exotic and very different mental world in which my Ixtepejano friends and informants lived and which I was fascinated to document and to explain. Never for a moment did I doubt that these fantastic concepts and experiences of theirs were anything but the contents of a "nonscientific" world view. Ixtepejanos live in a world where death, suffering, and economic misfortune are common. Crops often fail, and dysentery and other diseases are endemic, and mortality rates of children and adults are high. These are conditions that demand explanations. To my mind they were all concomitants of "underdevelopment": the Ixtepejanos attributed these misfortunes to airs, witches, or the will of God because they did not have in their ethnoscience any notions of germs, much less an appreciation of the relationships between contaminated drinking water and dysentery. Nor, I surmised, did they have any sense of class analysis, nor any perspective on their lot in life that is afforded by a knowledge of Mexico's colonial past and its position in the modern global economy. In short, it never occurred to me that their fantastic world view might have anything more than a certain metaphoric validity. It well reflected their precarious and dangerous existence, but did not, I was certain, accurately explain it. My complacence was soon to be shattered.

One morning after I had been living in Ixtepeji for about six months I was walking across town to resume talking with an old man who had been telling me his life history. I was lost in thought about the direction I wanted our dialog to take when I looked up to see a very anxious woman standing in front of me in the rock-strewn street. Wringing her hands she spoke to me in whispers with furtive glances to one side and then the other. I recognized her immediately as Doña Delfina, one of the two most notorious witches in town. Because I was interested in witchcraft and folk medicine I had tried some months before to get to know her, but she had rebuffed me in no uncertain terms. But now here she was seeking me out. "Señor Miguel, you're a stranger from far away and you certainly have much knowledge. You can perhaps help us with a terrible problem that we have in our house." I immediately forgot about my planned chore for the morning as my mind raced with expectations of getting to know this formidable woman and having her reveal to me the most esoteric and profound beliefs and practices associated with witchcraft.

"Well," I said, "I don't know, perhaps I can do something, but first please tell me what this bad problem is."

"Oh Señor Miguel, it's my sister-in-law, my brother's wife. She has a very bad disease in her arms, and she is going to die soon unless someone does something for her right away." Although it was a cool morning, she wiped perspiration from her face with her apron and implored me to come and look at her sister-in-law. With a naiveté born of inexperience and exuberance I agreed and followed her into her house where with little ceremony she presented the sick woman to me. Both of her forearms were ulcerated with deep ugly lesions that looked like infected third-degree burns. They were raw and oozing with pus and serum. The woman was in great pain and did not speak to me. Delfina explained that the condition was getting worse day by day and that her sister-in-law was now unable to grind corn or do any other household chores. I asked what they thought the cause could be, and she replied with the platitudinous "Only God knows."

I was at a loss to explain to them or to myself what this condition was and said that they should go and see the young doctor who was doing his tour of social service in Ixtepeji after having just graduated from medical school, but they said that he had left town for a few days. I then told them that the best thing I could do for her was to drive her down to Oaxaca City to see some other doctor. All they would have to do is get her several kilometers up the trail to the highway where my truck was parked.

"No, no. That's no good," said Doña Delfina. "Something has to be done right now. And anyway we're not going to take her to the doctor because they're no good for these kinds of things." Delfina was adamant about not going to a doctor, and when I asked her sister-in-law if she wanted to go to a doctor she morosely shook her head back and forth.

Since a doctor was out of the question, I remembered that I had up in my house an old can of army surplus sunburn ointment that I carried in my backpack. It had benzocaine in it, which takes the pain out of superficial burns and other skin traumas. I told them about it and suggested that we might put some on her arms for temporary relief. They both acted as if I had offered a miracle drug to a terminally ill patient and beseeched me to go and get this medicine. I did and gingerly daubed it onto the poor woman's sores. The anesthetic took effect almost immediately, and first the sick woman and then Doña Delfina were astounded. This was clearly, to their mind, very powerful medicine. They thanked me profusely and beseeched me to continue "the treatments." I came back that afternoon to see my patient and found that not only her general disposition but her arms were greatly improved. The wounds had stopped running and were only slightly uncomfortable. I gave her another treatment then and another that evening. By the next morning healthy scabs had formed over even the worst sores, and the woman was able to do light work. The following day she was completely recovered, and I was given credit for a "miraculous cure."

At that time I had an arrangement to eat lunch and dinner in the home of a friend of mine, Celedonio, who later become my compadre. As we were huddled around the fire after dinner a day or so after the "miraculous cure," he asked me to tell him exactly what had happened with Delfina. Word of what I had done had spread all through town. Feeling some not small sense of pride, I explained to him how I had responded to Delfina's request to cure her sister-in-law and how grateful they were that I had "saved her life." He looked at me incredulously and to my surprise asked me, "Why did you do that?"

"And why not?" I replied somewhat taken back.

"Because it was not a good thing to do," he said.

"It was not a good thing to help this poor woman who was suffering so?"

"You just shouldn't have done it," he said with a seriousness that irritated me because he seemed so unappreciative of my notable results.

"And so what was I supposed to have done, let this miserably sick woman die without trying to do anything for her?"

"You just shouldn't have gotten mixed up with those people," he said.

"And why not? I know that a lot of people don't like Delfina, but her sister-in-law is a good person and anyway she was suffering a lot. I had to help her." It all seemed very clear to me.

Then he leaned forward and said quietly, "You really don't know what was going on there, do you?"

Still somewhat indignant I said that all I knew was that a poor woman was in terrible pain and was maybe going to die and that perhaps I had saved her life.

Then he said, "I'm going to tell you what really happened so that you will know. The reason that she was so sick was because of your neighbor Gregoria." Gregoria, who lived in a house just across a small cornfield and above my house, also had a reputation of being a bad witch. What had happened, according to Celedonio, was that Gregoria had used black magic to take Delfina's brother away from his wife. Part of her strategy was to make his wife very sick and possibly to kill her. Just about everyone knew this except the contested man who was probably made dumb by poisons in his food and by other effects of Gregoria's powers. The proof was that he had been hanging around Gregoria's house and giving her money that should have gone to his wife and sister and also that his wife was dying. Delfina had been doing everything in her bag of evil tricks to get him back to their household, but to no avail. As Celedonio described it, these two titans of black magic were laying down artillery barrages of evil forces across the town and Gregoria, my neighbor, had been winning. Winning that is, he said, until I stumbled onto the scene and tipped the balance of power back to the other woman. Celedonio was thus not discrediting my cure but only taking me to task for my folly in having effected it.

"Until you came along Gregoria was winning. Now things have all changed. The husband is back with his wife and sister, and his wife is well again. Everyone knows what you did, and because of it Gregoria is very mad at you and you better be careful. Because she is so mean and hateful she will try and get you. You better be very careful."

"Oh come on. You don't believe in those superstitions, do you?" I said, appealing to his masculinity and budding sense of modernity.

"No, I don't—not very much," he said without conviction. "But just the same it's a good idea to defend yourself. Maybe you should leave town for a while until Gregoria calms down."

"Ah come on, Celedonio," I said, "you know that none of that stuff works, that it's all just a bunch of superstitions. That old woman can stick pins in dolls and burn them all year long for all I care. As long as she doesn't come after me with a gun I don't care what she does."

"You may be right," he said, "But just to be safe, you better be careful, because who knows what she is doing to you."

I went home that night and didn't think again about what Celedonio had told me. The idea that Gregoria could actually harm me did not even occur to me as something worthy of much further thought. As it was I had plenty of other things to keep me occupied.

About this time something else happened in Ixtepeji that I later realized was to be part of my encounter with these malevolent women. A cargo truck went off the road above the town, and as it crashed down through the forest on the side of the mountain a man riding on the back was killed. Since Ixtepeji was the seat of the municipality in which the accident occurred, the dead man's body was brought to the town. To be removed from the accident site, the body was lashed onto two branches and carried in this fashion. One night and part of the next day passed before the body was removed from the site, and in the cold air it had frozen into its final posture—eyes open, knees bent, and one arm raised in front of its chest as if gesturing. Since the doctor had returned, the authorities directed him to do an autopsy. Because I was a friend of the doctor and had expressed considerable interest in his work in the town, he invited me to assist him with the autopsy. On a dismal and cold afternoon the cadaver was placed for the procedure on a rough-hewn table in a low adobe building behind the courthouse.

When the time came to begin the autopsy, the doctor cleared the room of all but myself, the municipal secretary who was to take the doctor's dictation in a corner of the room as far from the cadaver as he could get, and two women in their late teens whom the doctor had been training as his assistants. These two young women were to do the main work of the autopsy. As the doctor instructed them, they began by cutting the dead man's clothes off and then sawing off the top of his cranium. The doctor had no bone surgery instruments and had to improvise with old rusty carpenter's tools. It was only after considerable exhortation and cajoling by the doctor and finally his help that the young women were able to finish the task of removing the cranium. One of their lesser difficulties was watching the action of the saw and yet avoiding the cold anguished stare of the cadaver's lifeless eyes. But the worst part was the opening of the chest and abdominal cavities with the crude shears and saw. The cold, rigid arm of the cadaver was constantly in the way, and the girls were not put at ease by the doctor's jokes about how they were going to wake up in the night and feel that same cold arm around them in their beds.

I had dissected animals and human cadavers and seen any number of surgical procedures but found myself feeling progressively more uneasy as the autopsy continued into the night, which was only lighted by a couple of smoky lamps. This unembalmed, unshaven body with its foul odors in this lugubrious setting was altogether too disagreeable for my tastes. When at last the final stitch was sewn in the cadaver's leathery skin with a large needle and twine, I was more than ready to escape out into the night air and see the reassuring glow of fireflies. But for the next few nights my sleep was disturbed by the dead man's swarthy face with its dark purple contusions and crown of Frankenstein-like sutures.

After about a week or so I stopped thinking about both Gregoria and the dead man, as I became absorbed in my work. In Ixtepeji most of the town goes to bed with the chickens, and I was accustomed to sit up late in my one-room adobe house on the edge of town and write and read at a small table that I had the local carpenter make for me. One particular night was not unlike most others in the late summer. Dense clouds blanketed the town blotting out the moon and stars. Cornstalks rasped against the wall of my house in the cold breeze that blew down the mountainside. Inside drafts made my oil lamps flicker and throw bizarre shadows on the walls. Mice scurried about in the rafters, and dogs barked and howled both near and far. But aside from these noises all other sounds in the town were dampened by the fog. I was writing some notes or possibly a letter when I became aware of an itch on my left forearm that eventually demanded scratching. My first thought was that I was being bitten by fleas again—a recurrent problem that required dusting my bedding with flea powder. The two cotton shirts, a sweater, and a jacket that I wore against the damp cold prevented me from scratching well and eventually I had to remove the jacket and roll up my sleeves to get at this persistent "fleabite." What I saw when my arm was exposed caused me to fall into a state of stark terror.

There on the side of my arm were several large angry welts. And not only that, they seemed to rise up and grow as I looked at them. Immediately the image of the chancrous arms of Delfina's sister-in-law exploded into my mind and right after that the realization that Gregoria's house was only some fifty yards away through the fog. The immediate assessment of the situation that, against my will, spontaneously rose into my consciousness was that "she's got me!" While I had been sitting complacently in my little house she must have been, as she was probably at that very moment, doing something to kill me. A weak voice that I recognized as my rapidly fading rationality said, "Bullshit." And then there came into my mind's eye the horrendous, contorted, and bruised face of the cadaver and the overwhelming fear that tomorrow I would be lying on that rough table as the ribald doctor directed my autopsy with those crude carpenter's tools. One part of me castigated another by saying, "Why didn't you leave town while you had a chance like Celedonio told you to, while you were still alive?" My mind began to race like a motor with its throttle stuck while I witnessed the disintegration of my own rational, scientific, materialist world view. The unsuppressable assertion rose into my mind that it was all false, that the people among whom I had been living with what I had assumed were quaint backward customs and superstitions were aware of and in touch with knowledge and forces with which I was in no way prepared to deal. I feared for my life as I never had before. It was going to take more than some sunburn ointment to save me.

This state of absolute terror lasted for I don't know how long, perhaps thirty or forty seconds, perhaps several minutes. Then slowly I began to struggle against it. I thought about fleeing to Celedonio's or to one of my neighbors. But I didn't want to go out into the pitch black darkness and have to stumble through the steep, dripping cornfields around my house. There was no way of telling what was out there—perhaps even Gregoria. But at the same time I desperately wanted to do this, to go to people who understood what was happening to me and who could possibly do something to save me. But another much weaker voice in me said, "What kind of nonsense is this; are you really going to capitulate to these superstitions?" And then too I thought that if I went for help, what would I say—"Help me, help me. I'm dying of witchcraft?" This seemed rather ridiculous—me the scientific anthropologist banging on someone's door and raving about being witched. But then as I looked at the welts on my arm I said to myself, "These are not superstitions." They were indeed very real facts, the kind that science is based on. And the inescapable hypothesis was that they were evidence of witchcraft. I was too preoccupied to think of it at the time, but much later I realized that I was then in a state of extreme cognitive dissonance. Reality was all askew. I had the most intense sense of being suspended between two different worlds. One was that of the rural Mexican Indians that I lived among, the other was my own world view, which until now I had never seriously questioned. But now it seemed different, not in me but back very far away in Berkeley with its abstract intellectual life and security. But now I wasn't in my comfortable little cottage in the Berkeley hills. I was deep in these dark foreboding mountains of dangerous and mysterious forces.

After I don't know how long I began to calm down as my own basic world view feebly started to come back into ascendancy. I heard a voice in the back of my mind asking in what other way could this bizarre phenomenon be explained and then I heard myself saying, "Maybe I've been hypnotized." My father had used hypnosis in his medical practice and had taught me how to attain anesthesia and deep relaxation. And, on my own, I had attained complete anesthesia for extensive dental work. I knew that by using hypnosis it was possible to moderate heart rate and even the temperature of the extremities. I was also generally aware of the hysterical conversion reactions that sometimes underlie cases of presumed witchcraft. I started to think that perhaps, just perhaps, I was suffering from such a conversion reaction and wasn't going to die a miserable death in these lonely mountains after all.

As I regained more composure I began to review my encounter with Delfina and her sister-in-law and what Celedonio had told me. I also started to think about all the cases of witchcraft that I knew of and the people who were said to have been made sick and died from it. I started to realize that while I had presumably been cataloging these events as interesting ethnographic data and then letting them fall from my conscious mind they must have been registering somewhere else in my memory to emerge on this night and to manifest themselves as this strange body language on my arm. I found this explanation to be extremely comforting since it continued to sweep away more of the fear and anxiety. Little by little the reality that I was experiencing became more structured by my own world view. And within a half-hour or so I had effected another "miraculous" cure.

But gone now was the cavalier insouciance and pride that I had after curing Delfina's sister-in-law. More than this, though, I now had a much deeper appreciation of world view and of cultural differences in general. Whereas before these were intellectually interesting and analytically powerful concepts, now that I had seen my own world view temporarily shattered and in some way overwhelmed by another, the concept of world view and especially a concern with differences among world views took on a new significance for me. The next day, as I was thinking about my experience, I recalled a passage I had read a year or so earlier in Lévi-Strauss's *Tristes Tropiques*, which chronicles his fieldwork in Brazil. Somewhere in this very personal book he says that a person who had done ethnographic fieldwork is forever afterward a "marginal man." The ethnographer will never completely become a native because he will always acquire his new cultural perceptions as an overlay on his own natal culture. But then too, when he returns home to his own milieu, he will be seeing his world through eyes that have lost their innocence and now refract reality differently.

After my experience I was left with an appreciation of witchcraft that lent a new dimension to what previously had been a strictly intellectual grasp of it. Now the anxiety of Delfina, the terror of her sister-in-law, and Celedonio's concern for me were emotions and ideas that I had briefly experienced much as they must experience them. And furthermore, this appreciation of their realities gave me a new and much deeper appreciation of the intellectual task in which I was engaged. I became more enthusiastic about my fieldwork. It now was more real and exciting. I felt that my own disease of the arms was an important milestone in my work, that it was an indication that in some important ways I was starting to understand the reality of the people with whom I was living.

This experience has also colored fieldwork that I have since done in other settings. For example, in the 1970s I worked with a cult of spiritualists in Baja California, the main figures of which are mostly older women who in all essential ways are shamans (Kearney 1977, 1978). One of these remarkable women, Micaela, who was also one of my key informants, lived in a lonely shack in the hills outside of Ensenada. She was engaged in a constant struggle with a "bad woman" down the road. I first became aware of this conflict one morning when I walked from my campsite to have my morning coffee with Micaela. She was haggard and disheveled from not having slept that night. When I asked her what was the matter she said, "Didn't you hear that owl in the tree outside my house? It was Josefa who was doing that to worry me and make me sick."

For country people in Mexico owls are harbingers of death, and for Micaela the presence of this one was a serious assault. On another occasion I arrived at Micaela's to find that she had spread a ring of ashes from her stove all around her shack and the little chicken house along side it. When I asked her what the ashes were for, she said they were to see tracks and confirm that Josefa was coming in the night in the form of a coyote to steal chickens.

These perilous ordeals of Micaela and the fear and hatred she had of her neighbor made me think back to the battle between Delfina and Gregoria. Had I not gotten caught up in it I don't think I would have been able to appreciate as well as I did the intense, florid shamanistic experiences of Micaela and her spiritualist sisters.

In the first years that I knew Micaela, she lived with a man who was a hopeless alcoholic for whom she would buy pure grain alcohol in a drug store when we went into town. Eventually his health disintegrated, and for some weeks before he died he was incontinent and had severe dysentery. As he was unable to leave his bed, Micaela kept him in improvised diapers.

By chance I arrived in Ensenada the day after he died. Neighbors down the road had sent for an undertaker, and the graduate student with whom I was working and I found Micaela in the mortuary with several of her spiritualist sisters. The hearse was just leaving for the public graveyard as we arrived. At the cemetery we found a grave that was almost completely dug and got gravediggers to come and finish it. Since there had been no money for a coffin, his body was in a battered cardboard box tied together with strips of an old sheet. The sun had already set when I finally found two boys to help me and the elderly undertaker carry the box to the gravesite. The box kept coming apart such that our friend's head dangled out. The first time I saw his head come out of the box the face of the dead man in Ixtepeji came into my mind and with it a shivering remembrance of the intense awe and fear that gripped me the night I had the problem with my arm.

It was almost dark when we finally got him into the ground and found the gravediggers again and had them come and fill the grave. As we were zigzagging around the mounds of freshly filled graves on our way to the car, I was almost certain that I saw an owl silently float through the black silhouetted trees and out of the graveyard in the direction of Micaela's house.

REFERENCES

KEARNEY, MICHAEL

1972   The Winds of Ixtepeji: World View and Society in a Zapotec Town. New York: Holt, Rinehart & Winston.

1977   Oral Performance by Mexican Spiritualists in Possession Trance. Journal of Latin American Lore 3:309–328.

1978   Spiritualist Healing in Mexico. *In* Culture and Curing. Peter Morely and Roy Wallis, eds. Pp. 19–39. Pittsburgh: University of Pittsburgh Press.

1984   World View. Corte Madera, CA: Chandler & Sharp.

SIX

What Drives the Birds? Molting Ducks, Freshman Essays, and Cultural Logic

PHYLLIS MORROW
University of Alaska, Fairbanks

I once heard a rather succinct statement about differences in cultural logic from a Yupik Eskimo: "Before the white man came, we used to build our houses underground and bury our dead above the ground. After he came, we built our houses above ground and buried our dead below. We haven't been warm since." After a dozen years in the Arctic, I increasingly appreciate his observation, as I see more and more ways that each culture's assumptions about the way life "ought to be organized" create disorganization cross-culturally. What follows is a story not so much about unraveling the logic of another culture, which is never fully possible, as about discovering its pervasive, entangling presence.

But let me back up. I need to tell you how I came to be here, physically and philosophically, in the first place. I have vivid childhood memories of a favorite series of books about people around the world. I must have been very small when I first became fascinated with them, for their texture—a tactile, coated cloth—is as strong in my recollections as their content. Two, in particular, I studied over and over again. One showed pictures of classical Egypt, and the other "Eskimos of the Far North." Some days I imagined myself slaving away over a hot pyramid. Other days I wrapped myself in my mother's old fur coat and pretended to mush my dog team. I spent a lot of time wondering what life was like in such contrasting places. When my father returned from a business trip to Alaska in 1956, I was six years old. He brought me a seal-fur belt, adding more layers to my associations with the North, for I loved the distinctive smell of the leather, as well as the sleek, honey-colored fur. Although I never thought of going to Alaska myself, the place certainly had pleasant associations from the beginning.

Looking back at that childhood, it is no surprise that I chose to major in cultural anthropology when I entered college, but it was not until I was in graduate school, five years later, that I rediscovered the North. That summer, a trip to southwestern Alaska rekindled memories of the

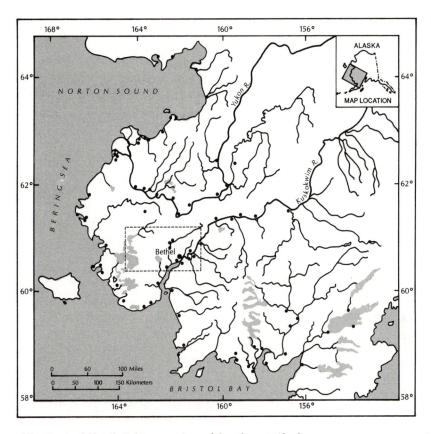

The Central Yupik Eskimo region of Southwest Alaska

ripe, oceany small of seal oil, introduced me to real people—Yupik Eskimos—and taught me that cultures are very complicated when met outside the pages of a textbook. I realized that this was where I wanted to do my fieldwork. I had no premonition that "the Bush" would be my home for the next decade and that I would soon marry and settle in Alaska permanently, although a friend of mine, accurately sensing that I might never return, begged me not to go. As I learned the Yupik language, I gained a deep respect for a group of people seeking a healthy integration of tradition and change and very tired of trying to explain themselves to "outsiders." This explaining seemed to take a lot of time when people would rather be out hunting or fishing. After a year in a village, I found myself enmeshed in language issues and particularly concerned with improving the interface between cultures through improved translation and cross-cultural communications. I took a job there, and I stayed, wrenching myself away only briefly ten years later to finish my Ph.D.

Now, as I reread my "field notes" (a motley collection of carbon-copied letters to friends, journal entries, maps, and errata) from that first

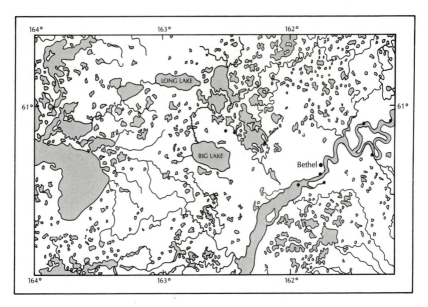

Big Lake and the "Tundra Villages"

year of living in a Yupik village, I feel a mixture of nostalgia and empathy for the hesitant outsider who tried so hard to make sense of what was happening to and around her. My training in anthropology had prepared me to look for the cultural patterns inherent in everything people do, yet my own patterns and those of the people with whom I lived were so subtle as to defy notice. Often, they just didn't seem to be there, until—but that's what my story is about.

It was our last day in the village, and we were packing to leave. Among our friends were John and Anna, a young couple who were still childless, like my husband and I, and who lived nearby. Anna and I frequently picked berries together, jigged for fish, and took long sociable steam-baths in the evening with her sisters and cousins. She was not a talkative person, but we had grown close simply through this companionship, and now she lingered around our disordered house, watching me sort possessions with an expression of regret. At one point she had gone home for a while and then returned to tell us that she and John were going on the communal drive for molting birds, out on Big Lake. This was the first we had heard of the drive, and by then familiar enough with communication styles to recognize an invitation, we decided to forget the packing and join the expedition. Soon we heard Gregory, a man of about fifty, announce the drive to the neighboring villages over CB radio, and another neighbor, having heard that we planned to go, had sent their young son over to accompany us. As we were to find out later, this was a standard way of assuring his family a share of the catch.

In a few hours we set out in a caravan of four skiffs: ours, John and Anna's, and several younger members of Anna's family. We were not going far as the crow flies, but the tundra is a flat expanse of marshes and tortuous sloughs, doubling back upon themselves so often that you seem to spend as much time facing your point of departure as your destination. We corkscrewed endlessly up the river, stopping our boat frequently to help John repair his eternally broken engine (at one point he had to hand-fashion a new pin with his pocket knife), to pole through shallow spots, and to wait there for others who would need our help. Whenever we pushed one of the heavy wooden boats through the shallows, we expected someone to act as the leader, to give us some audible cues—counting, grunting, or heave-hos—which would concentrate all of our efforts at the same moment. Either we missed these cues, or coordinated labor was not really critical, because somehow we all made it across. This should have given us faith in the apparent disorder to come, but at the time it just seemed curious.

Toward evening, we made a final bend in the river and found ourselves facing a vast expanse of water. It loomed like a gray inland sea, the bushes on the closest shores mere blips on the horizon. The far shore was invisible; we stared out over the curvature of the earth. For the first of many times we began to wonder exactly how the bird drive would be managed. A century-old account had told us that, on the marshes:

> Salmon nets are arranged by means of stout braces and stakes to form a pound with wings on one side; the people form a long line across the marsh and, by shouting and striking the ground with sticks as they advance, drive the birds before them toward the pound. As they approach it, the line of people converge until they reach the wings, and the birds, thus inclosed, are driven in and killed with sticks. (Nelson 1983:135)

We had no idea how this would translate into motorboats on this large lake.

We stopped, got out of the boat to stretch, and then hitched our craft to John and Anna's. We fired up our Coleman stoves in the boat, ate dried fish and drank tea, and then headed out to the middle of the lake, where we waited for the drive to begin. Eventually, from the lack of concerted effort, it became obvious that the drive would not happen that night, and John pointed out a spot across the lake where we would camp with several other boatloads of people about our age. A standard eight-by-twelve-foot canvas wall tent was set up with a tundra "tree" serving as a pole at one end and an oar, which was somewhat taller than the tallest available tree, at the other. Some people hooped other trees over their boats, lashed them to the sides, and covered them with tarps to make quonset-shaped shelters. Our little backpacking tent was viewed with interest but some skepticism by the younger boys. A smoldering fire of tundra moss set upwind from the wall tent provided a dense cloud of smoke, which gave some relief from the mosquitoes if you were willing to sit in the middle of it; the men quickly monopolized the tent, the only other spot that was relatively mosquito-free. After we tired of donating blood to the insects, one of the women decided to smoke the men out of the tent, which we did by discreet but assiduous applications of damp moss and waving of jackets. After they moved out, one by one, thinking that the wind had changed direction, we occupied the tent. At around eleven P.M., a young boy waved a freshly shot duck in the tent door, and we toyed with the idea of eating again, but decided that we should get some sleep before the drive. The boys, however, had figured out our earlier trick and decided to smoke us out of the tent, so we emerged, only to find a pile of feathers and six ducks in various stages of nakedness and disembowelment. The message was clear: We sat down to finish the job that the boys had decided was "women's work." After finishing the ducks in total darkness, a brief commodity in August, we fell into our sleeping bags, only to be awakened by daylight at four A.M.

Tired, but eager to begin, we broke camp and motored back out on the lake. By six A.M. we had not figured out what, if anything, was being organized and where the other boats were. We scanned the horizon with binoculars and pulled up broadside to other boats to ask people. "*Naamell*" ("I don't know"), they would shrug unconcernedly. When Gregory, who had originally announced the drive, passed, John asked if he was going to be the leader. Gregory said no.

John finally spotted boats some distance from us, and we decided to join them. Half an hour later we were sitting in midlake on a sickeningly pitching boat. It was a nasty windy day, with big swells and whitecaps. For a while we stayed with John, then stationed ourselves between some boats that seemed to be lining up across the vast expanse of water. And then we waited for something to happen. One hour. Two. Who was calling the shots here?

It was chill and the wind stiff. By 10:30 we were craving some familiar sign of action, rank, organization, command. We began to feel lonely. We had long since separated from John's boat, and the boats nearest us—still at some distance—were filled with strangers from other villages. At eleven o'clock, Gregory's boat plowed over to us, and he shouted that our end of the line was too slow and that when he passed again we should advance some distance. This was a great revelation, since we did not know that we were supposed to be moving.

Across the lake's great diameter, we could just barely make out boats, stationed at intervals of up to a quarter of a mile, stretching all of the way to the horizon. Wet and cold, we began a process whose end and progress we could not gauge. Most puzzling of all was the absence of birds. We had seen only four ducks all day, and they were flying, not being docilely herded across the water. It was only later that we learned that the number of birds in molt follows a bell-shaped curve and that it is possible to sweep the same lake three times over the course of a few days to maximize the catch.

Fighting the waves, which sometimes washed over the stern, and my stiffening fingers, I spent the hours trying to convince myself that the horizon was really horizontal, as it pitched and rolled rhythmically with the boat. Totally disoriented, I struggled to find the pattern to it all. What would this look like from the air? Why did everyone else still seem as uninformed as we? Like us, the occupants of others boats seemed to be just passing the time, hunkering under tarps trying to keep warm or dry.

For the next four hours we continued to sweep slowly over the lake. By four P.M., in an excess of fatigue and near-hypothermia, we pulled over to shore to rest and make tea. There, we discovered that others had dropped out for lunch much earlier; in fact, many had simply slept until noon. Others had just arrived that day; they had not camped. Discouraged, we realized that we had maximized all of the possible discomforts of this operation, including positioning ourselves on the roughest part of the lake.

Having seen a few other boats zipping toward the far shore and back, we decided, for lack of a better plan, to try that for a while. I had some fears that we were about to drive into the middle of the ducks, but since we had not seen any ducks that seemed vaguely unreasonable. Giddy with fatigue, I began to enjoy what had become an exercise in meaninglessness.

As we powered into the center of the group, we suddenly saw a thousand black, bobbing heads ranging across the bay and clearly moving toward a cliffed shoreline. Excitedly, we returned to our position in the line. This was obviously not the time to quit!

Over the next hour, boats began to converge. We counted seventeen craft. The apparently aimless boats moving across the front of the line and darting in and out of the center turned out to be "runners," whose job, we now saw, was to scare up the birds and to keep the boats moving in a uniform pattern. There had been difficulty in maintaining an unbroken line, we realized, because we were about the only ones dumb enough to stay in the midlake waves for long.

As we began to close in, more and more boats appeared, and there was a rush of excitement. Suddenly, from formless anarchy, sprang a precisely orchestrated structure. As we converged on the ducks, the runners began to shout and beat on the bows of their boats, drumming with taut wet anchor lines. Others joined in, a few at a time, beating on pots and pans. Now there were more than seventeen boats in a fairly tight arrangement across the end of the lake. It didn't seem cold to me any more, but I was reminded of the intensity of the wind by the fact that I could only hear the shouts and beating of sticks of those quite close to us. We drew in closer and closer, dropping anchor for a few minutes and then hoisting it to move in a few yards at a time. At long last we spotted John and Anna; John's motor had given out again, and this time we supplied him with fresh sparkplugs. It was good to be surrounded by familiar faces.

As we moved within about 150 yards of shore, I saw young boys picking up ducks that had escaped from the water and wringing their necks. The shouting and excitement increased. Now other boats began to dart in and out and around the swimming birds. The frightened animals dove and resurfaced, popping up and down in some confusion but still moving in a concerted pattern. By now we were in the shallows, and as we fought the water weeds tangled in our prop I understood why their Yupik name meant "imitation hair." The roaring outboards and the exuberant shouts made a great joyous din. This productivity, after twelve hours of suspense, this hungry anticipation of ducks in the cooking pot, excited us all.

Quickly, those who had brought salmon nets—six or eight boats—began to feed them out into the water. The other boats parked around the perimeter, and the occupants held the nets a few feet out of the water or tied the floatlines to their own boats. Yet others drove the birds into the one end left open. Then, in one swift move, the gap was closed and the nets encircled the prey. The rest of the boats moved in and ranged themselves broadside, and suddenly the boats and people, nets and ducks, seemed choreographed. The women and children held up the nets, facing in, low to the center, wringing the necks of trapped birds. Two men fired shots into the center from both sides, which frightened me since we were all facing each other. But this was merely to start the ducks diving into the nets, in a frantic effort to escape, for immediately we were wringing necks and disentangling ducks and tossing them rapidly into the boats, while the men stood facing out from the net in all directions, shooting at the escapees in a mad free-for-all of shotguns and whooping. The men were having a carnival time, the little birds popping up for a fraction of a second, while everybody fired at once, many at the same duck, and then immediately firing at some other bobbing head as they simultaneously teased each other about who had hit the previous one or who had hit it first. They shot again over and over, as fast as they could reload, their shotgun barrels heating up from the rapid fire.

After all of the netted ducks had been caught, several boats ranged off to catch, shoot, and retrieve missing ducks, while the boys continued to snatch those that had made it to shore at the base of the cliffs. We disengaged the final birds from the nets, and the net owners pulled them in. In each boat, there was now a random assortment of ducks, whatever the occupants had managed to grab.

I was totally fatigued, and gray from motion sickness. It had been twelve hours since I had been on land. Still, there was only a brief respite, for the ducks had to be distributed. We all sped back to the mouth of the river. Surprisingly, we were not far from where the drive had begun.

Disoriented by the apparent randomness of our long drift and by the enormity of the lake, we had not realized how systematically we had swept the lake's surface in the course of that long day.

Where we had stopped to eat the night before, people lounged on the ground near five piles of ducks. As each boat arrived, people tossed their ducks on shore, where two men rapidly sorted them according to species. Although we could tell that they were distinguishable, we did not know the species names in any language. For an hour, boats continued to pull into shore. When everyone had assembled, Gregory, whom Anna now pointed out with a slightly deprecating tone as "the boss," instructed one representative from each household to come forward. At first, only men approached, forming a big semicircle. Again, Gregory asked people to come forth, and the more reticent women and girls there as sole representatives of their households moved into the ring. Anna and I, represented by our husbands, sat back to watch. Near the end of the drive, I had counted thirty-eight boats; now there were over fifty people from seven different villages waiting for their shares.

Gregory directed three men from different villages to pass out the ducks. There was absolute equality of distribution, each family representative receiving the same number of each species, a total of eight, regardless of age or work contribution. Near the end of the distribution, when there were not enough to go around evenly, the lucky people who happened to be at one end of the semicircle got an extra bird, but it was clear that the goal was equality. Some people stayed afterwards to cook a communal feast, while others dispersed into smaller kin groups to camp another night or to drive back to their village. There were stories of earlier bird drives, of a lake now abandoned for drives because the supernatural humanlike beings called *issinrat* always spirited the birds away at the last minute, and speculation about why this drive had been less successful than others. Some drives yielded as many as fifty birds per household. Perhaps, people thought, it had been the combined effect of large waves, gaps in the line, and the earlier indecisions. Drives on Big Lake were often problematic, it seemed, when the wind came up. There was talk of doing another drive, on a longer, narrower lake, the following week. Exhausted, we went home to bed.

Later, I was to spend a great deal of time puzzling about how the bird drive had all come together in the end. Obviously, there were certain minimum requirements in my mental model for organizing a large number of people into a working group: acknowledged authority or leadership, efficient use of time, and a means for disseminating information and dividing tasks. Yet in the bird drive, the "leader" had denied being a leader, time had seemed irrelevant until the last hour or so, and everyone was about equally uninformed. On the other hand, none of this bothered anyone else, so the problem was clearly with my model.

The key seemed to lie in the characteristic tension in Yupik society between an egalitarian and consensus-based ideal and the need for leadership in many situations. On the one hand, experienced individuals are respected and emerge as situational leaders. On the other hand, putting oneself ahead of others is socially unacceptable, and anyone who professes leadership borders on hubris. In short, at the same time that individuals are pushed forward as leaders, simply because the need for structured organization is appropriate in some situations, those people are discouraged from acting like leaders. In this way, Gregory became both the leader and not the leader.

Second, a critical mass of people with the same goal in mind, enough of whom have done a similar task in the past to be familiar with it, is necessary to do the job. Each participant freely uses his/her own judgment (e.g., joining the bird drive at various points in the process, dropping out temporarily when the waves become too rough, and so on). If conditions are such as to permit the task to "happen," enough people will stay committed to the job to accomplish it. If not, they will vote with their feet. This amounts to an effective form of consensus decision making. There is no need for the group to gather, discuss and overtly plan a course of action; in fact, given the need for a flexible adjustment to wind, weather, geography, and equipment, such plans and discussions would be either impossible or counterproductive.

Emotionally, there was general acceptance of the assumption that things would happen when it was time for them to happen. In short, there was no frustration, because there was no arbitrarily imposed notion that the drive should happen within particular time limits. No wait was "too long," no conditions "too frustrating." One always had the options of leaving, of joining the process late in the day, or of simply sticking it out until the time was ripe. The bird drive, as random as it had appeared, was as orderly as it could be under the physical and social circumstances.

Not all visitors to the Kuskokwim region, however, come to appreciate the effectiveness of local ways. Over my year in the village, for example, I had heard villagers privately express innumerable frustrations at the insistence of various visiting bureaucrats that people commit themselves to attending meetings and making binding decisions about everything from school policies to land management.

This was, of course, simply not an appropriate way to decide important issues. People generally preferred to make decisions using a more time-consuming, but more participatory, process analogous to the one I have described. Even when this fact is explained to the bureaucrats, which it rarely is, being quite taken for granted, the bureaucrats have a difficult time adjusting their system to facilitate local control. Often, the outsiders go ahead and make decisions based on limited input and then draw mistaken conclusions about why more villagers do not participate in their forums. Meanwhile, the villagers feel that their opinions have not been solicited.

It is not just the process of decision making that makes me recall the bird drive, though. Oddly enough, I think of it in connection with the papers that Yupik Eskimo freshmen write when they enter the university. When I hear other instructors condemn their writing as illogical, I wish I could send my colleagues out on that bird drive, to give them some faith in the internal logic of systems other than their own.

For the principles of essay organization are as implicit in their "correctness" as are the principles of work organization. And, in order to appreciate that fact, you have to be willing to make the a priori assumption that the illogic may be in the mind of the beholder. How is it possible to develop such an appreciation? In addition to participating in such events as the bird drive and discovering that there is a happy ending despite your suspicions, one way is to become sensitive to the way stories are used in the culture. These oral forms give clues to the ways words may be used in written texts, at least by students who have not yet learned their professors' expectations.

Two simple examples may serve to illustrate this potentially complex point. One relates to the fact that many Yupik stories rely on an "if the shoe fits, wear it" sort of impact. Eating dried pike at a respected elder's house, I was once regaled with the story of how her sister came into a room where her children were eating and scolded them for not finishing everything except the scales. The story was not overtly addressed to me, but then again, I was the one person present who was not eating my fish skins. Remembering that fish and game return to be caught again only if humans show them respect by, among other things, using them fully, I dutifully peeled off the scales so that I could chew up and swallow the skins. Similarly, student papers often contain stories that, to the non-native reader, seem only tangentially related to the topic. The writer assumes that the connection will be clear; in a culture that honors individual autonomy by allowing people to either acknowledge or ignore a message, stating the point explicitly would be culturally equivalent to bludgeoning the reader. An added problem is, of course, that even if a non-Yupik reader realizes that he is being told to eat his fishskins, he is not likely to know why. The answers to this sort of question are in the broad context of cultural knowledge that the writer assumes, incorrectly in this case, to be shared. The answers are not in the text.

Having been surrounded by books all of my life, this lesson was a hard one for me to learn. It was brought home to me the day our outboard engine refused to stay in gear. Neither my husband nor I are mechanical wizards, but we have faith in our ability to figure things out, at whatever plodding pace might be required. So we did the logical thing.

We sat down in the boat, opened our owner's manual carefully on top of the covered engine, and were beginning to make some headway in identifying the problem on the trouble-shooting page when a Yupik friend walked by. "Maybe I should help," he offered, using a standard polite phrasing in no way meant to imply that we obviously needed it. He came over, moved the book, removed the engine cover, and revealed, to our immediate embarrassment, a broken part lying in lame isolation from the rest of the machine. "Maybe this is the problem," he said helpfully, with a pleasant smile. The incident certainly taught me something about mechanics—and about Yupik communication styles (we were thankful that he had spared us humiliation). It also made our differing orientations toward literacy quite clear.

The way that students corroborate objectively stated facts is another case in point. The analogous case in the oral tradition is illustrated by the story of a woman and her baby who were turned into rocks by a shaman: "This is true because I saw the rocks and they are indeed shaped like a woman with her child on her back." In the academic context, I have read papers that say such things as this: "Uayaran was a great warrior who lived a long time ago. He was trained to drink only the water which dropped from a feather dipped in it. When I was little, my grandmother never let me drink water when I wanted to." The apparent non sequitur is intended to explain Uayaran's training in the context of Yupik methods of toughening young boys. The writer saw no need to explain how the two thoughts connected; culturally, this is a straightforward juxtaposition and needs no elaboration. Furthermore, in this context, the traditional justification for the water restriction—"Too much water will make the flesh soft instead of firm," or couched in more obviously pragmatic terms, "A person must be self-disciplined in order to survive times of hardship"—may not be stated at all. To the writer and his presumed audience, these reasons are, in some ways, less important than the fact that the teaching itself is so time-honored. The message is: "It was done in Uayaran's day, and in my day, too. We have perpetuated this tradition, and therefore it is valuable." In this telling, too, the tradition is passed on.

If, at this juncture, you are beginning to feel that you could walk into an Eskimo village and interact with people, showing some understanding of Yupik ways, then perhaps I have done both you and Yupik culture a disservice. I began this essay with the statement that it is never fully possible to unravel another culture's logic, and I conclude with a repetition of that warning. In fact, there are layers upon layers of possible explanation here. The density of reality is always much greater than even the most subtle exegesis, and mine has been quite superficial. Just to add perspective to this statement, let me add that it is part of my cultural tradition, and not the Yupik one, to attempt such an analysis in the first place. "What drives the birds?" is not a Yupik question.

My point, too, is not that I can answer that question but that the question and my need to ask it are important things to ponder. This essay is not merely an interesting description of somebody else's way of thinking: Implicit differences in cultural logic make explicit differences in the way people are treated. If my colleagues see chaos where there is merely a different sort of order, then Yupik students get low grades. If bureaucrats see indifference to public issues where there is actually a preference for a different decision-making process, then public policy does not reflect public input. Try substituting the name of another ethnic group for "Yupik," and the point becomes a general one.

Fortunately, even a partial understanding of differences, such as the one I have sketched, helps me to understand my students' papers and to show them ways to structure their writing for non-native audiences. Perhaps it will make my readers, too, suspect that books—and essays like this—cannot sufficiently explain cultural systems. It always helps to try a different strategy, such as taking the engine cover off. At the moment you notice that something works for the participants although it seems to defy your logic, it may be time to look for another logic.

REFERENCE

NELSON, EDWARD
1983   The Eskimo About Bering Strait. Smithsonian Institution reprint.

PART TWO

Lessons from Fieldwork

SEVEN

Not a Real Fish: The Ethnographer as Inside Outsider

ROGER M. KEESING
Australian National University/McGill University

It was to be my first night in a Solomon Island village. . . . At Bina, on the west Malaita coast, where I had been dropped by a government ship, I unpacked my two backpacks before the gaze of all the village children and many of the adults. Out came the mosquito netting, then the Abercrombie and Fitch air mattress and its foot pump. I spread the mattress on the ground, screwed the pump into the valve, and pumped, but nothing happened, in front of the expectant crowd as the sweating white stranger pumped away. Finally, after endless fiddling with the valve and sotto voce cursing, Western technology at last unfolded its mysteries.

Awakening on the thatched verandah to find a steady rain, I watched where the locals were going off, along the beach and around the point, bent under pandanus leaf umbrellas, for morning pees. I followed the same path. I discovered only by later observation that it was the women's latrine; the men's latrine, separated (as I was to learn) even in such Christian villages by strict rules of gender segregation, was a structure built over the water. My hosts were too polite to comment on—or claim compensation for—what I later realized had been a massive breach of propriety.

There had been no way to learn any Pidgin in advance, and after less than a week in the Solomons I could scarcely communicate at all with the villagers (although a couple spoke a bit of English). By midmorning, the carriers arranged by the district officer to guide me across the middle of the island had not arrived. Eventually, in late morning I succeeded in persuading two young men to carry my bags and lead the way; but after an hour and a half of walking into the foothills they announced that they would take me no further. Not until I had spent another reluctant night in a Christian village could I persuade anyone to take me further.

The still pagan Kwaio of the mountains above Sinalagu on the east coast, who had perpetrated the 1927 massacre of a district officer and his

entourage,[1] were feared by the colonial government as wild and dangerous. Their hostility to outsiders, especially missionaries and government,
was legendary in the Solomons. Yet the lure of the mist-shrouded Kwaio
mountains had been reinforced a few days earlier as I had traveled down
the coast on a small ship with a Malaitan government clerk. "You
wouldn't want to go up *there*!" he advised me. "The people live in houses
on the bare ground, like pigs, and they don't wear any clothes!"

After conferring with the district officer, who claimed to know the
Kwaio and their mountain fastnesses well, it seemed that their potential hostility might best be defused if I approached their heartland from
a different direction than Europeans usually did: by land rather than
by sea. But with no maps, little information, and no way of communicating effectively, I was relatively helpless in seeking to enlist
cooperation and explain my intentions. All I knew was that I was supposed to get to a place called 'Aenaafou, which the district officer had
told me was the key midpoint on the path to "Sinerango."[2]

My guides the next morning set off, but not toward 'Aenaafou. "You
can't get there from here," an English-speaking Christian man had explained, translating for me. "The river is up." I had been in no position to
argue, and at least I was moving inland—and upward. For the next nine
hours, I struggled and sweated up and down precipitous paths: an hour
and a half of climbing straight upward to a long-deserted mountaintop
settlement site, then a plunge down the other side, on slippery red clay,
into the gorge below. Looking back at the maps (which in 1962 did not
exist), the maze of elevation lines shows this to be the steepest, most
broken terrain in the Solomons, almost vertical in many places. Rather
than following the contours, the path zigzagged from peak tops to water-
ing places a thousand or more feet below.

We did not pass a settlement all day. But exotic it was, not least of
all because my tour guides were two cheerful and pretty teenage girls,
smoking pipes and stark naked. They bounded up and down the path
like mountain goats; my fifty-pound packs were a trifle. At the end of
the afternoon, exhausted, I was led into a mountaintop clearing with
several thatch buildings. It was clear from the response of the men
gathered there, surly-looking and carrying long machetes, bows and
arrows, and clubs, that I was neither expected nor particularly welcome.
Trying to explain my presence through linguistic filters, I learned that
this was a marriage feast. I was told I would have to stay inside one of
the houses, from which I could only peek through narrow gaps in the
thatch. Having been warned by the government that I might well be
killed by Kwaio warriors, who had dispatched a dozen Europeans
through the years (and were to dispatch another, a New Zealand missionary, three years later), I was less than relaxed.

What followed through most of the night was uninterpretable and
often terrifying. Perhaps two hundred people, the women and many of
the men naked except for shell ornaments and woven pouches, streamed

into the clearing as dusk fell. Several times, a warrior clutching a machete or club ran screaming around the house from which I was peering, shouting with what seemed hostility; one chopped down a banana tree beside the house with fierce whacks. Shouts and speeches, then falsetto screams echoing out on all sides, naked bodies back and fro in the flickering firelight. Eventually, persuaded by the sheer lapse of time that I was not to be the main course and numbed by physical exhaustion, I strung my mosquito net in a corner of the house and collapsed into sleep, only to be awakened in terror when someone stumbled into my net and he and it collapsed on top of me.

In late 1964, after almost two years of fieldwork, I could look back and smile at my early anxieties and innocence. I had been to a dozen wedding feasts, had helped to finance some with my own strung shell valuables, and knew now about the conventionalized mock threats and food distributions that had terrified me that first time. I spoke Kwaio fluently and had been received by these fiercely conservative mountaineers with a warmth and enthusiasm that had been amazing. (Only later did I more clearly understand the extent to which I had, through accidents of history, been incorporated into their historic project of anticolonial struggle; when I arrived they were trying to write down their customs in emulation of colonial legal statutes, and I was to be their scribe.)[3] Taking part in feasting prestations, incorporated into kinship and neighborhood networks, allowed into shrines to take part in rituals,[4] I felt like a comfortable "insider."

But of course, I wasn't. I could never leave my own cultural world despite my partial successes in entering theirs. In fact, the lonely isolation, after ten months with scarcely a word of English (and mail service only once a month), was taking me near the edge of psychological balance. I choose two small episodes late in my fieldwork to illustrate both my precarious state and the unbridged and unbridgeable gulf between their world and mine. Both began while I was sitting in my thatch house typing field notes (I was very good about that in those days and have been degenerating every since).

As I sat typing one day, a wizened little man I hadn't seen before—he turned out to be from the mountains ten miles down the coast—slipped rather furtively beside me and whispered, "Come outside, I want to tell you something important." I put him off several times while I finished my journal entry, but eventually I followed as he led us secretively into a dark corner of an empty adjoining house. He leaned over to me and asked me portentously, in a hoarse voice scarcely loud enough to be heard, "Do you know where we all come from?" "What do you mean?" I asked. "Do you know where we Malaita people came from?" "Not exactly," I said, "but we're finding out something about that." "We all come from the same place, you Americans and we Malaita people. Do you know that?" Aha, I thought. A visionary glimpse of the human past. . . . I shifted into lecturing mode, and for five minutes or so I gave him a condensed explanation of the evolution of humankind and the prehistory of the Pacific. He heard me out politely. "I didn't think you knew," he said. "I'll tell you. You know that mountain at Iofana, beyond 'Ubuni—that's where we all came from. We Malaita people and you Americans." And then he gave *his* five-minute lecture, about the snake ancestress 'Oi'oifi'ona from whose eight human children the Malaitans—and Americans, by way of a migration to and beyond Tulagi—are descended. He was right. I didn't know.[5]

A few weeks later, I was again at my typewriter. I heard a commotion in the harbor a thousand feet below and went out to look. Loud voices, splashing of human—and other—bodies in the water. "They're driving *kirio* [dolphins] onto the beach and killing them," explained a local lad. A couple of minutes later, some young men from a settlement just up the hill came bounding down. "We're going down to kill a dolphin!" they announced. I was horrified: I had just been reading Lilly's early accounts of dolphin intelligence and had spent hours with my former teacher Gregory Bateson before I left California, discussing his plans for dolphin research. "Don't kill a dolphin! They're intelligent! They're like people!" I called out. But they paid no heed and went bounding down the precipitous path to the harbor.

Two hours later, they were back, carrying a huge leaf package. "We got one!" they called cheerfully. I was still horrified. Although Malaitans eat dolphins, that is a fringe benefit; they kill them for the teeth, which are used as exchange valuables and ornamentation. The young men unwrapped their package, to display a big butchered dolphin. I confess to a moment of ambivalence at the sight of red mammalian steaks—I had had no meat but an occasional strip of pork fat for months. But my outrage on behalf of a fellow sentient being far outweighed my urge for steak, and I abandoned my typewriter in favor of rhetoric.

"Don't eat that thing! You shouldn't eat *kirio*. They're not fish [*i'a*, in Kwaio]! They're like people, not fish! Look at its blood—it's red, and warm, like ours!" My friends went on cutting logs and building up a fire to heat the stones for a leaf oven, oblivious to my rhetoric (but giving me odd glances). My rhetoric was impeded somewhat by language problems. Dolphins may not be fish, but they are *i'a*. "But they're not *i'a to'ofunga'a*, 'real *i'a*,' I insisted (but they are: The category includes dolphins and whales as well as fish). The locals were unimpressed, so I reiterated the argument about warm, red blood. "And look," I said, "they can talk. *Kirio* can talk, they way we do."

This was too much, and they stopped building the fire. "What do you mean, they can talk?" I remembered that in the *Life* magazines in my house, there was an issue with a Lockheed ad showing a scuba diver tape-recording dolphin squeaks; and I bounded into the house to look for it. A few minutes later, I returned in triumph to the fire-builders, who had returned to the task and were heating stones. The ad was perfect. Fortuitously, the microphone the scuba diver was holding looked exactly like my tape-recorder microphone. "Look at this," I said. "The *kirio* is talking onto the tape recorder. They talk just the way humans do. That's why you shouldn't eat them."

At last, I had their interest. "We didn't know they could talk! How do you talk to them? What language do they speak? How can they talk under water?" I explained as best I could about dolphin bleeps and the efforts to decode them. But they went on with their stone-heating and then put the tasty-looking meat into a leaf oven. "You shouldn't eat them," I pressed again. "They're not like fish, they're like us. They're intelligent. They talk." But after the possibility of humans talking with dolphins had faded, so had their interest. But not their appetites. Eventually I went back to my typewriter, wondering why my logic and rhetorical force hadn't persuaded them to bury the poor kindred spirit rather than eating it.

Only after typing fretfully at my notes for another fifteen minutes did it dawn on me that until 1927, when the government imposed the *Pax Britannica* after the massacre, the Kwaio ate *people. . . . .*

Last year, a quarter of a century later, on my eighth fieldwork trip into Kwaio country, chewing betel and squatting around a fire reflecting with Maenaa'adi about the outcome of the divination he had just performed and the ritual about to be staged, I was still all I will ever be: an outsider who knows something of what it is to be an insider.

NOTES

1. See Keesing and Corris 1980.
2. The government had been getting all the place names wrong for fifty years.
3. See Keesing 1978, 1988; and Fifi'i 1989.
4. In the category of small-boy-who-doesn't-know-any-better, a status into which I was inducted after my wife's return to the United States at the end of 1963.
5. This episode was brought back to mind in 1989 during a session taping stories of ancient ancestors and human origins with the brilliant young pagan priest Maenaa'adi and my longtime Kwaio collaborator, the late Jonathan Fifi'i. During a pause, Fifi'i turned to me and said, "When I was in California with you [in 1966–67], I met some people who said they were descended from apes and monkeys. I thought that was really interesting. I'm descended from a snake."

REFERENCES

FIFI'I, J.
1989   From Pig-Theft to Parliament: My Life Between Two Worlds. R. M. Keesing, trans. and ed. Honiara: University of the South Pacific and Solomon Islands College of Higher Education.

KEESING, R. M.

1978   'Elota's Story: The Life and Times of a Solomon Island Big Man. St. Lucia: University of Queensland Press (2d ed. 1983, New York: Holt, Rinehart & Winston).

1988   The Anthropologist as Messiah. Etnofoor 1:78–81.

KEESING, R. M., AND P. CORRIS

1980   Lightning Meets the West Wind: The Malaita Massacre. Melbourne: Oxford University Press.

EIGHT

🌀 Centering: Lessons Learned from Mescalero Apaches

CLAIRE R. FARRER
California State University, Chico

INTRODUCTION

In 1974 my daughter, Suzanne, and I moved to the Mescalero Apache Indian Reservation in southern New Mexico where I was, with Tribal Council approval and partial living support, to do dissertation fieldwork for a Ph.D. in anthropology and folklore. The reservation is largely mountainous, although there are some high plains; elevation varies from 3,400 feet to just over 12,000 feet. The area was familiar to us: From 1961 through 1971 my former husband and I had lived in Alamogordo, a small town about thirty-five miles from the reservation, and our daughter had been born there in 1962.

The reservation covers roughly 720 square miles and is the homeland of approximately 2,500 people, of whom about 85 percent reside there at any one time. Three ethnic/linguistic groups (Mescalero, Chiricahua, and Lipan) live at Mescalero; they are self-consciously separated by speech and designs used on clothing. But, in truth, the languages spoken are mutually intelligible and the design differences function as markers of family pride. These Eastern Apaches are matrilineal but have no clans, as do their Western Apache and Navajo "cousins." Fathers' lines are important and remembered, too, especially if one has a famous warrior or head man in one's lineage. But it is to the matrilineage that one owes primary allegiance and where the majority of affective ties are reported.

While there are a few wealthy people on the reservation, most people work at wage-labor jobs in nearby towns or at Holloman Air Force Base near Alamogordo. The Tribe has the goal of providing jobs for everyone who needs one, but that is not yet reality. Many do, however, work for the Tribe directly: in the Tribal administrative offices or in Tribal enterprises such as the cattle industry, sawmill, or fish hatchery. But most who work for the Tribe are involved in tourism. The Tribe owns and operates a large, elegant resort, the Inn of the Mountain Gods, and a very popular ski area, Ski Sierra Bianca. Additionally, some people work as conservation officers or big game guides with a few also working for the Bureau of Indian Affairs (BIA) or other federal agencies, such as the Bureau of Land Management (BLM). Preferred jobs, however, are with the Tribe.

My first contact with the Mescalero came through my former husband, who had employed a reservation man in his lab. The man invited us, in 1964, to the reservation for a summer ceremonial where I met his wife. That contact began what was to become the focus of my anthropological work. I still return to the reservation each year and, in between visits, maintain contacts with our adoptive family as well as with friends.

"Centering: Lessons Learned from Mescalero Apaches" is taken from my field notebooks and personal journals over a twenty-five-year period, for I do not always learn quickly.[1] At the request of the individuals, all names have been fictionalized except for Second and Evans, those in the family that adopted my daughter and me in 1975.

1964: THE FAMILY AND THE CENTER

Annie Brownfeather had told me to meet her after lunch the next day when we parted the night before, as my little family left the ceremonial grounds to comply with the Anglo curfew. She didn't tell me where to meet her or what I was supposed to be doing. Yet my curiosity had been piqued sufficiently during that girls' puberty ceremony as we watched the spectacular Mountain God dancers, with their tall headdresses and bodies completely covered with paint, masks, kilts, and moccasins. So, with Suzanne on my hip, I showed up the next afternoon looking for Annie. One of the women cooking in the long, oak-boughed cooking arbor directed me to a camp just to the south and east of the ceremonial mesa.

Camps, erected for the summer ceremonial, consist of tipis, tents, and arbors oriented toward the ceremonial mesa. Although the mesa is over 6,000 feet, still it gets hot during the day and everyone appreciates the coolness of an arbor, with the ever-present winds from the desert below blowing through the freshly applied oak boughs. Those same boughs keep one from seeing inside the arbors so that they become quiet and cool family refuges. Tents and tipis, with their canvas walls impervious to vision, are used for sleeping or storage.

As I entered the indicated camp, there seemed to be no one present, save a group of toddlers sitting in the dirt passing around a much gummed and chewed piece of fry bread. A man emerged from a large tent. "I'm looking for Annie. She said to meet her here," I said to him rather tentatively.

"Come in; I'm her uncle. She said you were coming."

I walked toward the the tent, Suzanne still on my hip but looking longingly at the other children. The uncle barred my way with arms folded and looked directly at Suzanne. In what I was later to learn was *'inch'indi'*, communication without words, he indicated I might go into the tent but Suzanne would have to stay outside. The only place to leave her was in the dirt with the other children, roughly in the center of the family camp area. As soon as I placed her in the dirt, with much foreboding I admit, a child handed her the communal fry bread, which she quickly pronounced "Good!" A woman who came out of the tipi said *"Shił łika"* ("It tastes good to me") to Suzanne before addressing me, "I'm Annie's sister; I'm watching them. She will be all right."

(As indeed she was; when I emerged from the tent several hours later, I was met by another woman who came out of the tipi with my sleeping daughter in her arms; Suzanne had been fed, washed, and dressed in warm clothes, for cold comes with the setting of the sun in desert country.)

Entering the tent behind Uncle, I watched the painting of the Mountain God dancers, a ritual that women are usually forbidden to see.[2] At the time, I did not appreciate the significance of my being there or the honor being bestowed in my being allowed to watch the body painting. But I did learn that almost everyone in the camp was related to each other and that the area where the children sat with their fry bread was the joint responsibility of all who camped there. It was the center of the family, occupied by those upon whom the family centered: the children.

1974: LIVING AT THE CENTER

Parking the U-Haul truck in the Indian Health Service Hospital lot, I got into the car with Suzanne and the dog to look for someone who could tell us which house was to be ours for the next year. At the Tribal Offices in the Community Center, I learned that a disliked Public Health Service physician was being evicted and that we were to have his house. The only trouble was that he was fighting the eviction and the Tribe had not yet solidified the contract with the Public Health Service (PHS) so that they, the Tribe, would pay PHS for the house Suzanne and I were to occupy. From graduate school to the center of a controversy: I wasn't sure I was prepared for that. So I announced I would be in Alamogordo at a friend's house. Leaving the telephone number to be called when things settled down, we went back to the U-Haul to get a couple of things and check the lock before heading down the mountains and into Alamogordo.

A woman's voice startled me as I closed the doors to the U-Haul; I'd not heard her approach and, anyway, my mind was on eviction notices and controversy and starting off on the wrong foot and on my plants dying in the back of the truck before I'd be able to unpack them. The woman said, "I remember you. You put her (with a lip gesture toward

Suzanne) with our babies; you trust us. You respect us. We will take care of you. No one will bother your things. You will live in the center of us."

And so we did. We lived in the first (easternmost) PHS house; ours was the one intended for the head of the hospital and, as such, was the only single-family house among duplexes. We were quite visible, perched on the north face of the precipitous canyon and were in a direct line with the home of the president of the Tribe. But our house was on a terrace below his home. Symbolic statements were being made by our living place: We were in the administrative center of the reservation, centered below but within eyesight of the leader of the Tribe, yet also centered in an Anglo enclave with PHS physicians, nurses, and dentists as our immediate neighbors. Across the street, in the BIA houses, there were both Indians and Anglos with the latter predominating. The choice was to be ours, whether we would maintain our center with the Anglos or with Apaches. We chose the latter, and our center became *ⁿdé*, The People, as the Apaches call themselves.

1975: DREAMING FROM THE CENTER

I'd been trying to find Bernard Second for almost four months; everyone said I should work with him to learn the language and the other things I needed to know. Bernard was a young man who was reputed, as a Singer of Ceremonies, to be a Tribal resource, the one to whom people turned to learn the old ways, hear the old stories, learn the old ways of saying or doing things. Everyone said he was central, not only to the running of ceremonies but also to my work. But finding him was difficult, especially, as it turned out, because he did not wish to be found by me.

One day, when my planned activities at the elementary school had been postponed, I walked into the Tribal Museum, where Bernard's wife was director and curator. She and I chatted for a few minutes, for we'd become friends during the months I was trying to find her husband. She startled me by saying, "He's waiting for you in there," with a lip gesture indicating her office.

"You're late," he chided me when I walked into the office.

"How can I be late when I didn't know I was coming here?" I queried.

His only response was, "You are here because I called you."

I, thinking only of telephones, denied having been called. He shrugged and repeated that I was there because he had called me. (So much for my understanding of synchronicity!)

Bernard, whose own family later adopted us, said he had dreamed me before I arrived on the reservation but that his dream had been only that someone was coming with whom he should work to record some of the things he knew about his people, their history, and their language. He had been disappointed to find I was a woman for he had assumed his dream referred to a man; his knowledge was men's knowledge, not to be shared with women. As a consequence of matrilinearity, almost everything at Mescalero belongs to women, save religious and ritual knowledge. The men jealously guard the religion, its associated ritual, and the ritual language in which religious activities must be conducted. Bernard had decided not to be found until he was sure I was the one he had dreamed, for that person was to become a central point for him for some time to come. While he made no pretense of knowing why Power would chose a woman for what he believed to be a man's job, he nonetheless was finally convinced that he should work with me. And so he did. My center became Bernard, the center of the Tribe's ritual knowledge.

1978: CIRCLES AND CENTERS

^{n}da$^?$i bijuu$l$, the circle of life, is formed by a quartered circle:

The visual metaphor it presents is a rich one for Mescalero people (Farrer 1977, 1980). It is simultaneously many things: the universe and its forces; the world and its four primary directions; the proper way to speak and construct speeches; the balance and harmony inherent in the universe and that which *^{n}dé*, The People, are pledged to maintain; the four stages of life (infancy, childhood, adulthood, old age); the four seasons enclosed by a year, measuring from one summer solstice to the next. The visual metaphor is all of this and more.

"Hmmmm. It looks like a floor plan for the girls' ceremonial tipi," I mused.

"It's the same thing! Pay attention!" Bernard responded.

The center crossing point, what I (Farrer 1987, 1988) call a chiasm (from the Greek chi symbol [χ]), represents the balance point of the universe, the firepit in the girls' tipi, and the girls' puberty ceremonial in the life of The People, as well as life in general within the created universe.[3] The center point is the metaphysical place where the Mescalero Apaches are no matter where they physically may be located. For they believe that their actions, both individually and as a group, are essential to the continued maintenance of the inherent harmony of the universe, as conceived and given genesis by *Bik'egudindé*, According to Whom There Is Life, the Creator. As long as they maintain their own centeredness, they generate the energy required to center the universe. The arms of the chi, as in chiasm, are hooked so action and thought can capture processes and essences from wherever and through whatever is encountered. By this means, the visual metaphor is transformed into the proper way to conduct formal speeches or the appropriate way to sprinkle salt on food or the four stages of people's lives or the four seasons. In all things, however, it is the center that is crucial.

Maintaining the center is a job that requires all people, Anglo or Indian or one of any other ethnicity, to be mindful of their assigned place and responsibility. The Mescalero Apaches believe that our human minds are too puny to comprehend the Creator. Thus the Creator, neither male nor female but both and neither, gave to each people in the world a set of responsibilities. Hopi must be true to the Hopi prophetic vision; Christians must be true to the Christian vision; Moslems must be true to the Islamic vision; Apaches must be true to the Apachean vision: Each vision, and the plethora of others in the world, is necessary to sustain the whole as set in motion and place by the Creator.

It is both a comforting and truly an awesome responsibility that the Creator has placed upon us. The primary responsibility of each person is the maintenance of the center that is within so that as we each live our life's circle we will contribute properly to the universe's center.

1984: COSMOS AND CENTER

"If our religion goes, we go as a people," Bernard had told me some years before. The more I learned of the religion, especially that focused around the girls' puberty ceremony of which Bernard was Head Singer, the more I was forced to learn to pay attention to the sky, as well as to the rest of the natural universe. This summer I'd brought an astronomer to the field with me, as my own training in astronomy was minimal and I was not sure enough of our own Western European scientific dogma to feel on comfortable ground with comparisons and contrasts with the Apachean version.

We sat around the dining table at Lorraine Evans's, Bernard's youngest sister and my youngest adopted sister. The star charts were spread on the table, but they turned out to be useful only to the children, who delighted in exposing them to sunlight and then dashing into a closet to watch them phosphoresce in the darkness. Bernard sees the sky in its natural shape and colors and could not relate to the flat charts with their skewed perspective nor to the arbitrary lines we use to define constellations. Where we see Auriga, a six-star constellation (and also use it as a part of Taurus), Bernard talks of The-Three-Who-Went-Together (meaning three who died at the same time), a three-star constellation that includes Capella as well as Beta and Iota Auriga. Comparing knowledge systems is much more difficult than I had originally imagined.

Gene Ammarell, then the education officer of the Fiske Planetarium at the University of Colorado, Boulder, was with me thanks to a grant from the American Council of Learned Societies. He and Bernard could talk man-to-man about men's knowledge and their contrasting views of what constituted proper science. Yet, always before beginning, Bernard said to me, "Are you ready? Is it [tape recorder] on? Do you have your notebook?" And, then, bragging on me as though I was not there, he would say to Gene, "She takes notes in the dark, too. Now, what does she want to know?" Finally, I had provided him with a way in which he could directly teach me men's knowledge without violating his own cultural canons against instructing women in the esoteric knowledge of men. Why, I wonder, did it take me so many years to think to bring a man to the field with me?

In the beginning, Bernard relates, there was only the Creator, who in four days brought the universe into being. On the last day people were created, for we are the weakest link in the chain of being and are dependent on all of the rest of Creation for our own sustenance. This genesis is made visible to people through the natural workings of the universe. It is seen in the four seasons, the circularity of the stars, the circles described by the motion of the universe around us, the stages of life through which we all should pass—unless we die prematurely. It is all there for us to see, if only we will open our eyes and pay attention, if only we remain centered. $^{n}da^{\gamma}i$ *bijuu∤*, life's living circle, provides both template and center for each of us.

1986: GENERATING THE CENTER

Again an astronomer came with me to Mescalero; this time it was Ray A. Williamson of the Office of Technology Assessment in Washington, D.C. We had a specific protocol and particular things to check from my previous work. Bernard was very ill and, as it turned out, was unable to finish singing the ceremony. We were able to work together only a couple of nights. But, perhaps, there were more important things to learn than specific star and constellation names and how they are used to time the ceremonial and life itself.

Each girl having a puberty ceremony has her own Singer, in the ideal at least. The Mescalero number fewer than 3,000 now and there are not always enough Singers to go around; oftentimes, two girls, usually sisters or matrilineal cousins, will share a Singer. All Singers follow the Head Singer, who is still Bernard Second. Even if a Singer learned a different version of a particular song or ritual sequence, he will follow the lead of the Head Singer during ceremonial time. When the Head Singer does not perform, or cannot do so, there is movement toward entropy and a threat of chaos.

Lorraine and I, and other women in the extended family, took turns caring for Bernard, who insisted upon staying in the tipi on the ceremonial mesa rather than going to a hospital where we women all felt he belonged. He had started the ceremonial, had sung for three of the four nights, but could not sing on the fourth, and most important, night when Singers and girls stay up all night performing various rituals. Bernard, the center of the year's ceremonial, was missing, and the re-creation of the universe that the Singers recapitulate during the four nights' singing was going to be missing its final time—the time when people assume responsibility for maintaining their own individual centers and, thus, the universe's center.

The last night moved toward ten P.M., the latest beginning time if all is to work out correctly the next morning with *haigha*, the pulling of the sun; still Bernard did not appear. Three of the other Singers came to me, as I sat just outside the tipi entrance, close enough to hear calls for assistance but far enough away to allow Bernard to rest. As they approached, I was silently screaming, "I'm an Anglo, an outsider, a woman; don't ask me anything!" But the Singers approached me as a woman of Bernard's family, since I was obviously barring the entrance to the tipi where he lay.

"Can he sing?" one asked.

"No," I said emphatically.

"Will he sing?" they persisted.

"Perhaps in the morning, if he can rest," I responded.

I wanted to run and hide so they would have to ask real family members, not a fictitious adopted one like me, what to do. But it was my turn to stay with Bernard. Then came the realization that perhaps this, too, was a lesson for me if only I'd pay attention, as Bernard had so often chided me to do.

The center is where the person assumes responsibility for the on-goingness of whatever may be in progress. It is not necessarily entrusted to the most able, the most knowledgeable, the most wise, the most deserving. It may well be given to the least among us. As Bernard had told me, in each generation there is one who carries the weight of the world; no one ever knows who it is, so it is wise to help all to the extent of our own ability for we never know if it is the fool, the crazy, the leader, or the everyday person who has been chosen in that generation. Only the Creator knows who the person is. As long as each of us performs our assigned task, no matter how trivial it may seem, we are contributing to the centeredness of the universe. The balance begins, and ends, with each of us.

1988: ASSUMING THE CENTER

It was particularly warm for a November day, as perhaps two hundred of us trudged up the side of the canyon deep in the mountains of the reservation. We, Lorraine and I, were being led by cousins who cautioned us of slippery places and who formed a phalanx around us. She and I were holding hands and trying to talk of everyday things so that neither of us would cry any more. As we came into the clearing, with its mound of dirt from the very deep and narrow hole that had been dug, the lump in my throat made it impossible to breathe until the tears started to flow. Now that we were there, Bernard's funeral service and burial could begin.

Although I have over forty pages of notes on the next little while, what I remember most are the sky as screen for memories; the eagle who flew over, almost as a salute; statements Bernard made when I first met him that he would die before me, although he was ten years younger than I; the tall body, dressed in his Indian clothes and wrapped in a tipi cover, lying on a board—no elaborate coffin, for Bernard had outlined the elegant simplicity that was to be his funeral.

What I hear is the voice of Wendell Chino, longtime President of the Tribe, in an impromptu eulogy saying, ". . . Claire Farrer, a good friend to Bernard for many years. Now it is time to write all those things you two talked about for now they are important to my people."

In addition to fighting grief, I had to fight fear—fear of perhaps not being able to do what was expected of me; fear for being sure I did not know half as much as they thought I knew; fear of dying myself before I could write what little I did know; fear of not being able to fulfill, or even wanting, the role of being custodian of a portion of Tribal history and memory.

Then, I "saw" in my mind's eye a time when I was talking with a Mescalero woman my age who wanted to know what would happen to my notes, tapes, and photographs when I died. She had just introduced her granddaughter to me with the words, "This is the white lady I told you about. When your grandma can't remember, you ask her." I told her then of the instructions in my will concerning my professional material and reiterated that my material really belonged to the Mescalero Apache people. That same woman had been one of those consoling me just before we began the climb up the mountain side to the gravesite. And I realized my center had shifted yet again and now I must also husband the core of knowledge with which I'd been entrusted through the years. I felt as though I was the center of a Tribal round dance, but while it was my body in the center of the dance, the persona was much larger than, and different from, the personal me. I had finally joined others in securing a center.

1989: THE CENTERING PROCESS

At various times in our lives, our centers move. As infants we are centered on our own needs and desires—even if the fry bread is much gummed when it comes to us, it still tastes sweetly. As we mature, our center switches to our relatives, to our own children, and to outside others for some of us. We always live at the center of our own little universe; sometimes we can see it in spatial terms as we draw cognitive maps centered on our own egocentric perspective: *I* am here—everything else is out there.

Our dreams can shift our center from one awareness to another. And some of us get lost in the chasm and chaos as we try to inaugurate a new center through a chiasm. Shamans, intuitive dreamers, healers, and maybe even me: All are chiasms effecting a movement from one reality to another, sometimes consciously and sometimes serendipitously. Perhaps our own consciousness is but a speck in the center of the cosmos; perhaps it doesn't exist unless it is consciously created and re-created in each encounter.

In reflecting I have found it strange that I, born in New York City and reared in a thoroughly Anglo way, should learn a tenet of my own Quaker faith in the mountains of New Mexico under a brilliant night sky marred only by the haze of the Milky Way and smoke from camp and cooking fires while sitting in the dark in front of a tipi worrying about an Indian man ill inside. But perhaps not so strange after all: If I am to believe what I have been taught and have learned through observation during the years I have spent at Mescalero, then I must allow that the balance and harmony each of us desires must begin in our own beings. I am the center, and so are you. Each Mescalero Apache who is properly attentive contributes to the essential and inherent balance and harmony of the universe. Each Anglo who is properly attentive has the same potential. Quaker or Mescalero Apache or layperson or Jungian analyst: Each begins the universal connection through a centering of one's own self. Some choose to begin by meditation; others choose to begin by drawing $^{n}da^{\gamma}i\ bijuu\lambda$, life's living circle, and in so doing, drawing their own center. It really is the same thing, as Bernard averred, and as he insisted, I would learn as soon as I could properly pay attention.

The center is always with us. And, if we reach out as in the arms of a chiasm, we have the potential to merge with another's center. By so doing, we *become* the process of centering.

ACKNOWLEDGMENTS

I sincerely thank the members of the Mescalero Apache Tribe for their forebearance through the years. Particular thanks are due my daughter, Suzanne, who shared many of the field experiences with me.

This article was first presented as a slide lecture at the C. G. Jung Institute of Chicago on November 22, 1987. An earlier, shorter version of it was published in *Friends Bulletin,* a monthly journal of the Quakers.

A NOTE ON ORTHOGRAPHY

I follow a simplified Roman alphabetization of Apachean words. Low tone is not marked on vowels, while *é*, for example, indicates a high tone e. Nasalized vowels are represented with a hook under them: *ǫ*. *ⁿ* indicates syllabic *n*. Fricative *l* is represented as *ł*. The glottal stop, which is sometimes phonemic and sometimes attached to consonants, is *ʔ*.

NOTES

1. Fieldwork has been supported by several agencies: The Whitney M. Young, Jr., Memorial Foundation, Inc.; The Mescalero Apache Tribe; the American Council of Learned Societies; the Phillips Fund of the American Philosophical Society; the Research Board of the University of Illinois, Urbana/Champaign; the Graduate School of the California State University, Chico. Grateful acknowledgment is tendered to each. Obviously, in so personal an article, I am solely responsible for its content.

2. See Opler's *An Apache Life-Way* (1965:100) for a brief discussion of the reason for the prohibition against women and children watching the painting of the Mountain God dancers.

3. While I have only recently published on the notion of chiasm, I have presented it in professional meetings on a number of occasions, including the 1983 Eleventh International Congress of Anthropological and Ethnological Sciences held in Vancouver, British Columbia. In a session entitled "Play and Ritual as Communication," chaired by Dr. Alyce T. Cheska, I read a paper on the ritual clown and chiasm—"Łibayé: Chiasm and Continuity." It is fully presented in a chapter, "Clowning and Chiasm," for my forthcoming book, *Living Life's Circle: Mescalero Apache Cosmovision.*

REFERENCES

FARRER, CLAIRE R.
1977   Play and Inter-ethnic Communication: A Practical Ethnography of the Mescalero Apache. Unpublished doctoral dissertation. Ann Arbor, MI: University Microfilms.
1980   Singing for Life: The Mescalero Girls' Puberty Ceremony. *In* Southwestern Indian Ritual Drama. Charlotte J. Frisbie, ed. Pp. 125–159. Albuquerque and Santa Fe: University of New Mexico Press and the School of American Research, Advanced Seminar Series.
1987   On Parables, Questions, and Predictions. *In* special section, Parables of the Space Age, M. Jane Young, ed., of Western Folklore 46:281–293.
1988   Generating Balance. Friends Bulletin 57:89–91.

OPLER, MORRIS E.
1965   An Apache Life-Way: The Economic, Social, and Religious Institutions of the Chiricahua Indians. New York: Cooper Square Publishers.

🌿 Of Teamwork, Faith, and Trust in West Sumatra

C A R O L   J .   C O L F E R
Sultan Qaboos University

A VILLAGE CALLS

We'd lived less than ten minutes by car from Pulai village for over two years, and I'd driven within a stone's throw of it many times. That day, together astride my husband Dudley's yellow Suzuki trailbike, we were out for a joy ride. In truth, we were seeking a bit of ever-elusive privacy, an escape from the public nature of our home in nearby Piruko.

The September day was beautiful with blue sky and white puffy clouds overhead. The road was neither a morass of mud nor a mass of billowing dust, both conditions to which we'd become accustomed. We headed across the Batang Hari River to the forests. Driving through the cool shelter of the trees was our relaxation, our joy.

The last few months had been difficult. I was the anthropologist on a team of soil scientists; and one of them—a dedicated, hardworking, and bright one, at that—had been unjustly accused of doing Christian missionary work in the area. It was becoming clear at that time that Jim and his family might be asked to leave the country, meaning a huge loss to the project and to us personally. They had become good friends.

As we rode along, Dudley and I were discussing my need to do some research in a Minang community. I felt I knew a lot about transmigrants from Java, but I wanted a clearer picture of the differences between the transmigrants and the indigenous population of West Sumatra. Our project had worked only with transmigrants (because of governmental interest in them), and I felt we were neglecting an opportunity to make use of indigenous experience. It also seemed possible to me that the Minang people might have noticed the lack of benefits from our project for their own local agricultural system. This could have been the factor that led to the accusation about the Christian missionary work. There were obvious problems with interethnic equity and, having recently become Chief of Party, I wanted to rectify these problems if at all possible.

The gist of our conversation prompted my husband to veer toward Pulai at a fork in the road, leading us onto a narrow path exactly wide

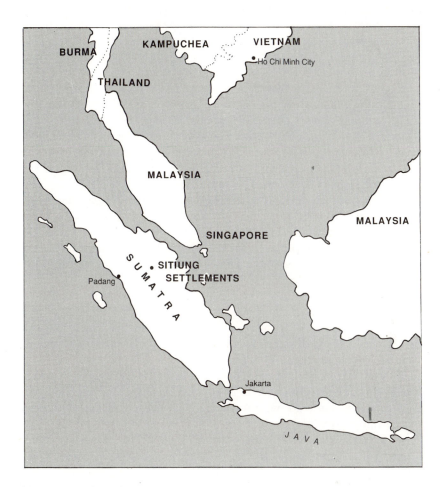

Sumatra, Indonesia

enough for a car. This turned out to be the axis along which the village was situated, paralleling the nearby river. We were greeted by a profusion of trees, hiding the community thoroughly from casual detection and also hiding the curious but friendly stares of children and a few adults in village yards.

Piruko, where we lived, was a planned transmigration community with every home replicated four times on every block, every yard exactly one-quarter ha in size. Although eight years of human occupancy had altered the once identical houses, the original square wooden structures were often still visible. Even the placement of trees in the yards attested to the standardization that characterizes such settlements.

Pulai was different. Brightly decorated concrete houses were interspersed with traditional wooden homes built on stilts, with Minang roofs, the outer peaks reaching skyward in the shape of a water buffalo's horns (or according to legend, a canoe). The houses were generally aligned along the road, but in a haphazard, natural fashion. They seemed a part of the surrounding forest, which gradually blended into the fruit trees and other greenery. Yellow flowers sprinkled the yards in abundance highlighting the brightly painted windows here and there, contrasting with the many shades of green that characterize the whole area. The profusion of trees gave the village a cool, refreshing air. I was enchanted.

We drove on across the river and proceeded into the forest in search of monkeys, boars, peace, and other natural phenomena. From that moment of discovery, I resolved to return to Pulai.

A few days later, Megan (my teenage daughter) and I decided to go for a similar joy ride. She'd been in Kalimantan with me some years earlier, working with Kenyah Dayaks who lived along a river. We wondered if the people of Pulai had the floating platforms that the Dayaks had used for bathing, sociability, and all functions requiring water. So she and I headed for Pulai.

This time, we stopped at a cluster of buildings that turned out to be a Muslim religious school and its dormitories. The dormitories were made of woven mats, strung together into human size boxes, and set up on stilts. Little did we know at that time that some of these "boxes" were occupied by entire families.

We were immediately surrounded by interested boys and young men, ranging in age from about ten to twenty—a common occurrence in Indonesia. They chattered away in Minang, their native language. We could understand only bits and pieces of their speech. Though we knew we were perfectly safe, we felt uncomfortable, closed in. As we resolutely moved toward the river, the circle broke, granting us freedom to go where we wanted.

Very steep steps had been carved out of the cool, damp banks of the river. Regular use kept the steps firm and grass-free, but on all sides lush vegetation surrounded us. Clamoring down the steps behind us was an entourage of the younger boys, grinning mischievously or smiling shyly.

At the bottom we found only a shallow side channel of the river between the shore and an island. We returned to our motorcycle, grateful to escape the persistent stares, the alien language, and occasional laughter of the boys.

I realized, as I contemplated working in Pulai, that the chance to conduct research on my own again was a powerful draw. I had worked for two years in a very collaborative mode, with soil scientists and agronomists. The decision to do so had been a conscious one: I wanted to use anthropological information to help determine research priorities on the project. To do that effectively, I had to work closely with the agricultural scientists. It had worked well.

Yet the enthnographic loss was significant. I had chosen—like my co-workers—to live in a comparatively comfortable home (with a generator, running water, fans), largely to enhance communication with my co-workers, recognizing that this would have a negative impact on my communication with villagers. I had accepted the driver that had been urged on me for the same reasons. We lived close enough to each other so that a significant amount of my leisure time was spent with co-workers, again reducing my contact with the local populations.

Some of our work involved designing and doing experiments collaboratively with farmers. Although this process provided some useful ethnographic information, I was always wondering what the farmers would be doing without our collaboration. That this close association with other team members presented a potential danger to my rapport with villagers (should they act, or be perceived to act, inappropriately) was also clear.

My co-workers were remarkably aware and culturally sensitive. But they were not anthropologists. The degree to which this religious controversy, for instance, might affect my work was troubling me. I'd lived and worked under the constraints of teamwork for two years and now relished the idea of returning to "real fieldwork." I was confident that my rapport with team members was sufficiently good to allow me to go it alone for a while.

GETTING PERMISSION TO WORK IN PULAI

I returned to Pulai one morning a few days later, driving through town more slowly, hoping someone might invite me in, trying to get a feel for the place, wondering how best to proceed. The people were friendly, but more guardedly so than the transmigrants. No one invited me in, but I noticed a small shed, outfitted on three sides with benches, full of men, apparently just sitting around. One thin man about my age (forty) gave me a particularly friendly smile, which cheered me in the difficult first moments when fieldwork actually begins.

I drove on to the river, lined with lush tropical growth, its beauty and breadth always a source of strength and inspiration to me. Coming back, as I reached the village edge, I saw the thin man again. Again he smiled, giving me courage to stop and ask him where the headman might be. I felt a surge of relief that he understood and spoke Indonesian, as well as Minang. I was self-conscious but grateful when he led me back to a little shop near the shed full of men and called the headman over to me.

The headman turned out to be a young man in his late twenties. He (and the toothless old shopkeeper) listened to the explanation of what I wanted—to learn about their agricultural system, about their way of life, so that our project could begin to do agricultural experiments that would be more appropriate for their own system. We also hoped this would help the government develop policies that were more appropriate for Sumatran conditions. He smiled shyly and nodded with what I took to be reserved approval. I could understand enough of the Minang language to pick up his occasional corroboration of something I had said, addressing himself to the older man, who seemed to speak little Indonesian.

Then the headman asked what exactly I wanted to do in Pulai. As I spoke of coming every day, spending time in the village and in the fields with families, interviewing people, he began to look more and more uncomfortable. His youth led me to suspect that he held the position of village headman because of educational certification requirements of the central or provincial government and that he might be headman in title only (or mainly). I could see that I was putting him in a difficult position. He looked enormously relieved and grateful when I asked if he'd need to discuss the issues with the village elders. Yes, one person shouldn't make a decision like this, he said. We agreed that I should return in a week's time.

The following week I got my first lesson in Pulai politics (and kinship). I learned that the "elders" the headman needed to consult were the clan leaders of Pulai's three major matrilineal clans (Tigoninik, Melayu Satu, and Melayu Dua) and the religious leader (who was also head of the religious school).

How fortunate that Pak Munir, one of the leaders of Melayu Satu, was the thin man who'd first smiled at me. The leader of Melayu Dua was a distinguished-looking middle-aged man who was also the head of the village elementary school. The religious leader was a member of the Melayu Satu clan. The leader of the Tigoninik clan, who I later learned was by far the most influential, never came to any of our meetings, though the young headman was also a member of this clan.

Each time I came to the village for a meeting, I lingered, hoping to meet some of the village women. On one such occasion, an old, but still strong, woman beckoned me into a room adjoining Pulai's grandest house. Large and new, this house was beautifully constructed of elaborately carved wood, with the traditional pointed roof and stilts.

The woman's lips and teeth were stained red and black from years of chewing betel nut. She struck me as forthright, curious, friendly, and self-confident. I was to learn that this was the clan home and meeting place for the Tigoninik clan and that she was the mother of the clan leader. She could not speak Indonesian and I could not speak Minang. But three women in their twenties and thirties translated for us.

Her message was that I had been talking with men of little import, that I needed to speak with and get permission from Pak Datok before proceeding. Pak Datok was her son. I promptly went to his home, and kept returning until I could explain to him my purpose in being there and request his permission to proceed.

I suspected that I had been accepted, at least provisionally, one day when these influential men invited me to accompany them the following week to a village rice-planting party. Pak Munir quickly assumed the role of my champion, explaining my agricultural, *not religious,* motivations to all of the villagers.

The process of getting permission to work in Pulai underscored an important Minang (and perhaps pan-Indonesian) value. Interpersonal relations should be cordial; conflict should be avoided. In all of these formal meetings with the men of Pulai (and with the head of the sub-district), there was a strong undercurrent of concern. I could feel the distrust, the suspicion. They all asked me many questions and warned me, in polite, gentle terms, that they did not want any *politik* (political maneuvering) on my part.

They were, of course, referring to Jim's alleged religious activities. Missionary activity was strictly forbidden to our project by Indonesian law, and it was greatly feared by the devoutly Muslim Minangkabau of the area.

One of the rumors that seemed most absurd to us was that Jim had been paying a million rupiah (US $1,000) to anyone who would become a Christian. This was consistent with a common warning to children in West Sumatra to not take money from foreigners. Christians were reputed generally to pay people to convert. Pulai's inhabitants believed these rumors, and many feared that I had come to their village with similar intentions.

Despite these genuine suspicions and fears about my motives, no one ever brought up this subject directly. The villagers mentioned politics, they spoke generally against "carrying or bringing people from one group to another," but neither the alleged missionary work nor Jim was mentioned until I brought it up. I was then able to address their concerns directly, though it took months and a dramatic event before I truly won most people's trust.

ACCEPTANCE FINALLY COMES

By January, I was beginning to despair of ever getting beyond the villagers' suspicion that I had religious intentions. There seemed to be no end in sight. Pak Munir initiated almost every interchange, when we were together, with an explanation of my agricultural not religious interests, and he took every opportunity to point out the agricultural nature of my actions and questions—as did I. Yet the suspicion remained.

The people of Pulai brought up their own religion, Islam, continually. Pak Munir and I went out to Fahmuddin and Miryam's rain-fed rice field in early January. The rainy season was underway in earnest, and we had a difficult time getting through the many huge mud holes in the road. The same road we'd traversed so easily in October was now a quagmire, regularly entrapping the log trucks that moved between the highway and the settlements and forests.

There were three married women in their late twenties working together in the field—Miryam, Rukiyah, and Sam (all of the Peliang clan). They lived near each other and regularly traded labor. Sam was married to the influential Pak Datok.

I watched the women weeding, bent double over the sharply sloping hillside, and tried to copy them. The slope was so steep I regularly slid down a foot or two. Pak Munir, true to the local division of labor, sat on a log during the two hours we worked, fondling a weeding tool but never touching a weed.

The women asked about Christianity and circumcision. My explanation prompted a lesson in Islam. Pulai boys are circumcised between ages six and twelve and become real Muslims at that point. Girls are "circumcised" at six days after birth, though this involves only a light scraping of the clitoris, not its removal. People consider youth of both sexes under age fifteen to be too young to sin, not yet fully responsible.

Women are considered dirty during their menses and are forbidden to fast, to pray, or even to be touched by their husbands. Postmenopausal women are clean and pure, and for premenopausal women, menstruation has a purifying function.

This discussion led to concerns over family planning. The women knew something about and expressed interest in all kinds of contraception. We compared effects of the Pill in our respective countries. They said they were afraid of birth control. Sam told of a woman who'd gotten an IUD, which had worked its way up into her body and was approaching her heart. The woman had been taken to Padang for an operation the previous Tuesday. I was to hear more about IUDs in the near future.

They wondered why my husband had wanted to marry me, since I couldn't have any more children. Minang men, they all agreed, wouldn't want to take care of another man's children (though many, I'd noticed, do). How long was I divorced before I remarried? Islam required them to wait three and a half months before marrying again. Was adultery allowed in America? Prostitution? Premarital sex? I explained that, as in Pulai, none of these things was really allowed, but they all happened.

The next day we went to another upland field, this time accompanied by Pak Munir's wife, Niisah. This was my first chance to talk with her alone. Some twenty years ago, she had come from Sawahlunto, the district capital, about eighty kilometers from Pulai. But she was taken in by a family and the Melayu Dua clan after marrying Pak Munir, which was an exception to the usual matrilocal residence pattern. She rarely did agricultural work, partly because Pak Munir was successful at contract and other entrepreneurial work. They had no fields under cultivation, though he occasionally claimed partial ownership/interest in his clan's rubber orchards.

We went out the same slippery, muddy road to the area I'd watched the community plant in October. Niisah called to everyone we passed—a common practice—saying we were on our way to Nur's field. Nur was weeding her field with another woman, Yanti (both around forty years old). Yanti, like Nur's husband, is a Tigoninik, but the women consider themselves to be friends, not relatives. Nur is Melayu Satu. Their homes are quite close, their fields adjacent.

We talked about the "1001" names they knew for kinds of weeds. I was increasingly getting the impression that only the women weed. These women said the men fish and tap rubber and "look for money."

Again, family planning emerged as a topic of interest. Niisah had eight children, seven of whom survived; Nur had six children and one grand-child; and Yanti had three children (two boys and a girl). It's important in this matrilineal society to have at least one girl. They told me, wor-riedly, about a woman who'd become pregnant with an IUD in place, and they wondered what would happen. I promised to look in a book I had.

The next day I went out that wretched road again, with Niisah, this time to a field belonging to the headmaster of the religious school. There were almost thirty women weeding his field (no men, no children), many of whom were students. I learned to sharpen the weeding tools from Nur, who also lent me her head kerchief. The women worried that my "beautiful white skin" would darken in the blistering sun. Conversation, laughter, singing, all serve to lighten what is undeniably a dreary, hot, back-breaking task.

When Niisah and I returned to Pulai that afternoon, we received word that the woman with the IUD was not doing well. When I offered to go see her, Niisah accepted gratefully. The woman, Risani, lived in a small box in a row of similar boxes built on stilts between the regular houses on the road and the river. The entire dwelling was about two by three meters, and its walls were woven from forest fibers. The house, like the school's "dormitories," looked like a rice storage structure. I had thought that was what it was!

Risani and her husband and three children had come to Pulai from Solok (about one hundred kilometers to the west) in search of their for-tune. Risani was seven months pregnant, writhing on the floor in pain and hot as a firecracker. She had been passing blood and pus. Her young husband sat by, trying to look impassive, yet with anxiety etched deeply into his face. I too was afraid for her life.

I asked what had been done. Her abdomen had been smeared with charcoal, and the local healer had "read" over her. "To read," in this way, is to whisper magico-religious phrases over someone or something.

My own anxiety level was rising. I was doing fieldwork, and this was an opportunity to find out about how people made decisions regarding health care. From an academic standpoint, I knew that I shouldn't in-terfere. Yet it looked to me as though this woman might be dying.

I decided the pursuit of knowledge could wait for a more benign moment. I asked, "Has she been to a doctor?" No, not yet. I didn't know whether or not her husband approved of doctors. I said I thought she needed to go to the doctor. No response. "Is transportation the problem?" No response. "How about if I come and get her?" No response. Her husband stared unhappily and silently into space.

Finally I asked if the problem was money. His face riveted to mine— a strong yes. I offered to pay; and they gladly agreed for me to take her.

I went home to get my jeep and driver. After considerable maneuvering, we managed to get the vehicle through the narrow paths to her hut. Getting Risani's body, awkward with pregnancy and pain, into the jeep was another hurdle. She lay on the floor in the back, still moaning and writhing in pain, with her husband beside her. I sat in the front, twisted around, holding her hand.

The twenty-minute ride over bumpy roads to the health clinic seemed interminable. The tenor of her moaning informed us clearly that the bouncy ride was painful. I could monitor the depth of her discomfort by the pressure of her hand on mine. Her husband held her other hand. I saw him rearranging her sarong, but I wasn't sure what he was doing. My mind was on her struggle, her danger, and my own fear for her life.

As we drove into the clinic yard, I was surprised and dismayed to see a gaggle of foreigners (one of whom I knew) coming toward me with outstretched hands. I hated to leave the woman in my charge, but the clinic personnel were already opening the back door of the jeep to take care of her. Politeness seemed to dictate that I greet these people. I listened as patiently as I could to their reason for being there (they were in fact looking for me) and explained that I was in the midst of an emergency.

After extricating myself temporarily, I returned to the cluster of people behind my jeep. I was amazed to discover that Risani had given birth to a baby girl in the car on the way to the clinic! The baby, premature, was the tiniest I'd ever seen, though apparently perfectly formed. Mother and daughter were taken into the clinic, and I was required to turn back to the visitors.

Every effort was made to save the baby, within the capabilities of the small rural clinic. Risani's husband came to my home to fetch me three days later to bring her and the new baby home. I could hardly believe the baby was still alive, and I couldn't help noting sadly that her chances in that small crowded hut were rather slim. Indeed, a few days later I learned that the baby had died. But Risani was well. The IUD was never found.

This event, to my surprise and relief, brought to an abrupt end people's overt suspicion of my motives in the community. I was never again called on to explain my purposes in being in the village. The general concern for Risani, actually a stranger in Pulai, is reflective of a cultural ideal that strongly values human beings and welcomes them into the community wherever they come from. My concern for this unknown woman and my willingness to pay for her medical care (twenty-five dollars) seemed to demonstrate to the people that I shared this value. They were then responsive and able to accept and trust me as they could not before.

❧ The "Killing" of Neni Bai

PAUL WINTHER
Eastern Kentucky University

PART ONE

It is not an exaggeration to say that seldom does a visitor to India soon forget the experience. The number, variety, and intensity of feelings can multiply as a tour evolves into months and years. The contrasts between beauty and ugliness, real and disturbing, alternately assault and soothe your sensitivities. That these emotions may persist suggests that you don't so much travel in India as the place begins to occupy you. You don't "see" the country; you "feel" it. It is a phenomenon that can alter your consciousness in ways much more subtle and ultimately more profound than merely recognizing differences in wealth and reacting to deprivation.

For me India was, and continues to be, a surreptitious encounter that changed my attitude to existence. I want to relate to you how this happened to me. I want to tell you about a young girl who died. Or was she killed? Perhaps murdered is a better word for it. Maybe nothing really ever happened to her.

More than twelve years have passed, but the events are still vivid. I was a graduate student in anthropology, doing a participant observation study in north central India. Participant observation simply means learning the rudiments of a society's language prior to arrival, supplemented by intensive study of its history and culture, and then residing in a specific locale for one to two years—in my case, a village of approximately 2,000 people. You attempt to become "part of the furniture," so to speak, being very cautious not to violate any local rules of etiquette or taboos. As you ask questions, you observe, and in the quiet moments of the day you write about what you have seen, heard, and felt in the form of field notes. This is the material from which you abstract ideas for future publications.

During the innumerable walks I took through the village and adjoining land as part of my work, I often met people tending fields. These were landowners, sharecroppers, and hired labor, usually from the community. They would acknowledge my presence with a look or a wave or a smile. And, occasionally, I would stop to have a cup of tea with those

I knew particularly well. Boiled in prodigious amounts of buffalo milk and sugar, the beverage was compensated only by the relaxed flow of talk. I learned much about the village and its people from these encounters. It was as if the shade and the privacy in which we sat encouraged people to speak about things they would normally keep to themselves.

One series of meetings was particularly memorable. It involved two brothers, both Brahmans, a caste of high ritual status. The men were very friendly and always asked the same questions concerning me and the United States, to which I replied with the same answers. They responded with the same expressions of amazement or partial comprehension. I believe the inquiries were intentionally repetitious because they thought me to be a bit weird. Their questions, which I came to know by heart, were demonstrations of friendship, discreetly phrased in such a way as not to strain my apparently limited mental capacities. How else to explain and treat a foreigner 12,000 miles away from home, who sits and asks questions about such things as lineages, clans, and the like? Pancham Ram, one of the brothers, was an oddity for me as well. He wore a beard, and a bearded Brahman in the village was a rarity. We joked about this and compared respective lengths.

Pancham Ram was married and had six children, the oldest of whom, a girl, was deceased. Then there was another girl, Neni Bai, followed by four brothers down to the age of one and a half years. Pencham Ram, his wife, and children lived in a small dwelling with his unmarried brother. The family had a high ritual status but modest economic resources. The small amount of land they owned yielded sufficient produce to feed them, although it left little to sell at the market beyond the village.

Pancham Ram's daughter, Neni Bai, was in her early teens. I never talked to her or made inquiries about her until after her disappearance. An unmarried male, and a foreigner at that, does not ask questions about single females of high caste and marriageable age in the community and expect to remain in the village. But I noticed her each time I left my room above my landlord's cow pen and walked down the path to the village platform where the "important" men gathered when I took the short-cut to the highway where I waited for a bus to the nearest city. Often she would be there when I returned. She, like so many residents, became part of the animated scenery, stopping whatever was being done, the old women staring, the younger casting furtive glances beneath veils, the little girls giggling, and the boys shouting "White monkey!" and scampering away in good-natured mock fright. I grew accustomed to these acknowledgements of my presence, and cut off from everything resembling my previous American existence, they helped make occasional bouts of loneliness less difficult and prolonged.

Neni Bai was in that field the first winter when temperatures were unexpectedly low and I nearly froze; she was there in the incredibly dry heat of May and June, and she was there during the monsoon season, seemingly oblivious to the danger of the water-inundated gully threatening to engulf the village. And she was there the autumn day I left to visit distant New Delhi. It was a cool, clear morning. With the same dull, expressionless look she observed my departure. The only thing that ever seemed to move was her eyes, insufficiently striking to detract from her exceedingly plain face. A beauty Neni Bai was not, even less so because she had a club foot. Others said that she was retarded, and I believed them. It would cost her father much money to find her a husband. She was a human being, however, and I felt sorry for her.

Neni Bai was gone when I came back. But I was so absorbed in data collection that initially I only dimly sensed her absence. The people I met that first day seemed pleased to see me again. I felt good. I remember meeting one man who looked vaguely familiar and hearing him greet me. But I was in a hurry, said hello, and went to an appointment. I met the same man later with his brother in Pancham Ram's field. Then I realized it was Pancham Ram, but without a beard. I kidded him about the hairless jaw, and when I asked him why no beard, he and his brother laughed, Pancham waving his hand in that typical Indian way signifying so many things. I assumed he had become tired of the growth and didn't give my debearded friend's new appearance any more thought.

Only several days later did one of my informants mention the village meeting that had taken place during my absence. It had been called by the village headman (*sarpanch*). Other people's descriptions suggested that it had been a perfunctory occasion, serving to satisfy inquiries initiated by the police. I was sorry that I had not witnessed the events and issues prompting the meeting. I was politely insistent that they tell me more. The *sarpanch*, I was told, had ordered Pancham Ram's beard shaved. Furthermore, no one was to talk to him for three days, and if they did, their crops would fail.[1] I sensed that Neni Bai's absence, the village meeting, and Pancham Ram's beardless condition were related. In retrospect, maybe I should have left the puzzle unsolved, for what I was to discover was disquieting.

Neni Bai was indeed gone. She had become pregnant by a lower caste male. Her throat had been cut and her body thrown into a dry well on Pancham Ram's land. Pancham did not deny having perpetrated the act. My shock was intensified when I was told that he had strangled another daughter—the one he had mentioned months before—two years before my arrival. The same well had been used as a disposal site. The agitation I experienced during these sessions may have been evident, but my feelings did not appear to be shared by others. It is difficult to describe the villagers' reactions in exact terms, but they gave the impression of a perplexing indifference, a casually nonchalant attitude, and one I thought was merely a disguise affected so as to calm me. However, unobtrusive inquiries during the remainder of my stay generated similar reactions.

In those early days I was convinced that these people had been just as upset as myself. It was, after all, merely human to be ashamed of a fellow villager who had committed such a horrible act. I assumed without question that they felt as I did, and I strove to discover reasons why their reactions were not following these assumptions. I realize now how engrained in my consciousness were my assumptions about the act of killing called into question because of Neni Bai. The villagers' awareness of the girl, of her father, and of the significance their relationship attained in my eyes seemed to be predicated upon different principles, which hitherto I had had no reason to think differed from my own.

I eventually went to the local police station to find more details about the Neni Bai/Pancham Ram incident. The superintendent, whom I knew fairly well and who did not hail from the area, told me that he was aware of the village meeting and had sent a policeman to investigate. Since the case was closed, he showed me the files. He also perceived my incredulity. He volunteered that the police do not usually pursue these matters in the surrounding villages. It was not a "crime" in the sense that I understood the term. While it was a violation in legal theory, it was nothing very out of the ordinary for these people, he continued. I was becoming decidedly uncomfortable. The community meeting, the beard shaving, and the *sarpanch*'s warning were apparently little more than empty ritual designed to pay lip service to the power of the Indian state, its conception of legality based upon Western, Judeo-Christian–derived principles. The constable's investigation, the file sheets stamped and placed on record, prevented anyone from protesting insufficient implementation of the law.

So much for justice, I thought. But I was unsatisfied. Being able to comprehend the underlying logic intellectually is different from accepting it emotionally without feeling estranged. I had prided myself on beginning to understand how the villagers viewed the world around them. I was reacting to the contradiction between what I felt to be an exceptional event and my friends' treatment of it as less than exceptional. As I walked back to the village that day, I felt lonely, depressed, and apprehensive. The community appeared unappealingly foreign to me. They had become strangers all over again. The hard part of the research lay ahead, I thought—a realization that my concept of "human being" might not be shared by the people amongst whom I was living.

PART TWO

What I ultimately gained from trying to understand Neni Bai's departure and the milieu in which it took place was a heightened awareness of the power of culture to condition an individual's perception of reality. My informants, friends, and acquaintances and I shared perceptions of Neni Bai. For example, she was a female, young, unattractive. This overlapping made the disagreement regarding the significance of her death so disconcerting to me. Given my need and desire to remain in the community and accomplish my goals, I was impelled to examine engrained assumptions and modify basic attitudes typical of our society's world view. I was divesting myself of the cocoonlike security, the complacency such unquestioned assumptions provide, and was assimilating in subtle, albeit commanding, ways aspects of a fundamentally different consciousness. It is a trip I perhaps never fully returned from.

It is impossible to convey the complexity of thought my covillagers were employing in their interpretations of Neni Bai; only an inadequate attempt can be made. What they were articulating were themes found in the classical texts of Hinduism and their idiosyncratic interpretation at the local level. These ideas pertain to their notion of time and the phenomenal world it embraces.

One dominant idea in classical Hinduism is that of a transcendental reality underlying and sustaining all of the phenomenal world. While this does not discourage recognition of different objects, "in the end" all entities having status as "facts" and articulated by all languages are not *the* absolute. In the Hindu world view, the things perceived may not possess emotive potential identical to that of the Judeo-Christian world. Both Western and Indian cultures have the concept of time, but even a cursory reading of the texts of Hinduism suggests a different kind of sensitivity toward its nature and, by implication, those entities "occupying" time.

For those dominated by such ideas, things populating their world are seen as always in movement. Neni Bai's birth, for example, was not denied. Her actions during the course of her short life were acknowledged, but it was an acknowledgement of different significance from that I accorded her. For me her actions, all those qualities I had perceived as well as those I had not had a chance to observe but accorded her, *were her.* They defined her. Her uniqueness in time was my reality. But the villagers envisaged Neni Bai—as they probably do all human entities—as a surface phenomenon. Reality to them is something other than the outward appearance that I deemed as significant. Neni Bai, myself, them—and you, the reader—are part of a ceaseless flux, the underlying reality of which is left unchanged. Lives are created, lives are stopped, but the substance of things remains unchanged. And what I label dynamics, in motion, is perceived by my Hindu friends as but a manifestation of ultimate "unchange."

Although I could accept, rather than merely say I understood, that time was not a distinct entity and absolute in its independence, I still had difficulty seeing how Neni Bai related to this esoteric intellectual orientation. In other words, I was uncomfortable with their conceptualization of form. Gradually I realized that it is the "ultimate nonreality of any instant" that provides the foundation for their conception of human beings. I held a distinction between living and dead, between existence and nonexistence. These sets of contrasts are, for Westerners, facets of the human condition. We believe there exists a physical life, and the majority of us posit a spiritual existence also. The Western religions vary in how they perceive the latter after cessation of physical life, but the notion that one "lives on" after the other is familiar.

The people attempting to educate me in this south Asian community reflect an absence of this duality. For them existence and nonexistence are not different aspects of a thing residing in time and do not entail physical bodies evolving and culminating in cessation. Rather, existence and nonexistence are the thing itself, different manifestations of the same underlying, unfathomable sameness. Life and death, then, need not have the identical moral implications they do for us. Their indigenous cultural code conditions them to perceive, experience, and react in a manner I did not anticipate. The physical demise of a person can occur, the villagers perceive it, but the range of reactions does not automatically generate synonymous responses. Death taking place in time was not accorded the same status in regard to "reality" as I accorded it. The result was the curious, and for us probably unnerving, realization that Neni Bai's extinction was the dissolution of a "form," but her consequent "nonexistence" was coequal with her "existence." For them what was important was neither the death of Neni Bai as an event-in-itself nor a concern with the injustice I thought had been inflicted upon her.

The notions of the village people, while different from ours, are neither more barbaric nor more civilized. They do have definite perceptions of time and of the "human beings" populating it, but it is a concern with time on a cosmic order. While we attach importance to the passing events of a person's life and to grand historical episodes, they tend to see these events not as indications of change, progress, and evolution, but as revelations of the eternalness of the social order, of the world, and of the universe. On a far less grandiose level each person—Neni Bai, you, myself—is but a transient instance, an inconsequential "form" repeatedly appearing in a limitless "time."

Neni Bai and the milieu in which she lived forced me to become aware of how I had unquestioningly accepted one culture's definition of common sense. It now also enables me to recognize the usually unrecognized contradictions in the Judeo-Christian legacy regarding the creation, appearance, continuance, and cessation of human life. My problem is that I see and feel these contradictions in an environment not conducive to acting upon such realization; your problem may be that you see no contradictions at all. If you are among the latter, it will be difficult for you to accurately comprehend the phenomenon of violence and crime in a comparative perspective. You will engage in assigning labels to people and events that will be dramatically different from the interpretations of the participants themselves.

There is little in our genetic makeup that makes us prone, or not prone, to engage in ending human life. Rather, our responses are situationally defined. And it is our culture, through its numerous institutions, that conditions our consciousness. The irrationality of killing humans is transformed into the rational, the legitimate, and the acceptable, by society. Our institutions define when killing is to be condoned and when the annihilation of others warrants censure because of inappropriate circumstances. Stand aside for ony a moment and reflect upon how our society—or any society—constructs the proper setting for extermination of individuals or groups of humans.

There are probably many of you who, with some encouragement, would readily kill "for your country" or for your God. But we seem to be disturbed by merely killing, or by the label used to designate it. We feel better, we are ethical, if the institutional fabric of our society can satisfy our need for the legitimation of its performance. So killing for Christ and the U.S.A. is effectively conveyed to us in the form of protecting ourselves from some amorphous devil. One subtle function of the groups to which we belong is to lift us out of the emotional quagmire of morality. Not only do such institutions provide us with a sense of identity, security, and the satisfaction of human needs, they also alleviate us of the burden of serious reflection. We are free, but free to conform. Our institutions define the situations when we can kill with gusto, without debilitating feelings of guilt, or at least categorize the act(s) as unfortunate but necessary.

I could understand the phenomenon called Neni Bai only with an eventual willingness to recognize, and to shed, the ethnocentric tendencies inculated since my childhood. And only by engaging in a similar process can you begin to comprehend "crime" in your society and "crime" as it is defined and conceptualized by inhabitants of the many societies around the world. While all peoples may possess an intellectual category called *crime*, the contents of the compartment are shaped in numerous ways by their respective cultures. A heinous act in one culture may be a nonevent in another, or a performance of remarkably different emotional significance for those involved. This status is not due to any barbarism of the practitioners; it is a reflection of culture's ability to condition us and to invest acts with a multitude of equally logical, sensible interpretations. No one explanation is correct or constitutes a more perfect approximation of some ultimate "truth" existing independently of us, residing "out there." There are, according to the wise men in that Indian village, merely many diverse ways by which human beings express their self-deception.

NOTE

1. Nobody refrained from talking with Pancham Ram during this period, and no crops failed due to the infringement of the *sarpanch*'s admonition.

ELEVEN

❧ Turning Tears into Nothing

MILES RICHARDSON
Louisiana State University

You've been to Mexico before, haven't you? Anthropologists travel. It's part of their work, their work in the field, their work in the field of anthropology. It's their profession. But I wasn't certain, because at times they are so distant from their traveling, as if a part of them never travels, no matter how many miles, how many smells, how many sights, how many sounds, and how many hurts they may have walked, smelled, seen, heard, or bled from. It's the distant part that I am trying to contact. The distant part, you tell me, is that part of you that counts, groups, and orders. Constantly engaged and busy at work, it puts the uniques together, factors out the untidy, and bestows an elegant evenness to all. If it does that, it must be wise. Since it is wise, I want to ask it a question, a question about Mexico, about the people there, and especially about a little girl crying in the streets.

Now, don't be modest. You direct graduate students in their pursuits, you organize symposia at professional meetings, and you present ideas in learned journals. Having accomplished those things, you must know at least a little about a small girl with tears in her eyes.

Before I ask the question, I have to make certain that you are within the circle of my asking. I have to define the universe of discourse, as they say. The universe of discourse, the location of my asking and your responding, is not the country of Mexico, that ribbed land sucked dry by different peoples' struggles to be even before Cortés met Montezuma. The universe where we are to meet is the only one left as soon as you cross the border at Matamoros, Laredo, Juárez, Mexicali, and Tijuana. One step south of the border and the many Mexicos resolve into one, the city.

If you don't think that is true, and as an anthropologist you are prone to doubt—that's part of being wise—ask any driver of *Transportes del Norte*, "*¿En qué dirección está México?*" and he'll point south, where the city is.

Mexico City. How is its is? How would you characterize its being? Would you cite government statistics that more people live within its urbanized area than live in London, Paris, or even Tokyo? Would you point to the debate concerning the push-pull effect of rural to urban migration and then refer to the third-world phenomenon of urbanization without industrialization? Would you speak not only of unemployment but also quote estimates of underemployment? After presenting data on water quality, air pollution, and vehicular traffic, would you conclude with remarks about the explanatory inadequacies of both modernization and dependency theories? You would, and you would be correct, or as correct as your terms would allow you to be.

Were you to ask me, I would tell you to watch the sun struggle to shine through the filthy air, squint against the grit that comes up from the gray streets with each new swirl of chilling wind, hear the screech, the squeal, and the roar of traffic hurdling endlessly through the streets, smell the heavy sweat of the poor accented by the delicate perfume of the rich, and feel the small hurt of a tiny child fretting in his Pet Milk carton while nearby his mother offers a box of chewing gum to impassive pedestrians hurrying from here to there. If I were to say all of this, I too would be correct, or as correct as my words would let me.

And we both would be wrong. Even if you defined your terms with precision, they would err. Even if I chose the perfect word, it would mislead. This is true because Mexico changes. It doesn't stay constant. What was correct and firm yesterday at noon, the afternoon rains have washed away, and today there is a different city. Like the day I saw the little girl.

That day, the rains had done their job, and it was a new Mexico. The sun had risen with the vigor that it must have had on that first day the Aztec rekindled the world, and its rays came through the cleaned air to caress the city. A drop of moisture, left over from the rain, ran down the leaf of a plant springing up from a crack in a wall and then dangled in ecstasy as the sunlight gently touched it with a sparkle. With nature so transformed, the city was forced to follow. The traffic, which the day before was a snarling monster, became, under nature's spell, an exciting spectacle of courage and derring-do, and you wanted to applaud the skill of the individual drivers as they wove in and out, a gas pedal here, a gear shift there, and horn, a lot of horn everywhere—but with the magic of the morning the deafening honks become taunting calls that dare opponents to meet the challenger at the next red light. You admired the mother on the corner, her strong face, her black hair, her *rebozo* gracefully draped on sturdy shoulders, and you marveled at the way she lent her dignity to hawking gum on the streets. You had to smile at the baby sitting up in his cardboard carton, his enormous brown eyes exploring with trustful curiosity the world beyond the edge of his Pet Milk universe and his face constantly prepared to break into a big grin at the wonderful joy of it all.

I say "you" because the world that I was in had so changed that for a minute I thought that you were there, with me, as I walked down broad Juárez Avenue, passed the greenery of the Alameda, and approached the Hotel Prado. I wanted you there, to share the wonderful adventure of simply being, of being right then, at that point, together, in our lives.

Of course I was mistaken. You were off, somewhere, lost in a book by the anthropologist Claude Lévi-Strauss, enchanted by the elegant curvature of his logic as he orchestrated it through a symphony of binary contrasts. Foolish me. How could simply being there, on Juárez, passing the Alameda, and approaching the Prado, compare to such an exotic journey? Well, to each his own trip, and I was on mine, enchanted too, by all I could see, smell, touch, and even taste. Then it happened, the scream, the look, and the tears.

Only a few minutes before, she had been sitting against the wall of the theater next door to the Prado. In front of her, she had neatly unfolded a white square of cloth and on it arranged piles of pecans. She had placed the pecans equidistant from one another and from the edges and corners of the cloth. On top of each pile, she had with careful thumb and finger positioned a partially shelled nut in anticipation that the firm, yellow fruit thus exposed would entice a passerby to make a purchase. Unlike other street vendors, she did not harangue the crowds with calls to come and buy, but knelt quietly, her small body perfectly composed against the building's wall, and her livelihood positioned before her: yellow-topped, brown pyramids ordered into rows and columns on a square, white field. Rather than simply selling pecans, it was as if she had prepared an offering to the busy adult world that towered above her. At that moment, she screamed.

A van pulled up to the curb, and two men, the driver and his companion, got out, and without a glance or moment's hesitation, walked purposefully through the sidewalk crowd, passing just in front of me, and stopped before the little girl. She remained kneeling, her hands folded in her lap, her body pushed against the building, her head thrown back, and her mouth open, and from her mouth poured out a sound that rose above all other sounds in that world of sounds, dominating them, subduing them, and turning them into insignificant squeaks. If God, sitting on his throne in heaven, ever heard utter despair, he surely heard that girl's soul as it broke apart.

One man reached down and scooped up the cloth, made it into a bag, and handed it to his partner. The two turned back into the indifferent crowd, tossed the bag into the back of the van, and drove off.

A young attendant came out of the foyer of the theater and knelt beside the girl, careful to tuck the skirt of her uniform away from the dirt of the sidewalk. She put her hand, not unkindly, on the girl's shoulders.

"*No llores, niña, no llores,*" she quietly pleaded and began picking up the few pecans left scattered about. She reached for the brown paper sack the girl had near her, and as she hurriedly threw in the pecans, she whispered again, "*No llores.*"

Two well-dressed, older ladies, their fat purses held safely against equally large bosoms, paused on their high heels to look down.

"*¿Qué pasa?*" one asked the attendant.

"*Nada*," came the reply, and to ensure they understood and would go on wherever they were going, the young lady replied again, "*Nada, nada. Nada pasa aquí.*"

The attendant, glancing back into the foyer and in answer to a querulous command coming from its darkness, got up, and pulled the child erect as she did so. She handed the girl the paper sack, and told her once again, this time her voice a hiss as she scurried back to her station, "*No llores.*"

A chauffeur, standing beside a Mercedes awaiting its passengers from the Prado, crossed over to the girl and gave her the change from his pocket. When he came back, I asked, "*¿Qué pasa?*" "*Nada*" was his first word, but he added, "*No tiene licencia. "¿Cómo?*" I asked. "*Licencia. Licencia. Los derechos. No paga. Ella,*" came the closed-mouth answer, the sounds barely escaping the drawn lips as if the chauffeur were afraid of his own words. "*Nada pasa*" was his final statement, the words punctuated by the firm shut of the Mercedes' door, the driver now finished with both me and the girl.

She was still there, against the building, holding the sack with both hands, the tears flowing, but soundless, not a sob or even a sniffle.

I reached into my pocket, took out my billfold, thumbed it open—the face of my own sixth-grade daughter staring at me in the precious rigidity of a school photograph—and took out several bills. The girl saw me, and her face hardened like the gray concrete behind her. She stuck out her hand, and when I reached out to give her the money, she snatched it away, curling it in her fist, stuffing it in her skirt pocket, and not giving it a glance—her eyes fixed on me, cased in tears which she was bringing, through a stubborn hardening, to a stop. Only little girls cry, and she was now knowledgeable in the ways of adults.

Don't cry, little girl. Don't cry. Nothing has happened. Nothing has happened here. The attendant, not much older than you and already in uniform, says so and has so informed the well-dressed curious. They, who have done so well in their lives, believe her, so shouldn't you?

No, nothing is happening here, little girl. The chauffeur says so, and he drives an expensive Mercedes carrying important people on their important trips from here to there and back again. He says it's nothing. You simply don't have permission to earn a living. To get permission, to have that right, you have to pay a fee. That's all. It is nothing.

Nothing is happening, so don't cry. Adults don't want you to cry. It makes them uneasy. It makes them think that something is not right, that something is happening. That's the reason they gave you the money, to keep anything from happening. They don't like things to happen, like little girls crying in public, on busy Juárez Avenue. That's the reason they always say that nothing is happening and give you money to make sure it doesn't.

Having finished accusing me of every sin I ever committed and some of yours too, the girl's eyes became completely dry except for one small and stubborn tear refusing to fall from its perch on an eyelash. Then it too dropped, a last rivulet of her childhood, and she brought up her hand to wipe it away in disgust. How could she have ever cried! She turned to join the other adults, busy with their business, and became one of the many figures moving away into their going, and so disappeared.

The sun, having spent itself in the procreation of the morning, now grew pale, and the afternoon promised in its small future to revert back to yesterday's stagnant past. With the sun so weak, the traffic beast rose again and curled its obnoxious body around the remains of the day, squeezing out the last ounce of its freshness. At the street corner, the little boy twisted his small body into a corner of the milk carton where he fought to preserve his tiny self even as a dark ooze spread between his legs. Her dignity burned away by desperation, the mother thrust out her hand at those moving past to become a pitiful demand in a city of such demands.

I too turned away, turned away and left, left Juárez, the Alameda, and the Prado. I turned away and left, and now I'm here, and I turn to you with my question.

You already know the question. You are smart as well as wise. But wait. Wait before you tell me that you don't know the answer because there isn't one, and turn away too. At least let me be certain that you see the question itself and that you recognize the way in which it asks itself, how it circles around us and includes all within its encompassing accusation: the attendant in her uniform, the well-dressed in their easily convinced high heels, the chauffeur back in his Mercedes with the door firmly shut, and the two men in the van, certainly them, in their officialdom of *licencia* and *derechos*, and more; the city in its absorbing enormity, the country in its dull poverty, and the Glorious Revolution in its studied corruption, and more yet; our country and its insatiability that bites off greater and greater chunks of the world's wealth, leaving less and less and eventually nothing at all; and finally, you and me and our profession, the terms you define and the words I choose, responding to the hand offering a package of gum, to the tiny body tossing in a cardboard carton, and to the tears now all dried under the harsh light of adulthood, responding to these happenings by calling them fieldwork and so making them into an everyday, workaday *nada*, a normal nothing; just so that is clear, I'll ask you once more, "Who's to blame?"

 # "Did You?"

WARD H. GOODENOUGH
University of Pennsylvania

When I was on Onotoa in Kiribati in the summer of 1951, I learned that, like most other Pacific Islanders, people there routinely greeted one another with "Where are you going?" or "Where are you coming from?" to which such replies as "North," "South," "Ocean side," or "Lagoon side" were customarily acceptable answers. The questions and answers were routine greeting exchanges among people who had lived their lives in the same community and already knew one another well.

The novice Westerner encountering Pacific ways may at first react to the opening question as an intrusion into his or her privacy, feeling called upon to explain where indeed he or she is actually going. Not so. When asked "How are you?" at home, we are not called upon to explain our actual state of health. "Fine, thanks!" ends the exchange. The same held in Onotoa.

More disconcerting to the Westerner learning to live with Onotoans was the routine exchange that took place when someone in a group rose to go out to relieve himself or herself. As one stood up to go, one heard the usual question, "Where are you going?" In this case the appropriate answer was "To the sea." Someone returning to a group after "going to the sea" was greeted with "Did you?" to which the appropriate reply was "I did."

Urination might take place almost anywhere that was a little out of the way, appropriately with one's back to anyone else nearby. The beach was the place people went to for more serious relief. Hence the expression "To the sea." There was no attempt at privacy. Indeed, a person squatting on the beach might be holding a conversation with someone at a house forty or fifty feet away without regard to gender. When finished, one completed the toileting by wading out into the water for a quick wash. It was all done very matter-of-factly.

Western colonial officials and missionaries had been unwilling to accommodate to this easy approach to defecation. For their convenience, each village had been required to construct an outhouse over the water in front of the village assembly hall. It was customary for visitors to beach their canoes there and to be housed in the "sitting place of strangers" in the assembly hall, a large, sacred public building whose use was

Kiribati (Gilbert Islands)

hedged by many formalities. Before there were outhouses, those approaching from all directions had an unimpeded view of this imposing building, which sat just above the beach. Now visitors were greeted by a small hut on piles out over the lagoon's shallows interposed between them and the assembly hall. It did not enhance the majesty of the approach. Even so, when visiting another village with Onotoans, I could sense a contagious, excited tension among my companions as we approached the beach before the assembly hall.

The outhouse itself made few concessions to privacy. Its square frame, resting on the piles, supported two parallel pieces of wood on which to place one's feet. There was a screen of coconut leaf thatch about two feet high, at the most, so that the user's body from midriff down was shielded from outside view in squatting position. About four feet of open space extended above the screen to the roof, providing the user with an excellent view of the beachfront and the various activities taking place along it. It also provided people on the beach with an excellent view of the occupant of the outhouse.

On Onotoa, to reach the outhouse in front of the assembly hall where I was housed, it was necessary to walk out on two long coconut logs, laid end to end. There was no handhold; it was a balancing act all the way. At the beach end of this walkway, the log was about two feet above the sand, requiring the user to clamber up on it, rise to a standing position, and then get into a state of balance before tightroping out the nearly fifty feet to the business end.

Except when the English lands commissioner came to work in the village, I was the only user of this convenience for toilet purposes. I found that, as a Westerner, I was expected to use it. The Onotoans had been required to build it to accommodate the modesty of people like me. My habits in such matters made me happy to use it, in any case.

The structure had other uses, however. It was a place much favored by children for fishing with hook and line when the tide was in. They would stand in the outhouse, hanging over the low thatch wall, or sit on the log walkway just in front of it with their handlines or improvised fishing poles. Their efforts were not signally rewarded, but occasionally they came up with a few small fish. Thus, when I had need to use the outhouse, it often happened that children were out there fishing. I would come to the end of the log, precious roll of paper in hand, and make throat-clearing noises. The young anglers would look up, see me standing there, and quickly scurry in to the beach, clearing my access to the outhouse and giving me such little privacy as it afforded.

Because I had expressed an interest in learning the then-popular form of dancing known as the "Multiplication Tables," which had been imported from Tavalu in postmissionary times, the Onotoans decided that the proper way to keep me entertained and, perhaps, out of possible mischief was to involve me in nightly informal dance sessions in the village assembly hall. Thus, I soon became well schooled in giving the answers "To the sea" and "I did."

There was an occasion when the schooling served me well. One afternoon I was seized with an urgent need to use the outhouse. As I rushed to the beach, clutching the toilet roll, I saw that someone fishing with a pole was sitting on the log about four feet in front of the entrance. It was one of the village's loveliest fifteen-year-old girls. My urgency did not permit the usual throat-clearing routine. I leapt onto the log and proceeded as quickly as possible up to the outhouse. As I approached the girl she reached behind her with one hand to keep from falling off the log while she leaned over to let me step around her. She then serenely resumed her fishing while I entered the outhouse, dropped my pants, and squatted. My performance must have announced itself a good hundred yards in either direction along the beach. The girl remained politely oblivious to it all, seemingly intent on her fishing. At length I finished, pulled up my pants, and emerged to return to the beach. Again, she grasped the log with one hand and leaned over to let me step around her. As I did so, she turned her head, looked up at me, and in a sweet, matter-of-fact voice asked, "Did you?"

Thanks to what I had learned, I managed to keep my balance and replied as offhandedly as I could, "I did."

SUGGESTED READINGS

GRIMBLE, SIR ARTHUR
1952   We Chose the Islands. New York: Morrow. (English Edition: A Pattern of Islands. London: John Murray, 1952).
1957   Return to the Islands. London: John Murray.

MAUD, H. E.
1963   The Evolution of the Gilbertese Boti: An Ethnohistorical Approach. Memoir No. 35. Aukland, New Zealand: The Polynesian Society.

THIRTEEN

🌀 Strange Laughter

BRUCE GRINDAL
Florida State University

ENCOUNTER BY THE SIDE OF THE ROAD

When I was living among the Sisala people of West Africa, I had many occasions to visit with old men in their homes. In fact, most of what I learned about the Sisala came from the mouths of old men. The thick mudbrick walls of the houses resisted the intense sun; inside they were pleasant, cool, and sensuous with the odors of human living. Oftentimes I would sit upon a cowskin on the mud floor and talk for hours while sharing beer, boiled peanuts, and whatever other gift of food was brought in by some grandson or granddaughter. The conversation was always polite and never hurried.

The old men would talk about traditions and olden times, about the law and custom, about "what the ancestors brought down," about the ways and paths of right conduct. They talked of the times when men were masters, when they could kill their enemies without secrecy or a faint heart. They debated upon the disputes and quarrels of the day: the enmities between clans, enmities inherited by generations, enmities that caused wives to quarrel, children to fight, and babies to miscarry. They talked about "today's people"—about how everybody was out after their own selfish ends. They remembered their childhoods, the joys of being "herd boys" and taking lovers to their flesh in the grass; of crazy youth, of quarrels, about witches who threw "killer bees" at their enemies in public places. Among some, the sadder ones, they talked about their drinking, and a will to die. The modern world had taken away their sons and left them without immortality and purpose. As one said, "But for the singing of women, I am alone in this house."

One day in September of 1967, I was driving with my interpreter, J. B., to a village five miles to the west. The day was pleasant. The coolness of the night lingered in the morning air and the fields were ripe with the harvest and the wet-mown smell of grass, water, and earth. J. B. was in a good mood. We were going to his village, where he knew all the people. Thus along the way, I asked J. B. if he had heard any news or gossip. Had the crop been harvested yet? Was Dimua preparing to sacrifice to the village shrine? Had young Joha heard about his entrance exam

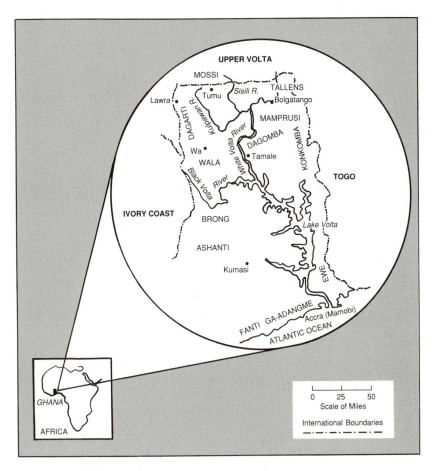

Ghana, with location of tribes

results? What was the health of old Hatia? Was her husband, Venu, still drinking?

J. B. especially enjoyed accompanying me to his village, for it afforded him an opportunity to respond to my questions in an intelligent and learned manner and to walk with pride as one of the successful products of the white man's education. To my queries, J. B. assumed an intelligent pose and, extending his jaw, assumed an air of authoritative erudition. Other times, however, especially when I asked about people whom he did not like or whom he found humorous, he exhibited a more mischievous side, which he expressed by contorting his face and assuming postures of surprise, mock indignation, or mimicry.

I inquired about one old man named Mummeni. J. B. at once looked stern, and in all seriousness related an unfortunate tragedy involving Mummeni's "brother." Apparently one of Mummeni's younger brothers had been living in southern Ghana, working as a fisherman on the Volta River. One day while he was fishing, his raft tipped over and he drowned. The body was never found. I asked J. B. whether there would be a funeral in the village. At this, J. B. appeared more deeply disturbed. "You know, when a man dies away from home, they must bring his body back to be buried. When they do, the eldest son must go down into the grave and say some words in the dead man's ear. Only in that way will his soul join the ancestors." J. B. stopped. There was a thought that would not leave him alone, and he remained silent for some time.

On a visit weeks earlier I had met Mummeni. I would guess his age to have been in the early fifties. Yet owing to his condition as a severly deformed cripple, he was an old man in his decorum. To describe his composure, I would say he appeared as if reclining on a sofa. His feet and lower legs were gnarled and foreshortened and had almost grown together to resemble the tail of a fish. This mass of his lower anatomy was neatly tucked into the grooves of his wooden sled. His left arm was similarly withered and extended like a flipper; yet his left hand held, in a most peculiar fashion, a block of wood that he used to propel himself about. His right arm was normal, and like his torso, muscular.

Mummeni lived as a solitary man. His house, which stood in the sun by the side of the road, was a visitor's first encounter with the village. Mummeni had had his house built in the modern style. Constructed of mud brick and thatch, it consisted of three rooms. Two were unoccupied, except for the presence of a western-made traveling trunk in one. In the main room, where the old man stayed, there was a posted bed with a kapok mattress and sheets. Also proudly displayed were a sewing machine, a bicycle, and a water filter. The house and grounds were well swept. The front entrance had a veranda that faced the road. A smaller exit in the rear faced onto a half acre garden with neatly tended rows of okra, groundnuts, guinea corn, bambara beans, and sweet potatoes. When we first met, he was in his garden tending to a row of bambara beans with his mother and a small boy from his brother's compound.

I was impressed by the man, by his honesty and forthrightness; but yet something about him I did not like. When we had entered his house and were seated on the cowskin, and having passed formal greetings, he abruptly stated, "You know, I am not a married man." I immediately felt embarrassed and did not know what to say. However, more than that, I felt angry. His statement was calculated for its effect. Having embarrassed me, he achieved control over the conversation, and he proceeded to tell the story of his life.

When he was a child of three, in a time that he had forgotten, he accidentally rolled into his mother's cooking fire. By the time he was rescued, his feet and lower legs had been burned severely as well as his left arm. As he grew older, it was realized that he would never walk again. Then two years ago, he became very sick and didn't know whether he would survive. In his own words, he was crazy with fever and talked in voices, praying to God all the time. When he recovered, he told his brothers that he would like to become a Moslem, and asked permission to build his house by the road so that if any Moslem passed by, the traveler could stop and say prayers with him.

He talked about his travels to southern Ghana and his appreciation of the civilized ways of city life. He proudly acclaimed his newly acquired trade as a tailor, and he displayed the gowns and mosquito nets that he had recently sewn.

Yet something about the old man was too down-pat, too perfect. He had, in a most obsessive and deliberate way, fashioned a life for himself that was both solitary and saintly. He was the proverbial man in a house by the side of the road, offering to others his generosity and wisdom. At the same time a strangeness would paint his face with a laugh and stifle his deeply felt history of pain, ridicule, and solitude. I had never met a saint, and at some level of my intuition, I distrusted what I saw.

Therefore, what J. B. said to me that morning about the drowning death of Mummeni's brother impressed me all the more. I kept in my mind that I would visit him and inquire into his brother's death.

J. B. and I arrived at Mummeni's house as the late morning sun had begun its steady glow off the east wall. The warming heat brought with it the sweet moist scents of the southerly winds, the storm clouds, and the possible brief return of the rainy season. The house seemed deserted and almost frightening in its austerity as the winds blew through the curtains that flapped about the doorway on the veranda. J. B. and I walked toward the rear of the house.

Suddenly, we heard an angry cry from the back of the house. As J. B. and I rounded the corner, we saw Mummeni hobbling through the garden, propelling himself on his sled, angrily pursuing a flock of black birds that had flown into his field. In his frantic pursuit of the black birds, Mummeni slipped and fell off his sled. Lying there, gnarled in the dirt, he frantically shook his stick at the birds.

J. B. laughed. More accurately he snorted in uncontrolled mirth. He shook so hard that he bent to the side in order to hide his embarrassment.

Mummeni saw us. At first he was startled. Then he quickly regained his composure, and grasping the shaft of his spear with his strong right arm, he righted himself. The spear trembled in his hand. The man was obviously embarrassed; however, I had no choice but to walk over and greet him. The hand he offered was limp and without direction. He averted his eyes and laughed in the obsequious manner often characteristic of some Sisala people upon meeting a white man for the first time. I disliked this, especially among elder men, whose dignity deserved better from them.

Entering his house, Mummeni immediately rushed over to the clay water pot in the corner of the room. Taking a calabash gourd, he dipped it into the pot. Raising it to his lips, he took a long draught, gulping the water, which trickled down his neck onto the seam of his garment. Having quenched his thirst, he moved to the center of the room. Successfully encountering the edge of his cowskin, the old man assumed a position of state. Only then did he acknowledge fully the presence of J. B. and me and begin the ritual of Sisala greeting. Now, everything about him seemed calm and composed.

After the greetings were finished, I bent over and again touching his hand, I said in a mixture of Sisala and English, "I am sorry to hear that your brother died." Mummeni apparently did not understand, for he turned to J. B. for a translation. J. B. then translated my words into his words, delivered with respect and authority. While J. B. spoke, Mummeni again drank from the calabash.

Suddenly, he bolted. It was like a hiccup or sudden burp. The water he had been drinking sprayed upon my forearm and shirt. I recoiled to witness the man laughing out of control. I looked at J. B. He was also laughing; this time J. B. made no pretense to hide his mirth. Instead, he rolled over on the cowskin, pointing his eyes and fingers at me and laughing again.

I was embarrassed. I failed to see what was funny about my remark, and not knowing what to say I continued along the same line: "I understand your brother drowned." As I said this, I illustrated in gesture the sensation of water.

Again, there erupted an uncontrolled spasm. This time, the old man hunched over, and hyperventilating, puffed up his cheeks, splayed out his arms, and extending himself forward like an insensible hulk, laughingly displayed the whites of his eyes. J. B. joined in the laughter as though he were celebrating a performance. He lightly clapped his hands and bowed to Mummeni. Mummeni, quietly retiring from his absurd pose, once again assumed his dignity. The conversation continued as if nothing had happened.

WHY DID THE OLD MAN LAUGH?

Why did the old man laugh? I do not know. I never again talked to the old man, nor did I speak to J. B. concerning the incident. I had no desire to pursue the subject.

No doubt my presence must have embarrassed the old man, as his bizarre behavior had embarrassed me. My reference to the brother's death may have called forth a memory, perhaps a morbid impression. Obviously, the query was inappropriate. Both of us were caught off-guard. The result was "strange laughter." It happened once; then it was over. Our mutual embarrassment and resulting estrangement prevented me from pursuing the subject.

To speculate what I might have discovered had I inquired further into the old man's laughter is purely academic. Had I asked J. B., I may have received a commonplace answer that would have allowed me to shove this experience into some comfortable corner of my mind and thereby forget it. Again, I do not know. The fact remains that I did not ask and thus the experience has remained a mystery, a mystery that has charmed me. Seventeen years later, I come to glimpse into this mystery, into the unexpected and darker side of laughter.

There is much I could say about Sisala laughter, about respect, decorum, the polite smile, and the flow of good humor in conversation. I could also talk about the more cruel sides of laughter, a laughter borne of the harsh conditions, endemic afflictions, and unsightly facts of Sisala life: the broken bones improperly mended, the milky cataracts of river blindness, the protruded swellings of guinea worm infection, and the demented ravings that result from organic brain deterioration. Incidents of human wretchedness and misfortune transformed into laughter. Each of these recollections, however, falls short of explaining the ritualized, hysterical laughter of a deformed man to queries about his brother's death. There is something lacking, a connecting tissue of structure, which would allow me to perceive the circumstances of Mummeni's laughter as homologous to other aspects of Sisala culture. One event, however, approaches this isomorphism. It had to do with killing a turkey.

KILLING A TURKEY WITH KOJO

After having lived in Sisala-land for a short time, I came to raise chickens and guinea fowl. For the most part, these fowl were offered as gifts from the various people whom I visited, and I would often return home from a village with a load of fresh vegetables and one or more fowl, usually with their legs tied together, squawking and shitting in the back seat of the car. I amassed a number of birds, ranging, at any one time, from five to fifteen. These I kept at the back of my house. I enjoyed watching them in the lazy afternoon.

On occasion I would ask my steward, Kojo, to kill one of the birds and prepare it for an evening meal. While I typed my field notes in the late afternoon, I observed him about his task. I was impressed by the ease and gentle manner in which he killed the fowl. Usually he would approach the flock quietly, making gentle gestures with his lips. As he approached, most would move aside. One bird, however, due to character, stamina, or confusion, always held its ground. It wouldn't move; instead it would stare up at Kojo, as though aware of the imminent threat but yet accepting of its fate. Gently Kojo would lift the bird from the ground, and cradling it in his arms, take it to the back steps of the house.

Sitting down, he would lay the bird in his lap and begin to stroke its throat. In this manner he would hypnotize the animal so that when he drew the knife through its throat, the bird would stand transfixed for a moment before it took off, flapping its wings madly about the yard.

They say that only a country boy (or girl) knows the pain of having to eat an animal which he (or she) has known ar.d named. While I could never share this intimacy with my birds, there was an awareness, a respect so to speak, whenever I ate one of them. The chicken was once a living creature; now it lay as cooked meat on my plate. Reflecting upon this, I decided that since I raised my own animals, I, as a proper anthropologist, should also butcher them.

A few days later, in the afternoon, I informed Kojo of my intentions. Kojo smiled, and together we walked to the backyard of my house. While I sat on the back stoop, Kojo walked over among the chickens, gently lifted the selected bird, and brought it back to where I was sitting. He sat down beside me and handed over the chicken along with his knife. He then drew back a few feet to observe.

Needless to say, I made a mess of the job. The bird was frightened to hysteria, and the more I tried Kojo's soothing manner, the more frantic it became. I was able, however, to hold on to the bird and to crudely cut its throat. I had never butchered an animal before, and the experience nauseated me.

That evening I ate the chicken which Kojo prepared, and afterwards, I felt sick to my stomach. Seeing my condition, Kojo approached me and said, "That chicken be too strong for you, master?"

"What do you mean?" I asked.

"Your heart too much like that chicken," he replied. "It beat too fast. The meat be tough, not good for stomach, master."

Over the next few days, I was troubled by occasional stomach cramps. This unpleasantness notwithstanding, I chose to persevere in the intent to slaughter my own fowl. Thus some days later, I again approached Kojo and told him I wished to butcher another chicken.

Again we went outside and Kojo repeated the ritual of selecting the chicken. Bringing the bird back to where I was sitting, he told me to hold it for a few minutes while he went back into the house. Thus I waited, holding the squawking bird tightly about the wings.

When Kojo returned, he was carrying a glass containing a small amount of apoteshe, a locally distilled spirit which I kept for the purpose of lighting my lanterns. He sat down next to me and reaching over to the chicken, began to softly stroke its throat. As he did, he gradually brought his fingers behind its head and coaxed the bird to open its mouth. With his right hand he lifted the glass and poured the spirits down the animal's throat. At first, the chicken convulsed slightly and tried to throw up the drink, but Kojo continued in his reassuring manner to stroke the throat. Shortly, the bird was completely relaxed. At this point, Kojo handed me his knife and, as before, withdrew a short distance. The knife passed through the chicken's neck like butter. Releasing the bird, it staggered about the yard, flapping its wings and spurting blood, until it fell over dead.

After that, I no longer slaughtered my chickens, but left the task to Kojo. I had succeeded in what I wanted to do, and discovered in the process that I did not have the heart to kill things. This resolution of mine was changed, however, by an unexpected event.

One afternoon, as I was typing my fieldnotes, a Land-Rover roared into my driveway and screeched to a stop. Out of it poured an Englishman named Dan, his girlfriend from Switzerland, a Pole named Andre, an American black named Seymore, and a cute English university student named Matsie. Matsie rushed up to me, planted a kiss on my cheek, and informed me that they had come to Tumu to have a "gang bang."

As any enthnographer knows, the unexpected arrival of friends at a field site can be disruptive. My friends were no exception. A year before, I had met them at the University of Ghana. Together we had enjoyed good times, particularly Matsie's "gang bangs." These consisted of going to a Lebanese restaurant, ordering five courses of food and drink, telling jokes and laughing, and getting stuffed and mildly drunk. Now they were on my doorstep ready for good times. Fortunately they were tired from the long trip, and that night retired early, spreading their bedrolls among the two available rest houses and on my living room floor.

The next morning J. B. arrived at nine. I introduced him to my friends and together we strolled to the open-air market in Tumu. J. B. was full of energy and curiosity; he was dressed in his best trousers and shirt. My friends were equally enthusiastic and eager to buy souvenirs. As we passed through the market, we came upon a man who was selling a large tom turkey tethered to a stake. Immediately, Dan and Matsie offered to buy it so that we could have a gang bang. I told them that they should give Kojo a dash for the extra work he would have to do to prepare the meal. Agreeing, they purchased the bird, and we led it home on a leash.

Now, turkeys are not given to being led on a leash, and especially not the big tom turkey we had bought. It strained fiercely, flapping its wings in defiance and proudly erecting the folds of red waddle on its throat. Attracted by the turkey's behavior, groups of children followed us as we walked back to the house.

I mentioned to Dan and Andre my custom of killing chickens by intoxication. Andre was particularly fascinated, and as we passed the government store, he rushed in and bought a bottle of gin for the occasion. We returned to my house to confront Kojo with an enraged turkey, and a crowd of curious spectators gathered to watch.

Kojo was not pleased by the carnival atmosphere; however, he stifled his displeasure and slowly approached the bird. As a result of its painful journey, the turkey had become very aggressive, and as Kojo moved in, it would dart at him. With sympathetic movements, Kojo gracefully avoided the bird's attacks while at the same time moving closer. As he did, he softly pursed his lips. The turkey gradually quieted, and soon Kojo was sitting at its side, caressing its chest and throat. Kojo's manner also quieted down my friends, the spectators, and the crowd of children who had followed us. Everyone waited in expectation.

I quietly sat down at Kojo's side with the bottle of gin between my legs. Kojo continued to stroke the bird's throat and gestured with his eyes that I should move closer. I reached over with my right hand and began stroking its breast. I could feel its heart beating hotly; its eyes were dazed, and froth was hanging from its mouth. The separate folds of red flesh on its neck had become engorged with blood, madly throbbing beneath the membrane of skin. Now under Kojo's gentle strokes, the terror gradually subsided like the sobs of a hurt child in the arms of its mother.

Kojo continued to stroke the animal's throat and brought his touch closer to the base of the turkey's skull. He gently nudged the head upward while at the same time prodding the bird to open its mouth. It was as though he were molding a bust sculpture, prodding the clay to look heavenward with puckered lips.

Kojo then motioned with his eyes that I should give the bird a drink. I put the bottle to the turkey's mouth and began to pour. The bird jolted. Its throat convulsed, and it choked up the harsh alcohol. I paused, and Kojo stroked its throat to bring the bird back into a calm state. I poured again, and again the bird jolted, only this time with less vigor. I was able to pour longer and longer draughts down its throat until one third of the bottle was gone.

The turkey now stood calm, solid and still like a rock ready to crumble. Kojo then passed me his knife. Taking it in my hand, I selected a point midway on the throat and began to draw the knife sideways through the flesh. The turkey's wattle was thick, and although the knife was sharp, it took two strong passes before I felt the bones of its throat. Before I could pull away the knife, the first spurt of blood fell upon my hand.

The turkey remained motionless. Then came another spurt, falling red like an exclamation mark upon the dirt. The bird then began to move, waddling to the left in a gentle arc. It was a clumsy waddle, and as the bird moved, its wings splayed out. The head remained erect in the pose that Kojo had molded with his caresses. The pose was one of complete indifference and arrogance as though the bird were staring down its nose at the spectators with disdain.

The absurdity of this pose caused the Sisala to laugh. J. B., in particular, was overcome, and clapped his hands and averted his head in embarrassed laughter.

The turkey completed the arc, whereupon it stopped and stood to face Kojo, its breast touching Kojo's parted legs. The turkey's eyes had become milky, and its mouth hung open with mucus and blood dripping down the sides. Its splayed wings now dragged on the ground and its legs trembled. It had lost control of its flesh and now stood helpless. Then, in a dramatic gesture of relief, the bird fell forward onto Kojo's lap.

For a moment there was silence, then the Sisala began to clap. The children jumped with glee; J. B. bowed and clapped his hands; and my expatriated friends, somewhat embarrassed, joined in. It was like a cheer at a bull fight when the matador performs a perfect coup de grâce, the moment of truth and death performed with finesse. Kojo was pleased, and he softly bowed his head in a humble smile.

Kojo roasted the bird over an open fire in the government cook house. He cooked the turkey long, and the aromatic spices and tenderizers in the stuffing thoroughly impregnated the meat, to produce a most succulent dish. That night, my friends and I had a gang bang. The feast lasted several hours, and the eating was interspersed by frequent toasts with Polish vodka. We laughed, and our faces became warm with drink.

Toward the end of the evening, Dan, the Englishman, left the table and returned shortly wearing his girlfriend's lace nightgown. This was particularly funny since Dan's girlfriend was small and petite while he was tall and lanky with funny-looking feet. Dan then proceeded to prance around like a fairy, and he danced with Matsie. Then he announced that he was going to make a surprise dessert, whereupon he took a half-finished bottle of brandy and disappeared into the kitchen. He reappeared with a plate of bananas he had generously covered with a layer of sugar and brandy. As we looked on, Dan ignited the dish with a match. Bananas flambé was the high point of the evening.

Afterwards, the conversations dissolved and my friends retired for the night. Kojo, who throughout the dinner had looked on with amusement and occasional bewilderment, asked his leave.

"Well, what did you think?" I asked.

Kojo shook his head. "The Englishman," he said. "He burn bananas." Kojo continued to shake his head in disbelief. "Your friends, they have good time. Man eat well," he said. Kojo then paused, and looking directly in my eyes, said, "The turkey be a man, a strong man. He make you laugh good and strong."

IN DEFENSE OF ANIMISM

How is the pathetic and bloody death of a turkey akin to Mummeni's bizarre imitation of his brother's death? The milky eyes of the turkey, the frothy saliva and blood hanging from its mouth, the desperation of its wobbly legs? A hunched over cripple, hyperventilating and showing the whites of his eyes? Do both events, in a strangely isomorphic way, stare into the tooth of death? What is the animistic moment?

To go further, I must slide back the screen which separates my person from the immediate reality of these events. I am no longer dealing with detached empirical observations and academically polite interpretations. I am dealing with events which have gotten into my guts and my soul. They are part of my poetry and my fiction.

That morning in September, the old man awakened to the moist scents of the southern winds. A strange day. A day of light and darkness. The rising sun beat hot upon the earth. The black storm clouds hovered ominously on the southern horizon, bringing with them the moist winds and the memories of summer rains and the wet earth. They were pregnant with memories.

The old man did not greet the day in a pleasant mood. Especially on humid mornings his crippled frame was penetrated by torture. To rise, to limber his crippled body, to face the day was the perpetual torture of his lot in life. And on this humid morning, with the possibility of rain before the harvest, with the potatoes and beans rotting on the vines, he cursed the sunrise.

There was a foreboding to this day. The old man felt it, but angrily he shook his head. The day was hot. The moist winds coming from the south blew the flaps about the doors. The winds stirred the dust on the floor and brought scents of the rainforests and the rivers and the electric anticipation of dark clouds and lightning on the southern horizon. A day full of strangeness.

The old man heard the call of black birds. A faint, but angry chatter of voices borne on the southern wind. Startled for a moment, the old man was consumed by a thought. A memory which would not leave his mind. He shook his head and labored to mount his sled. Grabbing a spear in his right hand, he propelled himself toward the back doorway facing onto the garden. Pushing the curtain aside, he faced the day.

Blowing in from the south, the clouds, dark and ominous, cast a shadow over the distant fields. He had to squint to see the black forms of the birds against the sky. The sounds came closer, and with each call, the scents: the dark marsh grasses, the new-mown crops, the rising mists of the firmament rich and sweet with the smell of decay.

Suddenly, the black birds flashed into the light of the sun and as quickly descended upon the garden. They strutted boldly about, the hot sun steaming moisture from their black bodies. They called on the old man in the doorway. They mocked his impotence and his deformity.

This wretched but proud man was consumed by anger. Propelling himself forward, he pursued the invaders. Scurrying among the rows of his garden, he had no occasion to be reminded of his premonitions and the strangeness of the day. The quickening rush of his blood dispelled the nagging fears which crippled his being.

Thus it is hard to say when the animistic moment came. Perhaps it was the beak of a bird angrily tearing into the flesh of his garden. Perhaps it was the silver eyes shining from a steaming black body. Perhaps it was the scent of the rivers and marsh grasses, the last gasp of a dying breath borne on the moonlight mists of a river, rising into the firmament upon the monsoon winds, to be carried on the breath of a crow, on the mists of its black body shining in the sun.

And so it was that the old man confronted his brother's ghost.

One, I, you, we would have had to be the old man to know the terror he felt. Was this the brother who troubled his dreams, who came to him in disguise, and who offered him water when he was sick? Was it the kind, the loving, the thoughtful brother who brought him gifts from his journeys? Or was it the brother who now mocked him in the angry and malicious voices of the black birds?

The old man felt his brother was everywhere about him. To have seen him transformed in the configuration of the maize and bambara beans, but then to see him vanish before his eyes. To have dared to talk to him, to command him to respond, but to have his words sucked away by the cold silence of the brother's presence. To have shivered in the fear of the touch of imminent death.

Into this scene came the white man and that ne'er-do-well interpreter. How absurd the old man felt. Lying there flat on the ground, while the black birds, which he strove so valiantly to drive away, now took flight in the presence of these visitors.

Who was this white man? Why does he come now to talk to me? These people from the sea, their skin bleached white by the water. How can you know what they think and feel? And that young interpreter. A rascal if there ever was one. Why is he not at home working with his brothers and taking care of his wife and baby son? A "white man's child." He walks about making the faces of the white man; he mocks us.

So it may have been that the old man thought these things as he composed himself within his house. Then the white man leaned forward and touched the old man, and spoke words which he did not understand. Then the pompous face of the interpreter, the stiffened jaw pointed upward in disdain, delivered the white man's words. A breath. It cut into the heart of the old man's lonely soul and rendered him naked, terrified and absurd.

Ghosts! The tooth of death!

My mind topples backwards over the years and at once I am a child again. Gathering blackberries in June and eating sweet corn, sweet peas, and watermelon raw from the fields. Catching crayfish, frogs, and snakes and believing that snakes bit you with the tips of their forked tongues. Running down paths and finding secret hide-outs. Once falling hands forward on a nail and wondering what it felt like to be Jesus.

And I recall old man Kech. His gray hair and small beady eyes, like a solitary and cruel rat. A rat, a man, who poisoned the neighbor's dogs and who in the imagination of children had murdered his wife, cut her in pieces, and fed her to the chickens.

On Saturday, he slaughtered his chickens with an axe on the block. We children gathered and watched. He dared us, he taunted us, he gave the axe to the eldest amongst us and made him cry. He murdered savagely. Then, in a flick of his eye, he picked up the chicken's head and threw it at me. It was alive. The blood splattered upon my leg.

On that night, after my friends had finished the sumptuous meal of turkey, vodka, and bananas flambé, I stayed up talking with Seymore. We sat in the living room of my bungalow, across from one another in my newly refurbished easy chairs. The night had turned cold. The dry air of the harmattan burned the nostrils and caused mucus to form in our sinuses. Both of us were bundled in hooded sweatshirts, illuminated by the burning of the kerosine lanterns.

Seymore was cool. He sat back in his chair like some moorish monk. He was distant. The words fell off his lips in a cool black jive talk, an impersonal style he could affect whenever he so wanted. He talked about Mao and the cultural revolution in China, about how revolutions had to be perpetual because the black man "be forever getting the honky off his back." And so he talked. I listened, intimidated.

Seymore described a play he was writing. A black mine worker and his white overseer were trapped in a mineshaft in a copper mine in central Africa. The black man stabs the white man with a knife in the ribs and then watches him bleed to death, while the white man confesses the story of his life.

"So what did the black man say?" I asked.

Seymore smiled. It was the sly smile of a superior person. "He don't say nothing."

"So why did the black man kill him?" I asked further.

Seymore paused, and with the same indifferent smile, replied, "Because he was there."

Then I got angry. "Why don't you kill me, then?" I asked.

Seymore didn't bat an eye. He continued to smile. "Hey man," he said. "It's only a play."

We both laughed. The tension eased. We talked about poetry. I told Seymore he reminded me of Salinger's character Seymore Glass, the Haiku poet child balanced on a street curb at sunset. Seymore laughed. We talked about Jack Kerouac, Allen Ginsberg, and the other angel-headed hipsters of the beat generation.

We talked in soft tones with long spaces for contemplation. We were warm and content from our earlier bout of heavy eating and drinking. Yet the cool dry night air awakened us from the stupor we had felt earlier. The night was alive with the possibility of conversation.

All the while we talked, the moths and winged termites flew into the dimming light of the tilley lantern, casting flickering shadows across the room. Throughout the house, the cats crouched in the dark corners and shadows, waiting with their glistening eyes for the mice, bats, and snakes that throughout the night descended from the rafters.

"Remember Aburi?" I asked, breaking the silence. "The birds?"

Seymore smiled. "Yeah man, that was poetry."

That previous April, Seymore and I drove across the Accra plains on our way to the town of Aburi in the highland forests to join Matsie, Dan, and a whole gang of expatriates for a night of high-life, drinking, and other crazy antics.

It was late afternoon. Ahead of us lay the Aburi escarpment, rising up from the plains like a walled fortress. The sea breezes from the south moved across the plains and up the escarpment to meet the black overhanging thunderheads of the forest.

Suddenly the white birds appeared, swept upon the updraught of the winds. They flashed golden into the sun and descending, disappeared into the dark forest.

FOURTEEN

Lessons from the Field: Gullibility and the Hazards of Money Lending

CINDY HULL
Grand Valley State University

In the months prior to my grand departure into "the field," I listened with awe and admiration to my mentors, those of the faculty, whose tales of trials and tribulations had inspired me to proceed with my academic endeavors. I also listened to my peers who had just returned, their faces still tanned, their memories fresh. Among the stories told at department colloquia and informal gatherings were scattered subtle warnings: "Don't drink the water, always soak the beans so you can scrape the bugs off the top before cooking, never step on a female tarantula, to kill a scorpion, separate its tail from the body, and never, ever loan money."

My husband and I took these warnings to heart. We promised to never fall into the traps that our predecessors had been foolish enough to experience. We would not be gullible. Our fieldwork experience would be flawless, our memories all pleasant, and my research extraordinary in its insights and conclusions.

Such, I suspect in retrospect, are the expectations of most graduate students, thrown, as it were, to the wolves, with no protection except those words of wisdom spoken in blissful reminiscence. However, like all anthropologists before me, I found the graduate student's concept of ethnographic reality, more often than not, falling short of that of their subjects.

We arrived in the small village of Yaxbé, causing a small stir as the 1,800 souls learned of the arrival of the gringos. Yet, in their usual generosity, they accepted us, or at least their children did. After a time the adults, too, began to come to visit to discover if all the stories of the strange gringo customs were indeed true. Did they really boil their water and soak their beans? Did they really sleep on cots and cook over a dangerous kerosine stove?

During those first weeks, the roles of anthropologist and subject were reversed. The villagers were understandably curious about our presence.

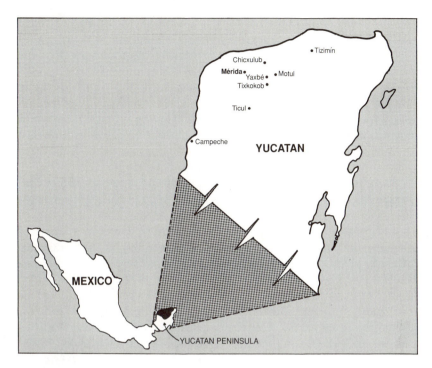

Yucatan Peninsula, Mexico

The braver of the villagers were persistent in their questioning. They wanted to know about our families and why they would allow us to journey so far from home. They wanted to know if we knew their cousin José who lives in Texas. They wanted to know why we didn't have any children. Nevertheless, by the end of the first month, they no longer thought we were complete idiots because we could not speak their Mayanized Spanish with any degree of fluency. They now believed we were only mildly retarded.

It did not take long for us to make friends, for the villagers were friendly and patient. Among our first visitors were a sister and her two younger brothers. Maria, the oldest and spokesperson for the trio, was a lanky ten-year-old with shoulder-cropped thick black hair. She wore skirts shorter than the norm for the village, and her shirts were too short for her tall frame. Marcos, who appeared to be around seven years old, was a subdued, middle child and Carlos, four, was the tagalong.

Since it was summer when we arrived, our presence was a special treat—a new diversion—for the children. Yet, for the duration of our stay, the Chan children and several others represented the core of our fan club, and they spent many hours in our nine-by-twelve-foot cement room. When they invited us to their home to meet their parents and grandparents, we were especially thrilled.

The Chan *solar,* or enclosed homestead, was one of the first that I had formally visited. It was located several streets off the two main intersecting roads, which I used to coordinate the four sectors of the village. As I stood outside the limestone wall, awaiting acknowledgment, I was moved by the austerity of the homestead. The wall, which surrounds all Maya homesteads and lines up with those of all the families along the road, was nearly nonexistent. The limestone boulders had fallen along the roadway, and no one had bothered to move or replace them in their proper spot. A gate, carelessly constructed of small sticks and rope, fell into the yard as I unhooked the latch.

Maria and her mother, Doña Carmen, met me at the opening where the gate had fallen in and, with an apologetic smile, picked up the meager door and replaced it behind me as I entered. Doña Carmen was dressed in a plain white *huipil,* which lacked the embroidered neck and hem characteristic of traditional garments. That she had been making tortillas was obvious by the raw cornmeal carelessly smeared on her dress. She wore her hair in the characteristic fashion of Maya women, pulled tightly and knotted at the back of the skull with a small comb. Her face had sharp, non-Mayan features. The nose was long and thin, the face quite narrow. Her smile was friendly and I estimated her age at fifty. I was later to learn that she was thirty-five and pregnant. Maria was dressed in one of three dresses that she wore continuously, and she was smiling widely as she introduced me to her mother.

Doña Carmen motioned me into the yard with a downward cupping of her hand, and as she led me to the main house she persistently apologized for their poverty. Indeed, the house was much poorer than those along the main road of the village. The mud and cement daub had fallen from the wattle sticks, exposing the interior of the house to view. The thatch on the roof was old and thinly spread, with gaping holes. Inside, the house had a packed dirt floor. Four hammocks were strung from a center pole and extended to the sturdier posts that supported the traditional oval structure.

At the rear of the main house was the cooking shelter, like most of those in the village but with a much smaller cooking area. Two pans hung from hooks on one of the supporting beams. On the ground, the cooking fire was smoldering under a large metal cooking sheet. Two low three-legged stools were placed on either side of the fire pit. A hollowed-out coconut shell covered with a small cloth indicated that she indeed had just finished making tortillas.

The yard itself was characteristic of the Mayan *solar.* Another house, as meager as the first, stood to the rear, slightly tilted and sagging. Further back a small shower building, made of wooden planks, was barely visible. The ground was packed from constant pressure of feet upon the hard limestone surface. Limestone rock jutted out from the ground at intervals, a danger to unaccustomed toes and very slippery after the rain. Between the two living houses, the children's maiden aunt, Fidelia, was extracting water from a well that was also in dire need of repair. Large chunks of limestone, once the body of the well, were now dislodged and laying haphazardly in the yard.

As we finished the tour, Maria's father entered the *solar.* Doña Carmen's husband, Gustavo, was a striking man, with mutant blue eyes that contrasted handsomely with his dark, Mayan features. He wore a panama hat and immediately struck up a friendly conversation. He introduced me to his parents, who had entered with him and stood timidly behind.

Gustavo's father and mother lived in the small house behind theirs, and the children ran to bring them to meet their honored guests. The old man, Estebán, was stooped and moved with the help of a homemade cane. He spoke to us in Maya, interspersed with Spanish. He smiled a toothless grin and even though I did not understand his words, I knew that his mind had known more coherent days.

We met many people in those first months, some poorer, many more affluent than the Chan family. Because of the obvious poverty of the Chan's, we both felt sympathy and compassion for them. When cold December winds blew, chilling our cement house, we took blankets to the Chan house and hung our army tarps over the most blatant gaps in their walls. When Don Gustavo asked for a small loan, thirty pesos, for some thatch, we gladly loaned it to him. With that first loan we fell headfirst into the trap.

After the second small loan, we began to feel uncomfortable. I recalled the warnings about loaning money, though I had forgotten who had made them, revered faculty with many years in the field or embittered returning graduate students who had one negative experience. Yet, something began to eat at me. Something had gone awry. We had crossed an invisible line between friendship and patronism.

Don Gustavo talked often about the many hours he worked in the *ejido* (village-owned fields) cutting and weeding the henequen plant, which is the backbone of the Yucatecan economy. He complained about the poor pay and the corruption by the team leaders, who often cheated the workers. We sympathized with him for we knew how hard he worked—he had told us so. We also knew that he sold vegetables in the village and was involved in both the legitimate and the illegitimate lottery. The children sold enchiladas and other prepared foods within the village, and we were told how his father, old Estebán, had to sell limes and other fruits in the surrounding towns and in Merida, the capital.

One day Doña Carmen came to our door with a letter she wanted to send to an *ejido* official in a nearby *municipio.* She asked that I type it so that it looked better. My better judgment told me that I should decline, but my curiosity about the contents of the letter overcame my reticence. In the letter, Doña Carmen was denouncing certain actions by village *ejido* leaders, several of whom we knew. Because I did not want to be implicated, even indirectly because of the use of my typewriter, in the denunciations, I refused to allow the Chan family further use of my machine, even though they were fairly prolific in their complaints about the local henequen leaders.

Meanwhile, some of our newly found friends began to speak to us about a certain man, whose *apodo* (nickname) was Flojo (not his real *apodo*). It seems Flojo was a deceitful man who took advantage of people who helped him. He was poor, but the money that he borrowed did not go to the care of his family, but to his own uses. He did not work in the fields, but spent his time in neighboring villages, selling lottery tickets. We thought this interesting but did not think it concerned us, since we did not know who Flojo was.

It was when Doña Carmen had her baby that we began to put together the pieces of our ethnographic puzzle. Don Gustavo came to us one day to say that Doña Carmen had to be transferred from the local medical clinic to the hospital in Merida since the baby was *otra forma* (of another form). This sounded ominous, and of course, we sympathized. My husband drove Don Gustavo to the hospital to visit his wife several times until we realized that he had the habit of arriving at our house just after the Merida bus passed through the village.

Don Gustavo began to ask for money. He claimed that because he had to take care of the other children, he had not been able to work; his compadre was in Mexico and could not help with the family expenses. Could we please loan him three hundred pesos. This was an outrageous amount for us, for we were on a limited budget, and we had to refuse.

When Doña Carmen returned home with her new baby, we were asked for one hundred pesos for clothing and food. Again we declined, saying that we would be glad to buy some food and blankets but that we could not afford to loan them that much money. He refused the offer of goods and reiterated that he needed the money so he could buy the food.

After Don Gustavo left, my husband and I discussed these events. We wanted to help our neighbors yet, somehow, we felt trapped in an uncomfortable relationship. Generosity became obligation, and when I began to remember what other people had told us about Flojo, obligation transformed itself into humiliation.

During this time of rumination and depression, Don Gustavo's daughter, Maria, arrived at our house with a note that she had written. In the letter, she pleaded with us to help the family until their compadre returned from Mexico. She had included a list of goods that they needed and the cost per item. It totaled nearly one hundred fifty pesos. I asked Maria what her father's *apodo* was, and she turned red and said, "People call him Flojo."

Handwritten notes on scraps of paper glued to the pages of my notebook illustrate the steady stream of requests from various members of the Chan family. "When will you buy the *panuelos* [diapers]?" "Please take us to. . . ." Terse comments made in my field notebook reflect our growing frustration and eventual bitterness toward the family that we had nurtured and encouraged. We began to avoid them, yet almost daily one of the children or adults would come with yet another request or an inquiry about when we would comply with the last request. We were miserable and confused.

Once people learned about our problems with the family, they began to tell us stories, the usual village gossip concerning deceit in selling chickens, unpaid loans, and the fact that the children had to sell food in the streets to feed themselves. It was eventually disclosed that old Don Estebán, Gustavo's minstrel father, earned centavos as a beggar in various neighboring villages.

We learned later that Don Gustavo had been the *solidario* (work group) representative several times but had been fired for corruption and for stealing money. We were surprised to learn that he actually worked very little in the *ejido*, that he spent most of his time selling lottery tickets and vegetables. This information allowed us to fit together the pieces of our puzzle, for although we had been curious why Don Gustavo had spent so much time in the village and on the intervillage buses, we had never doubted his stories about the many hours he spent in the fields. We had always assumed him to be an industrious man.

As the days passed, I slowly regained my anthropological temperament. That is, I was able to laugh at myself, to accept my mistakes, and in doing so, I gained a new perspective on these events. We visited Doña Carmen regularly and brought small gifts of food and clothing for the baby, but we refused to loan them any more money. The older children continued to visit us, though Don Gustavo came less and less often, and after several months the letters pleading for money ceased.

We had hundreds of experiences in Yaxbé, some joyous, others, like this one, extremely disturbing. But none of the events taught us as much as this one did. It may have been because it happened so early in our visit. It could have been because we learned about gullibility. But mostly we learned about the villagers and about ourselves as visitors in their world.

Our stereotypes about the homogeneity and social perfection of rural villages were put expeditiously to rest. Although we never attempted to force the villagers into a Redfieldian utopia, we did have idealistic expectations about their behavior. And, with the exception of the Don Gustavos and the occasional drunk or malcreant, we were not disappointed. Eventually we knew the town drunks by name and we could recognize the village turkey thieves (one of whom stole our camera). These characters became part of the complex matrix of village life, not aberrations to a flawless equilibrium or evidence of conflict and tension.

We also learned about the impact of the researcher on the society. The suggestions that the researcher should not change the social or economic environment of his or her village are valid, but impossible to comply with totally. For what kind of human being is one who would not give a blanket to a cold family or give clothing, as we did, to a woman whose house burned to the ground?

To us, Yaxbé was our home, like Grand Rapids and Detroit and Ann Arbor had been homes to us over the past few years. We did not see ourselves as deus ex machina, dropping favors to the common creatures below us, yet we considered ourselves obligated in a strong sense to the villagers. They had, indeed, accepted us graciously and generously. We shared their water, imposed on their precious time, accepted their meals and food gifts, and most of all, lavished in their sometimes over-whelming attention. Above all, we learned from them more than they could tell us in words alone.

We wanted to be a part of the everyday flow of life in the village. As unrealistic as it seems in retrospect, we wanted to be Yaxbeños. We were excited, for example, when we had to stand in line like everyone else at the *tienda* (village store) and when the young girls or Don Juan took our order without giggling. We felt accepted when we could visit a home without having everyone scurrying around to wait on us, send-ing children out the back door to buy us a Coke. And we became very comfortable having children piled in our hammocks, listening to our radio and pounding on the infamous typewriter. We loved having the adults visit, women on their way to the store in the mornings and men in the lazy hot afternoons.

Yet we were not Yaxbeños, nor would we ever be, no matter how long we lived in the village. To the villagers we would always be gringos, "our gringos" as they would jokingly say. We were not like them, and our presence was always clouded in a sense of mystery and awe. To the villagers we were rich. We had no refrigerator or oven. No washing machine. But we were there. We had a 1974 Volkswagen Beetle, a short-wave radio, a portable typewriter, and no jobs. We had to be rich. And that perception had an impact on the villagers, especially those, like Don Gustavo, who already existed on the margins of their own society.

Had these events occurred in the latter days of our stay, their impact would have been negligible. The situation would not have reached the same climax had our initial expectations been more realistic and had our Spanish language skills been sharpened. As the days passed, we learned the subtleties of the verbal and nonverbal language. We learned to recognize innuendo and sarcasm, aspects of language we had never learned in the university classroom.

Yet, had this series of events not occurred, these valuable lessons would have been postponed and our misconceptions perpetuated. We would have lost a meaningful thread—one which, interwoven with many others, completed a brightly colored tapestry of the Maya.

FIFTEEN

Arranging a Marriage in India

SERENA NANDA
John Jay College of Criminal Justice

Sister and doctor brother-in-law invite correspondence from North Indian professionals only, for a beautiful, talented, sophisticated, intelligent sister, 5' 3", slim, M.A. in textile design, father a senior civil officer. Would prefer immigrant doctors, between 26–29 years. Reply with full details and returnable photo.

A well-settled uncle invites matrimonial correspondence from slim, fair, educated South Indian girl, for his nephew, 25 years, smart, M.B.A., green card holder, 5' 6". Full particulars with returnable photo appreciated.

Matrimonial Advertisements, India Abroad

In India, almost all marriages are arranged. Even among the educated middle classes in modern, urban India, marriage is as much a concern of the families as it is of the individuals. So customary is the practice of arranged marriage that there is a special name for a marriage which is not arranged: It is called a "love match."

On my first field trip to India, I met many young men and women whose parents were in the process of "getting them married." In many cases, the bride and groom would not meet each other before the marriage. At most they might meet for a brief conversation, and this meeting would take place only after their parents had decided that the match was suitable. Parents do not compel their children to marry a person who either marriage partner finds objectionable. But only after one match is refused will another be sought.

As a young American woman in India for the first time, I found this custom of arranged marriage oppressive. How could any intelligent young person agree to such a marriage without great reluctance? It was contrary to everything I believed about the importance of romantic love as the only basis of a happy marriage. It also clashed with my strongly held notions that the choice of such an intimate and permanent relationship could be made only by the individuals involved. Had anyone tried to arrange my marriage, I would have been defiant and rebellious!

At the first opportunity, I began, with more curiosity than tact, to question the young people I met on how they felt about this practice.

Sita, one of my young informants, was a college graduate with a degree in political science. She had been waiting for over a year while her parents were arranging a match for her. I found it difficult to accept the docile manner in which this well-educated young woman awaited the outcome of a process that would result in her spending the rest of her life with a man she hardly knew, a virtual stranger, picked out by her parents.

"How can you go along with this?" I asked her, in frustration and distress. "Don't you care who you marry?"

"Of course I care," she answered. "This is why I must let my parents choose a boy for me. My marriage is too important to be arranged by such an inexperienced person as myself. In such matters, it is better to have my parents' guidance."

I had learned that young men and women in India do not date and have very little social life involving members of the opposite sex. Although I could not disagree with Sita's reasoning, I continued to pursue the subject.

"But how can you marry the first man you have ever met? Not only have you missed the fun of meeting a lot of different people, but you have not given yourself the chance to know who is the right man for you."

"Meeting with a lot of different people doesn't sound like any fun at all," Sita answered. "One hears that in America the girls are spending all their time worrying about whether they will meet a man and get married. Here we have the chance to enjoy our life and let our parents do this work and worrying for us."

She had me there. The high anxiety of the competition to "be popular" with the opposite sex certainly was the most prominent feature of life as an American teenager in the late fifties. The endless worrying about the rules that governed our behavior and about our popularity ratings sapped both our self-esteem and our enjoyment of adolescence. I reflected that absence of this competition in India most certainly may have contributed to the self-confidence and natural charm of so many of the young women I met.

And yet, the idea of marrying a perfect stranger, whom one did not know and did not "love," so offended my American ideas of individualism and romanticism, that I persisted with my objections.

"I still can't imagine it," I said. "How can you agree to marry a man you hardly know?"

"But of course he will be known. My parents would never arrange a marriage for me without knowing all about the boy's family background. Naturally we will not rely only on what the family tells us. We will check the particulars out ourselves. No one will want their daughter to marry into a family that is not good. All these things we will know beforehand."

Impatiently, I responded, "Sita, I don't mean know the family, I mean, know the man. How can you marry someone you don't know personally and don't love? How can you think of spending your life with someone you may not even like?"

"If he is a good man, why should I not like him?" she said. "With you people, you know the boy so well before you marry, where will be the fun to get married? There will be no mystery and no romance. Here we have the whole of our married life to get to know and love our husband. This way is better, is it not?"

Her response made further sense, and I began to have second thoughts on the matter. Indeed, during months of meeting many intelligent young Indian people, both male and female, who had the same ideas as Sita, I saw arranged marriages in a different light. I also saw the importance of the family in Indian life and realized that a couple who took their marriage into their own hands was taking a big risk, particularly if their families were irreconcilably opposed to the match. In a country where every important resource in life—a job, a house, a social circle—is gained through family connections, it seemed foolhardy to cut oneself off from a supportive social network and depend solely on one person for happiness and success.

Six years later I returned to India to again do fieldwork, this time among the middle class in Bombay, a modern, sophisticated city. From the experience of my earlier visit, I decided to include a study of arranged marriages in my project. By this time I had met many Indian couples whose marriages had been arranged and who seemed very happy. Particularly in contrast to the fate of many of my married friends in the United States who were already in the process of divorce, the positive aspects of arranged marriages appeared to me to outweigh the negatives. In fact, I thought I might even participate in arranging a marriage myself. I had been fairly successful in the United States in "fixing up" many of my friends, and I was confident that my matchmaking skills could be easily applied to this new situation, once I learned the basic rules. "After all," I thought, "how complicated can it be? People want pretty much the same things in a marriage whether it is in India or America."

An opportunity presented itself almost immediately. A friend from my previous Indian trip was in the process of arranging for the marriage of her eldest son. In India there is a perceived shortage of "good boys," and since my friend's family was eminently respectable and the boy himself personable, well educated, and nice looking, I was sure that by the end of my year's fieldwork, we would have found a match.

The basic rule seems to be that a family's reputation is most important. It is understood that matches would be arranged only within the same caste and general social class, although some crossing of subcastes is permissible if the class positions of the bride's and groom's families are similar. Although dowry is now prohibited by law in India, extensive gift exchanges took place with every marriage. Even when the boy's family do not "make demands," every girl's family nevertheless feels the obligation to give the traditional gifts, to the girl, to the boy, and to the boy's family. Particularly when the couple would be living in the joint family—that is, with the boy's parents and his married brothers and their families, as well as with unmarried siblings—which is still very common even among the urban, upper-middle class in India, the girl's parents are anxious to establish smooth relations between their family and that of the boy. Offering the proper gifts, even when not called "dowry," is often an important factor in influencing the relationship between the bride's and groom's families and perhaps, also, the treatment of the bride in her new home.

In a society where divorce is still a scandal and where, in fact, the divorce rate is exceedingly low, an arranged marriage is the beginning of a lifetime relationship not just between the bride and groom but between their families as well. Thus, while a girl's looks are important, her character is even more so, for she is being judged as a prospective daughter-in-law as much as a prospective bride. Where she would be living in a joint family, as was the case with my friend, the girl's ability to get along harmoniously in a family is perhaps the single most important quality in assessing her suitability.

My friend is a highly esteemed wife, mother, and daughter-in-law. She is religious, soft-spoken, modest, and deferential. She rarely gossips and never quarrels, two qualities highly desirable in a woman. A family that has the reputation for gossip and conflict among its womenfolk will not find it easy to get good wives for their sons. Parents will not want to send their daughter to a house in which there is conflict.

My friend's family were originally from North India. They had lived in Bombay, where her husband owned a business, for forty years. The family had delayed in seeking a match for their eldest son because he had been an Air Force pilot for several years, stationed in such remote places that it had seemed fruitless to try to find a girl who would be willing to accompany him. In their social class, a military career, despite its economic security, has little prestige and is considered a drawback in finding a suitable bride. Many families would not allow their daughters to marry a man in an occupation so potentially dangerous and which requires so much moving around.

The son had recently left the military and joined his father's business. Since he was a college graduate, modern, and well traveled, from such a good family, and, I thought, quite handsome, it seemed to me that he, or rather his family, was in a position to pick and choose. I said as much to my friend.

While she agreed that there were many advantages on their side, she also said, "We must keep in mind that my son is both short and dark; these are drawbacks in finding the right match." While the boy's height had not escaped my notice, "dark" seemed to me inaccurate; I would have called him "wheat" colored perhaps, and in any case, I did not realize that color would be a consideration. I discovered, however, that while a boy's skin color is a less important consideration than a girl's, it is still a factor.

An important source of contacts in trying to arrange her son's marriage was my friend's social club in Bombay. Many of the women had daughters of the right age, and some had already expressed an interest in my friend's son. I was most enthusiastic about the possibilities of one particular family who had five daughters, all of whom were pretty, demure, and well educated. Their mother had told my friend, "You can have your pick for your son, whichever one of my daughters appeals to you most."

I saw a match in sight. "Surely," I said to my friend, "we will find one there. Let's go visit and make our choice." But my friend held back; she did not seem to share my enthusiasm, for reasons I could not then fathom.

When I kept pressing for an explanation of her reluctance, she admitted, "See, Serena, here is the problem. The family has so many daughters, how will they be able to provide nicely for any of them? We are not making any demands, but still, with so many daughters to marry off, one wonders whether she will even be able to make a proper wedding. Since this is our eldest son, it's best if we marry him to a girl who is the only daughter, then the wedding will truly be a gala affair." I argued that surely the quality of the girls themselves made up for any deficiency in the elaborateness of the wedding. My friend admitted this point but still seemed reluctant to proceed.

"Is there something else," I asked her, "some factor I have missed?" "Well," she finally said, "there is one other thing. They have one daughter already married and living in Bombay. The mother is always complaining to me that the girl's in-laws don't let her visit her own family often enough. So it makes me wonder, will she be that kind of mother who always wants her daughter at her own home? This will prevent the girl from adjusting to our house. It is not a good thing." And so, this family of five daughters was dropped as a possibility.

Somewhat disappointed, I nevertheless respected my friend's reasoning and geared up for the next prospect. This was also the daughter of a woman in my friend's social club. There was clear interest in this family and I could see why. The family's reputation was excellent; in fact, they came from a subcaste slightly higher than my friend's own. The girl, who was an only daughter, was pretty and well educated and had a brother studying in the United States. Yet, after expressing an interest to me in this family, all talk of them suddenly died down and the search began elsewhere.

"What happened to that girl as a prospect?" I asked one day. "You never mention her any more. She is so pretty and so educated, what did you find wrong?"

"She is too educated. We've decided against it. My husband's father saw the girl on the bus the other day and thought her forward. A girl who 'roams about' the city by herself is not the girl for our family." My disappointment this time was even greater, as I thought the son would have liked the girl very much. But then I thought, my friend is right, a girl who is going to live in a joint family cannot be too independent or she will make life miserable for everyone. I also learned that if the family of the girl has even a slightly higher social status than the family of the boy, the bride may think herself too good for them, and this too will cause problems. Later my friend admitted to me that this had been an important factor in her decision not to pursue the match.

The next candidate was the daughter of a client of my friend's husband. When the client learned that the family was looking for a match for their son, he said, "Look no further, we have a daughter." This man then invited my friends to dinner to see the girl. He had already seen their son at the office and decided that "he liked the boy." We all went together for tea, rather than dinner—it was less of a commitment—and while we were there, the girl's mother showed us around the house. The girl was studying for her exams and was briefly introduced to us.

After we left, I was anxious to hear my friend's opinion. While her husband liked the family very much and was impressed with his client's business accomplishments and reputation, the wife didn't like the girl's looks. "She is short, no doubt, which is an important plus point, but she is also fat and wears glasses." My friend obviously thought she could do better for her son and asked her husband to make his excuses to his client by saying that they had decided to postpone the boy's marriage indefinitely.

By this time almost six months had passed and I was becoming impatient. What I had thought would be an easy matter to arrange was turning out to be quite complicated. I began to believe that between my friend's desire for a girl who was modest enough to fit into her joint family, yet attractive and educated enough to be an acceptable partner for her son, she would not find anyone suitable. My friend laughed at my impatience: "Don't be so much in a hurry," she said. "You Americans want everything done so quickly. You get married quickly and then just as quickly get divorced. Here we take marriage more seriously. We must take all the factors into account. It is not enough for us to learn by our mistakes. This is too serious a business. If a mistake is made we have not only ruined the life of our son or daughter, but we have spoiled the reputation of our family as well. And that will make it much harder for their brothers and sisters to get married. So we must be very careful."

What she said was true and I promised myself to be more patient, though it was not easy. I had really hoped and expected that the match would be made before my year in India was up. But it was not to be. When I left India my friend seemed no further along in finding a suitable match for her son than when I had arrived.

Two years later, I returned to India and still my friend had not found a girl for her son. By this time, he was close to thirty, and I think she was a little worried. Since she knew I had friends all over India, and I was going to be there for a year, she asked me to "help her in this work" and keep an eye out for someone suitable. I was flattered that my judgment was respected, but knowing now how complicated the process was, I had lost my earlier confidence as a matchmaker. Nevertheless, I promised that I would try.

It was almost at the end of my year's stay in India that I met a family with a marriageable daughter whom I felt might be a good possibility for my friend's son. The girl's father was related to a good friend of mine and by coincidence came from the same village as my friend's husband. This new family had a successful business in a medium-sized city in central India and were from the same subcaste as my friend. The daughter was pretty and chic; in fact, she had studied fashion design in college. Her parents would not allow her to go off by herself to any of the major cities in India where she could make a career, but they had compromised with her wish to work by allowing her to run a small dressmaking boutique from their home. In spite of her desire to have a career, the daughter was both modest and home-loving and had had a traditional, sheltered upbringing. She had only one other sister, already married, and a brother who was in his father's business.

I mentioned the possibility of a match with my friend's son. The girl's parents were most interested. Although their daughter was not eager to marry just yet, the idea of living in Bombay—a sophisticated, extremely fashion-conscious city where she could continue her education in clothing design—was a great inducement. I gave the girl's father my friend's address and suggested that when they went to Bombay on some business or whatever, they look up the boy's family.

Returning to Bombay on my way to New York, I told my friend of this newly discovered possibility. She seemed to feel there was potential but, in spite of my urging, would not make any moves herself. She rather preferred to wait for the girl's family to call upon them. I hoped something would come of this introduction, though by now I had learned to rein in my optimism.

A year later I received a letter from my friend. The family had indeed come to visit Bombay, and their daughter and my friend's daughter, who were near in age, had become very good friends. During that year, the two girls had frequently visited each other. I thought things looked promising.

Last week I received an invitation to a wedding: My friend's son and the girl were getting married. Since I had found the match, my presence was particularly requested at the wedding. I was thrilled. Success at last! As I prepared to leave for India, I began thinking, "Now, my friend's younger son, who do I know who has a nice girl for him . . . ?"

SIXTEEN

Lessons in Introductory Anthropology from the Bakairi Indians

DEBRA S. PICCHI
Franklin Pierce College

The Bakairi Indians interacted with many types of non-Indians. Yet they had never worked with an anthropologist before I came to study in their village. I spent fourteen months with them, and at times, I am certain that my inexplicable customs frustrated them to the point of anger. I know I had plenty of opportunities to consider both the superficial and profound cultural differences that separated us. I, like so many who preceded me, found myself learning more than I ever thought possible about a people's traditions as well as relearning in more meaningful ways basic tenets taught in introductory anthropology courses.

I planned to study how the Bakairi used their natural resources and to compare their methods with those employed by other, similar groups in central Brazil. As an ecological anthropologist, I was less interested in such aspects of culture as child rearing than in modes of production and labor organization.

Yet participant-observation, still one of the hallmarks of anthropological fieldwork, disallows selective learning about a people. Adjusting to a new culture provides on a daily basis many different types of experiences that prevent anthropologists from concentrating too assiduously on any one aspect of a people's traditions.

I had done my homework before I entered the field to begin research. I knew that the Bakairi Indians inhabited a small reservation in Mato Grosso, a central Brazilian state. About 280 of them lived in a single village on the banks of the Paranatinga River. The village was made up of some sixty wattle-and-daub houses in which small extended families resided. A ceremonial men's house, where the men congregated to discuss politics and to perform rituals, was situated in the center of the village. The Bakairi were fishermen and horticulturalists, raising manioc and rice in gardens carved out of the gallery forests that lined the river. They also hunted to a certain extent. Their religion was animistic, and shamans, who were responsible for curing diseases and performing witchcraft, were the only religious specialists.

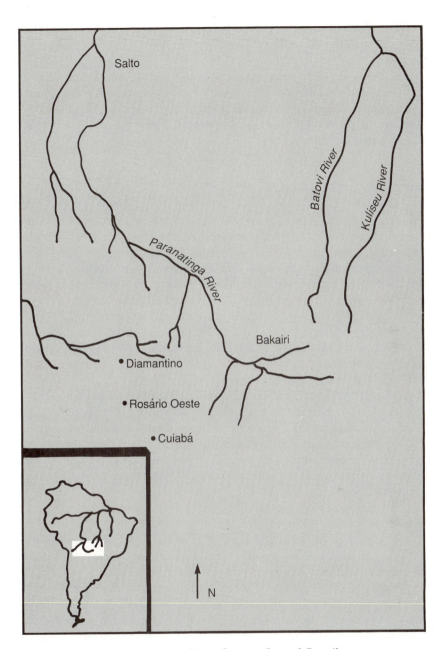

Bakairi Indian settlements in Mato Grosso, Central Brazil

I entered the reservation in March, the beginning of the dry season. I flew in a two-seater plane, carrying with me four hundred kilograms of supplies. Although I wanted to live with an Indian family, a technique I had successfully used in another Indian group with which I worked,

I brought enough food so that I could survive if left on my own. I anticipated staying two to four months before leaving the reservation to restock.

As the plane touched down on the grassy airstrip beside the village, I felt extremely nervous. I wondered if I brought enough trade goods and medicines. I speculated about whether my coffee and cigarette supplies would hold out. Yet, most important, I worried about whether the Bakairi would like me.

HUMANS AND LANGUAGE

Rays from the setting sun colored the water purple as I turned away from the river bank and clambered awkwardly up the steep path to the village. After only a month in the Bakairi village, I was still unsure of which stones were safe to walk on, so I moved slowly, not wanting to risk a sprained ankle. Indian women, agile and strong, passed me as if I were standing still even though many of them carried huge aluminum pots of water balanced on their heads. Snippets of a conversation spoken in Portuguese drifted back to me as I followed them to the village.

"She doesn't speak well," Cici, a young mother of two, complained loudly to her friends. "I think she must be as stupid as those giant anteaters that wander around the jungle."

Domingas, a frail old woman, answered Cici softly, "You ask too much. She has been with us only a few weeks. You cannot expect her to speak Bakairi as well as we do. Be patient and she too will be a human being."

They turned onto the main path leading up to the center of the village with me trailing behind. The warmth of the sun was gone, and dusky shadows crept toward the village from the Urubu Mountain, the home of the vulture.

Maisa, another young mother, spoke up. "I don't know. I'm worried. The *Alemao* really is not learning very fast at all. Geraldina told me that she tried to explain to her the story of how the jaguar copulated with a human to produce our people. Geraldina said she didn't think that girl understood two words of what she told her."

I made a mental note to record in my field journal the term *Alemao* as it was applied to me in this discussion. *Alemao* actually means "German" and refers to the nationality of the first Europeans who contacted the Bakairi in the late nineteenth century. I quickened my pace to keep up with the Indian women.

Domingas's placid voice rose again. "Brazilians visited here before. They stayed for as long if not longer than the *Alemao*, and they didn't even attempt to learn to speak our language. Why say hurtful things about this girl who at least tries?"

A flap of wings made me look up in time to see a black cloud of bats shoot out from a huge tree to the right of the path. They veered sharply upward, on their way to forage fruits and berries in the forest before returning to the tree before dawn. My mind automatically registered that they were too large to be vampire bats that suck the blood of animals and humans, sometimes communicating dangerous diseases such as rabies.

Then Inês spoke sharply, perhaps too sharply for a woman of her age when addressing an elder, "*Alemaes* and Brazilians are different, Domingas, and you know it. They are from different parts of the world. Your mother herself met one of the first *Alemaes* who entered our lands so many years ago."

Cici chimed in, "Yes, the *Alemaes* have always asked us questions about our ways and written things about us on paper that they take away with them. Brazilians are not like that. They bring us medicine and take care of the sick. How can you expect Brazilians to learn our language and become like us? That is the job of the *Alemao*, and I tell you, this girl will fail."

Domingas sniffed while the other women gave a collective sigh of discouragement. I had heard them give similar sighs in other contexts, such as when Maria's husband had come back drunk from a nearby town. He bought *pinga* with all the money he had made working for two weeks on a nearby ranch. The sigh meant something like, "The situation is impossible, but what can you do?"

We approached the first houses of the village. Children played outside while women and men conversed in small groups. Shouts of laughter rose from further down the lane as some of the girls flirted with eligible young men. The discussion terminated as the women separated to go to their own homes.

I slowly made my way back to my hut, calling out to those I knew and stopping to chat with those I especially liked. Inside my house, I lighted a candle and closed the shutters so that insects would not come in. Then I hung up my towel to dry and made some coffee on the alcohol stove. As I sipped the steaming beverage, I puzzled through what I had just heard.

I did not doubt that the women carefully planned what had just transpired. They spoke in Portuguese so that I could understand them, rather than in Bakairi, which they normally would have used among themselves. In addition, they had made certain that I would overhear them. This allowed for effective criticism to take place without a direct confrontation, which is avoided at all costs in an Indian village. In other words, their behavior was beyond reproach. They were disturbed about my performance and communicated their displeasure in a way consistent with Bakairi etiquette.

Yet I felt angry, believing they were being unjustly critical without giving me the opportunity to defend myself. It was true I was not intensely studying Bakairi. Most of my energy went toward gathering data on demographics and garden harvests, which were the focus of my research. What time I had left went toward language acquisition, but my progress was slow.

I blew out the candle and climbed into my hammock. I continued to feel perplexed about why my ability to speak Bakairi was so important to the women. Many people in the village spoke Portuguese, which allowed me to communicate in that language about most subjects. Why was Bakairi so important?

Then I remembered Domingas's comment about becoming a human. Perhaps to them, the ability to speak Bakairi was the essence of being a human. Without it, one would be relegated to the status of a Brazilian, who brought medicine, or an *Alemao*, who wrote things on paper. Although there was nothing intrinsically wrong with either of these identities, assuming a role closer to that of the Bakairi was preferable from the anthropological point of view.

The equation looked more interesting as I closely considered it. I knew from the anthropological literature that one of the key aspects of the definition of *Homo sapiens* was the ability to use language. The sophisticated capability to handle symbols and to move back and forth conceptually in time marked the beginning of a unique period in history. Cultural evolutionary rates exploded when our species began to use language.

The Bakairi were merely reaffirming a basic principle and extrapolating from it as they applied it to their culture. They believe that humans speak Bakairi. Without this ability, one could not understand Bakairi culture in all of its intricacies. The women were trying to tell me that a grasp of the language was a necessary precondition for an effective study of their traditions.

As I dozed off, I realized that I had just relearned a basic anthropological lesson—one that is discussed in the first month of every introductory course I have ever taken or taught. Yet somehow its significance had recently been obscured by other specialized considerations more germane to my research.

A pair of tarantulas caught my eye as they scurried across the earthen floor of the hut. I decided that I was too tired to care.

HUMANS AND SEXUAL MORES

The rains came. Torrential sheets of water fell on the village every day, transforming paths into muddy streams. My hut leaked but no more than any other. The palm thatch that served as a roof was relatively new so that it shed water easily. Other people with older huts complained of rivulets of water falling on them.

Everything inside was soggy or moldy. My cotton hammock, my clothes, my notebooks became limp in the humidity. A coating of mold covered the inside of the lens of my camera, and my leather shoes sprouted something that looked distinctly alive.

The humidity and heat were incredible. My shirt stuck to my back, and beads of sweat dripped regularly off my nose. Armies of mosquitoes swarmed audibly around me whether I was down at the river, in the forest, or sitting near the men's house in the center of the village.

I felt dejected and was not surprised when I came down with a cold. My symptoms were normal: a runny nose, aches and pains, and digestive tract disorders. I took decongestants and aspirin and waited for it to pass.

One rainy afternoon I was resting in my hammock reading a novel, a luxury I allowed myself on special occasions, such as when I was sick. Space was so limited on the small plane I used that I brought only a few books into the reservation. I treasured them and read them as slowly as I could.

When Maiare entered the hut, I had been absorbed in the dry and clean southern town described in *To Kill a Mockingbird*. I sat up with a start as he flicked the water from his hair all over me.

"Maiare, you're getting me all wet," I said severely.

"Sorry," he responded in a despondent manner. "I just got back from fishing and caught nothing as usual."

"I thought you said fishing was impossible when it rains because the fish don't bite. They are full from eating what washes into the water from the forest," I said. "Why did you even bother to go out on the river? Surely you must have just sat in a wet canoe and got rained on."

Maiare sat on the small plank of wood that I had pushed up against the clay wall of the hut. It served as a chair when visitors came to see me. He made an impatient gesture with his hand.

"Why?" he snapped. "You ask why? I'll tell you why," he continued with the frustration in his voice becoming increasingly apparent. "My wife is making me crazy. I had to get out of the house."

I made a humming noise that the Indians used to signal agreement or openness to hearing more. I started to heat some water on the alcohol stove. Clearly Maiare could use some strong sweet tea. As I moved around the hut, dodging leaks, his voice became bitter.

"And I'll tell you something. If she thinks I don't know what's going on, then she's dumber than a parrot in a cage. I know she's having sex with Jeremi."

I poured the hot water into a mug and stirred in lots of sugar, which I knew the Indians liked. Then I handed the cup to Maiare and went back to swing in my hammock. I tried to act in a casual manner, but I was excited. None of the Bakairi had ever confided in me about their personal problems. If I could get Maiare to tell me more about his situation, then I might understand better how sexual behavior was organized and how conflicts were resolved in the village.

"So," I said in a vague way, trying to disguise my interest, "Jeremi is sleeping with Balbina. Does Vita know about this?"

"Of course she knows. She's Jeremi's wife, isn't she? She'd be the first to realize it," Maiare said with surprise.

"Well," I replied, "it isn't always like that with my people. They say the spouse is always the last to know." I paused and then asked, "Is Vita upset?"

Maiare gave me a look of disbelief. "You ask the strangest questions, *Alemao*. Vita is very upset. A few days ago, she kicked Jeremi so hard he fell out of his hammock."

Maiare handed me back the empty mug, and I jumped up quickly to make more. I had additional questions to ask so I intended to ply him with tea for as long as possible. I again pumped up the alcohol stove and began heating more water. Maiare moped with his head in his hands.

I chose my words carefully as I asked my next question. "If you know and Vita knows, and you are both upset, then what can you do?"

Maiare's face brightened. "Vita could threaten to visit her parents, and Jeremi would get very upset because, without her, who would cook? Who would take care of the children? Who would wash his clothes?"

He chuckled gleefully as he pictured his enemy in such dire straits. The rains had stopped, and the cackle of chickens could be heard. One hen regally entered my hut, pausing on the doorstep as if to decide whether it was worthwhile to enter.

"Couldn't you go home to your parents?" I asked as I shooed it away. I didn't want it going to the bathroom on my floor.

Maiare shook his head sadly. "A man would lose face if he did that. No, we men must stay in the houses we build, pretending that nothing is wrong, even if it means we go hungry because there is no one to cook our food." He sighed as he stood up, "I guess I could beat her with my belt. Then she might stay home more often."

I was alarmed and asked quickly, "You would do that?"

Maiare turned to me and said grimly, "If I did, she would probably go to stay with her parents for a few months, and then I'd be stuck with no one to take care of the house. Plus she might leave the children, and then I'd really have problems." He turned and strode off down the path.

Later I sat in my hut, paper and pen before me, and tried to organize what I had learned. "Fact one," I said to myself, "the Bakairi have extramarital affairs." Both men and women were allowed to have multiple sex partners, unlike some societies where only men are allowed to have affairs.

"Fact two," I went on, "the Bakairi experience jealous feelings when they discover their spouses are sleeping with other people." Maiare was obviously very troubled, and hadn't he said that Vita had become so angry one night that she had kicked Jeremi? The reactions of the spouses suggested to me that the Bakairi did not casually accept affairs as many people believed they did.

Some anthropologists contend that jealousy is a function of capitalist society. That is, as people begin to control labor, the means of production, and capital, they view their own personal relationships in the same way and react possessively when threatened with loss. If a society lacks capitalist structures, as did Bakairi culture, then jealousy would be absent. "So much for that theory," I thought.

"Fact three," I continued, "the Bakairi appear to have few options when faced with infidelity on the part of their spouses." Men had fewer choices than women did, it seemed. They were able to beat their wives, but this was not considered an effective way to terminate an affair because the wife might leave. Or they could stoically wait for the affair to end, as Maiare seemed to be doing. I noted that he had not brought up attacking or killing Balbina's lover. Also, the option of divorce had not come up. Although the Bakairi recognized the practice, adultery apparently was not a legitimate reason for it.

A woman could leave the house of her husband and return to her parent's home for extended visits. Or she could wait for the affair to end, as I supposed Vita was doing. Violence and divorce did not appear to be appropriate responses for a woman either.

What puzzled me was what kept Bakairi couples together. Why was divorce not an option? It is in many cultures, especially in those cases where it is essential to know the father of a woman's child. For example, if the transfer of great wealth or title is contingent upon the identity of the child's father, then a wife's infidelity is a much more serious matter.

Then I recalled Maiare's parting words. He said that if Balbina left him, he would be responsible for housework and child care, as well as for his own duties. That suggested that the division of labor in Bakairi society was complementary: Men depended on women, and women on men, to perform specific key tasks. Divorce would rip the social tapestry apart. As Maiare said, he could not wash clothes at the river with the women. It was ludicrous to even imagine it. Furthermore, Balbina could not fish and cut down trees in the forest to make a garden. That was "men's work."

The rain began again, and I crawled back into my hammock. Another basic anthropology lesson had been endorsed by Maiare. He had reminded me that interlocking role definitions between the sexes are critical for the smooth functioning of a society. Much would be forgiven between men and women if they needed each other in profoundly basic ways.

Lightning cracked the sky. I wondered where Balbina was.

HUMANS AND THE SUPERNATURAL

"You know what I think?" young Marcedes asked darkly. "I think Bolo has bewitched me and that's why I'm sick and confused. I believe he got Vincente to cast a spell on me so that I'd be destroyed. I'm going to Paulino's tonight to be cured. Then he'll see."

I did not think this was the time to remind Marcedes that he had recently visited a nearby Brazilian town where he had gotten drunk, according to some of the other men who had gone on the trip. In addition he probably picked up a flu or a cold. The Indians always came back tired and sick when they left the reservation.

I kept quiet as Marcedes sat and brooded. We were perched on a plank of wood outside his hut. I heard his wife, Lita, pounding rice with a pestle in back of the house. The rhythmic thumping was relaxing.

"So Marcedes is going to be cured tonight," I thought. I was interested in seeing a Bakairi curing ritual. I had not witnessed one since I had been in the village. Curing took place regularly and openly in another Indian culture I had studied. However, the Bakairi viewed it as a secret practice that took place at night in private.

I did not know how to ask Marcedes to take me to Paulino's that night. I took a risk and asked, "I have some lovely red cloth Lita might like to have. Do you think I should give it to her?"

Marcedes cheered up immediately. I knew that Lita had been angry with him since he returned from town because he had spent so much money on food and liquor that he had little left over to make household purchases. He could give her the red material as a peace offering.

"However," I said slowly and then paused. "However, perhaps you could do something for me in return. I would very much like to go with you to Paulino's tonight to see you cured."

"I can manage that," he smiled as he helped me get up from the bench. "Let's go get that cloth."

That night was blacker than any I could remember. Usually a moon or stars provided some illumination. However, it seemed that a blanket had been thrown over the village preventing even my flashlight from helping us pick our way along the path to Paulino's hut. I was a little nervous because recently a snake had bitten a man as he was walking home on a dark night such as this. I walked slowly, hoping anything ahead of us would have time to get out of our way.

Paulino's wife, Judite, met us at the door and efficiently shepherded us inside. Paulino was waiting by the fire, already partially drugged from sucking on the huge green tobacco cigar he held in his hand. He started to say something to Marcedes but vomited instead.

Paulino's eyes were clearer after he had finished retching, and for the first time he seemed to notice me.

"Oh yes," he said with slurred speech, "I heard you were coming. Why don't you sit down with my wife over there."

He pointed vaguely in the direction of Judite, and we women retired to sit on a skin placed on the floor. Marcedes lay down on a hammock, while Paulino started to chant in a low voice. Soon he began to stamp one of his feet, circling Marcedes's hammock several times. Then there was quiet, and I saw in the glow of fire that Paulino was lighting his cigar again. He blew smoke onto Marcedes, muttering in a muffled voice. Then he discarded the cigar and began to massage Marcedes's arms and legs. The smoke-blowing and massaging continued for nearly half an hour.

My legs cramped, and my attention wandered as the curing ceremony wore on. I looked around the hut and saw that, although it was small and simple like mine, expensive machetes and rifles were hanging from the walls. They suggested that Paulino was wealthy by Bakairi standards. I knew that shamanism, or religious curing and sorcery, paid well, so I was not surprised.

Paulino sucked deeply on the cigar again and apparently became so dizzy that he fell on the floor. I saw his hands fumbling in a dark corner. He turned away from us and began to vomit again. After he had exhausted himself, Judite got up and put more wood on the fire. She helped him over to a skin that lay spread out. An eager Marcedes joined him there.

"What did you find?" he asked anxiously. "What did you discover?"

Paulino shook his head sadly. "It is good that you came because it is certain you were bewitched."

He opened his hand and showed Marcedes a small, smooth amber-colored stone, a piece of red material, and some fecal matter that looked like it came from an animal.

"The stone was lodged near your heart where it weakened you, and the droppings are from the spirit who chased away all your good luck," Paulino explained.

"And the red thing?" asked Marcedes, who was obviously strongly affected by what Paulino had just related.

"The red is from your blood, which has been poisoned by the sorcery of the enemy who tries to rob you of your life."

Judite began to bustle around, a cue for us to leave. Marcedes profusely thanked Paulino for saving him and gave him a small bag of fishhooks and line in payment for his work.

We started to walk home just as a light rain began. It was the end of the rainy season, and occasional showers still unexpectedly occurred. I wrapped myself in the plastic slicker I had gotten into the habit of carrying with me and asked Marcedes what would happen now.

"Happen? What should happen?" he answered. "Everything is going to be all right. I'll be better tommorrow. You'll see."

I groped my way back to my hut after waving good night to Marcedes. I lighted a candle and then found a cigarette, which I slowly smoked. The shamanistic curing ritual I had just observed was so obviously chicanery that I had trouble understanding how Marcedes, whom I considered to be an intelligent and perceptive man, could have been so easily duped. I realized that Paulino had really been drugged by tobacco and that the substance in such strong doses induced vomiting. However, I also knew that the stone and droppings were not placed in Marcedes's body through witchcraft and that Paulino had not removed them with magic. I believed Paulino hid them on the floor until he needed them. He picked them up when he fell down.

I was clearly not thinking like an anthropologist. Maybe the rainy season had sapped me of the energy I needed to emotionally grasp the cultural realities around me. I needed a break. Could I afford the time to take a few weeks off and go to Brasilia? I'd stay in a hotel, take baths every night, eat tons of chocolate, and go to the movies. I promised myself to consider the possibility of leaving the reservation for a while just as soon as I woke up in the morning.

I am not sure what woke me that night. It had cleared, and the moon was up. Some beams made their way through the cracks in the shutters and shimmered on my blanket. I thought some more about Marcedes and Paulino.

Maybe the practical reality of curing or sorcery really made no difference. "Did that really happen?" was not a legitimate question to ask because the scientific validity of Bakairi witchcraft was not the issue. Rather, what was crucial was how people like Marcedes related the supernatural to their daily lives. The vitality and significance of witchcraft were obvious when one observed Paulino's commitment to his art and Marcedes's concern about his personal problems. Theirs was a living ideological system that helped the men conceptualize and act within their cultural world.

The question of whether a spirit literally did leave those droppings was of no value. The central issue was whether or not the shamanistic ritual rendered Marcedes's experience comprehensible to him.

As the moonbeams climbed up the walls of my hut, I realized I had rediscovered another fundamental anthropological tenet as a result of my evening with Paulino and Marcedes. The supernatural plays a very real and critical role in the lives of humans. And we do not find anything comparable to it among other animals. We are unique in this way.

A shaft of moonlight illuminated the rafters of my hut. I went back to sleep.

BASIC LESSONS RELEARNED

I had given away everything that would not fit in the plane. The usual arguing about "who should have what" took place, but in the end everyone seemed satisfied. I was not too concerned about a completely equitable distribution of goods since I knew that kinship networks and ritual festivities would ensure a far more just allocation of my possessions than I could hope to achieve.

The past fourteen months had gone by rapidly. At first each hour crawled by, and I carefully marked off the days on my calendar. However, by the end of my field trip, I lost track of time. I would have liked to have stayed a few more months because it was the dry season again, and those were my favorite months. Yet I knew it was time to leave.

I had secured a great deal of ecological data, and I believed I would be able to complete my report as planned. I checked points off in my head. Yes, I had information on fishing and hunting catches. And I had weighed garden harvests. Plus I was lucky enough to secure some demographic records that went back some fifty years. I had verified them with the Bakairi for accuracy and knew I had some great material.

Nevertheless, other experiences I had undergone with the Indians somehow overshadowed my project. Weighing manioc in Geraldina's garden seemed far less significant than overhearing the women who had passed me on the river path complaining that I was learning Bakairi too slowly. Maiare's pain and frustration over his wife's affair had a greater impact on me than did my discovery that the Bakairi consume less high-quality protein than they probably should. Marcedes's attempt to understand his sick and confused feelings upon returning from a trip to a Brazilian town was more interesting than the natural and actual population increase rates I calculated.

These were the people who retaught me the basic lessons of anthropology. They took me to the heart of the discipline where it is affirmed that we are all human and that the differences between us are merely variations of the same theme.

I heard the engine of a plane and walked over to the landing strip. We said goodbye with little ceremony because it is believed that one must leave sorrow behind quickly. The plane took off, and I watched the huts that lined the big green river fade into the distance.

SEVENTEEN

Greasy Hands and Smelly Clothes: Fieldworker or Fisherman?[1]

PHIL DeVITA
State University of New York at Plattsburgh

Fieldwork should have been extremely simple. Even if stretching my imagination to the extremes, there was absolutely nothing to worry about. After so many years at sea, so many past preparations for lengthy ocean voyages, a single summer on a remote island off the coast of Atlantic Canada was approached as if it were a weekend cruise. I'd been to the island twice before. The last time, on a bitter cold evening in March 1976, I met the head of the fisherman's association, a fishing captain and lobsterman himself. We'd spent endless hours talking fishing and boats. After a bit too much Beefeater, he had agreed to let me spend the summer documenting the traditional life of Acadian lobster fishermen.

The island was, at reasonable speed, only fifteen hours from my home in the Adirondack Mountains. The entire project was worth a gamble. If I didn't like the people or the setting, I knew that after the summer I could continue writing grant proposals in hopes of returning to the warmer and more familiar islands of the South Pacific.

Now, however, with a small grant from the Canadian Embassy and a few dollars from a grant to study socioeconomic change in a rapidly changing environment, I had enough to cover expenses for the summer. I'd three times written to the head of the fisherman's association reminding him of my impending visit. I was explicit, informing him of the exact day that I'd arrive. Most important, each time I reminded him of his promise to locate a small house for me to rent for the summer. Not having received a reply, I remained confident that he'd keep his promise.

The Canadian lobster seasons are restricted by federal conservation rulings. In this particular area of maritime Canada, lobstering begins on the first day of May and ends on June 30th. I couldn't be there until the second week in May, after classes had ended, but I left as soon as possible, driving nonstop to the island. Recalling my last wintry session with the captain, with my own money I'd purchased two cases of Beefeater, a case of Scotch, and two cases of mixed French wines for his wife and, hopefully, to share over fresh fish dinners. Camera equipment, the tape recorder, my old sailing clothes, and the other professional baggage essential to the fieldwork enterprise were also crammed into the car along with my tools, since my mechanically sound, rusted out Datsun hatchback had seen well over a hundred thousand miles.

Once the small ferry had transported me to the island, I parked the car on the rocky bluff overlooking the wharf. The lobster boats motored up to the buyers' docks, unloaded their day's catch, and moved off to their permanent berths. The lobstermen were rushing to end the business of the fishing day. Squinting into the western sun, I strained, looking for some sign of the captain or his mate. I would have driven onto the pier, but from years at sea, I'd learned to leave fishermen alone and stay out of their way when they're working. Time passed slowly while I searched the dock for a familiar face. At the farthest end of the wharf, I thought I'd recognized the mate in the cockpit of one of the recently arrived lobsterboats, but I wasn't certain enough to approach. Then I recognized the captain in the same boat, and a sense of relief and excitement replaced the tiredness. The world was again in some comprehensible order. At last, there was someone not unknown, someone recognizable. The slight hint of the presence of friends from the earlier visit erased the uncertainty and aloneness in the strange, new environment.

The lobster were offloaded, weighed, and sold. The vessel motored around to the south side of the wharf, and I watched intently as the two men lashed the dock lines and secured the vessel. I walked down to the pier to approach the fishermen, both heading for an old pickup truck, each with a bottle of beer in hand. I called the captain's name. I didn't know if they recognized me. He stopped, stared, and responded with my name. We shook hands, and before I had time to shake hands with the mate, he informed me that he had bad news.

"Philip," he said, "I talk with the fishermen. We do not want you on the island."

I was, understandably, stunned. My immediate response was controlled. I composed myself, not even providing nonverbal clues to display the shock and sudden disappointment. After living most of my life either as a guest in someone else's home or as a guest in foreign countries, I'd learned by experience to deal with situations where you know that you're not welcome. You become sensitive to the most subtle hints of interpersonal conflict and know when it's time to pack your seabag. The unexpected pronouncement was far from a subtle hint. It was a simple and blatant declaration of their attitude toward my presence.

So much for the cottage. So much for the research and my well-developed plans for the summer.

That my immediate reactions to the initial events on the wharf were handled so calmly was, in reflection, primarily due to two facts. First,

I was too tired to respond immediately to a situation which I couldn't, at that moment, fully comprehend. Second, there was the manner in which the captain made the announcement. In the blunt, matter-of-factness of the statement, this five-foot-two package of vibrant Acadian friendliness and vitality, even after sixteen hours of lobstering, conveyed no sign of personal rejection or anger. He didn't apologize, didn't explain. There was no recourse.

Hell, the ethnographer is nothing more than an intruder anyway. Rarely is he or she *invited* to snoop around into the lives of total strangers. We make our own decisions on the fieldwork setting and then, most often, show up in unfamiliar places, fresh out of the sterile classrooms of graduate school, eager and naive but determined to conduct research in textbook fashion to satisfy absolutely no one connected with the research environment. Before I was ever an anthropologist, I'd had run-ins with every kind of intruder imaginable. From the many past experiences in the South Pacific and Central and South America, I still can't accurately rank the uninvited intruders whom I met on a personal "dislike" or "nerd" scale. True, the Peace Corps members, anthropologists, missionaries, and government officials most probably felt that same way about me. Except, however, on extremely rare occasions, memories of meetings with many of these neocolonial do-gooders still leave a bitter taste in my mouth.

I'd read Gerald Berreman's (1962) account of his own personal difficulties with initiating field research among members of a Himalayan village. I'd more recently read Jean Briggs's (1970) honest and insightful report on her ethnographic problems with the Utkuhik-halingmuit of the Canadian Northwest. In relation to their problems and my current situation, I might be well ahead of the game cut off from my research efforts at the very beginning.

From the moment he told me that I wasn't welcome, I realized that the captain was right. Not that he had the power to keep me from his island or that how he had acted was right. These weren't meaningful issues. He *had* the right to prohibit me from conducting research into his and his neighbors' lives. On my own, in the years that were to follow, I was able to learn of the motives for his initial action. However, at that moment, I had no problems reconciling the fact of that particular moment. I didn't know the facts and, in this case, the facts are unimportant. The fact of the matter was that he and his friends had, as the captain had informed me, decided against my presence as both an outsider and a researcher, not, as was the case, being aware of what my presence as an anthropologist meant.

In the next breath, after having informed me that I wasn't welcome on the island, the captain ordered me to follow him home for supper. This was not an invitation. It was an order! Without waiting for a response, he jumped into his truck. I stood watching as he jockeyed the battered pickup to turn around on the narrow dock. Passing where he'd left me standing, he waved, pointing inland toward the village. The option to drive directly to the mainland and take a room in the old hotel was, for the moment, rejected. The hotel and hot shower could wait until later that evening. The unexpected invitation, especially taken in the context of his earlier pronouncement, was offered as if he had never told me that I wasn't welcome on his island.

At his small home next to the Catholic cemetery, I again met the captain's wife and three children. After a handshake and an awkward hug, his wife asked a few questions about the trip. Obviously, she knew that my project was over before it ever began. It made no difference to her. She, as I remembered, and as she would always be, was all smiles and easy friendliness. Both she and her husband, and almost all of the Acadian fisherfolk had this disarming quality of genuine warmth and relaxed, natural openness.

"Ah Philip, we'll take a gin." The captain was on the porch pouring the last few ounces of an unknown brand into glasses for the mate, himself, and me. With a toast, each of us downed the booze. Returning the few feet to the car, I grabbed a forty-ounce jug of Beefeater, a bottle of Cabernet, and my corkscrew. He hadn't offered his wife a drink, and I suspected this was because the bottle was almost empty. I also recalled that his wife had, in our March meeting, spoken of how much she missed good wine. I handed the gin to the captain and offered the wine to his wife. Their surprise and pleasure was obvious. While thanking me, the captain opened the gin as I uncorked the wine for his wife.

We went into the house and sat in the small breakfast room adjoining the kitchen. Conversation was polite and unforced. No one discussed the decision announced at the wharf. His wife prepared supper while we drank and the children chased the dogs around the yard. I was tempted to return to the car for a bottle of Scotch but decided to remain and "take" the gin slowly. Knowing not to even ask for tonic or a lemon for fear of embarrassing my hosts, nor to cut the alcohol with water lest I embarrass myself, I nursed the gin. Well, I thought, I'll be gone before the evening's over. Why suffer for the sake of impression? Yet, I kept quiet and drank slowly as both lobstermen, smelling of fish, drank as if the Beefeater was water.

Over the meal of boiled chicken, potatoes, turnip, and green vegetables, they killed the forty-ounce jug. I brought in two more bottles and told them to enjoy and drink in good health. The conversation continued easily and remained warm and open. No questions about what I'd do now. They talked about the late winter thaw that didn't free the channel until a week after the beginning of the lobster season, problems with rough seas and bad weather when they finally were able to set the traps, how they had to hurry to get ready since they'd already lost valuable time. They complained about the price being paid for lobster by the merchants at the wharf—how the price was set by outsiders in Boston and Halifax and how they were being cheated from a decent wage.

Concerned about the lateness and the long drive back to the mainland village, I asked when the last ferry left from the island. Without hesitation, both the captain and his wife ordered, and it was another order, that tonight I was to remain with them.

Where would they put me up in this small house? There were three bedrooms, one for the parents, one for the son, and another for the two daughters. Arguing at the inconvenience, and soberly wanting to get into a hotel room with a hot shower, they, with their typical response of "No problem," insisted that I sleep on the small sofa near the kitchen entry.

The evening was filled with the same friendliness that I remembered from my winter visit in March. Visitors arrived frequently, each introduced to me, and each, like most every Acadian I'd ever met, was immediately open and congenial. That I was an outsider made little difference. Acadians have that remarkable quality of making a stranger feel instantly at home. A guest is naturally welcome and accepted—as family. Conversation begins without formality, without the feeling that you're being examined, more as if they'd always known you and that you'd just returned home from someplace else.

The mate had left before dinner and returned during the evening with photographs of his record tuna catch from the past summer. Like the captain and his mate, the other fishermen drank gin either straight from the bottle or from flowered jelly glasses filled to the top. Knowing that I wouldn't be driving because they had decided that I'd remain, I went to the car for another jug of gin and this time returned with the Scotch for myself.

I'd caught lobster before but not, however, in traps. I dove for them off Catalina and San Clemente islands and even snorkeled for them in the bays in the Galápagos. Late in the evening, I asked the captain if I could go lobstering with him the next day. Perhaps, because of the Beefeater, or in the spirit of the party, he agreed to take me with him.

Shortly before midnight, with the guests finally gone, the house quiet, I fell into a dead sleep on the small sofa. I was relatively sober but too tired for reflection, too exhausted to even attempt to analyze the events of the past few hours. In dirty clothes, in desperate need of a shower or at least a chance to brush my teeth, I slept for the first time in over twenty-four hours.

The captain shook me awake. "Hurry, Philip, time to go fishing." A light was on in the kitchen, but the rest of the house was dark.

I struggled to get up, wanting more than anything to go back to sleep. What time was it? Still dark outside. I focused on the kitchen clock. It was two in the morning. I'd gotten two hours of sleep. He wants to go fishing? Get me out of here! I need some sleep!

In the bathroom I searched for toothpaste and rubbed my teeth with my fingers. My shaving kit was in the car. I splashed some cold water on my face and dried myself with the first towel I saw. Returning to the kitchen, the captain handed me a cup of coffee. He was busy throwing food from the fridge into a paper sack. "We have to leave so we can pass through the Gully on the right tide."

Without giving me time to finish the coffee, he announced that we must leave. I followed into the cold, damp morning running to my car to find a jacket and a pair of deck shoes. I found a jacket but didn't even waste time searching for shoes in my packed seabags. The truck engine was running. We stopped a few houses away to collect the mate and raced down the unlit road to the wharf.

I don't remember much more of that first day. I was too tired, too cold. In the darkness, we powered out in line with other boats, through the narrow gully and out to the open sea. I'd stayed out of their way while they cast off and only when we were under way did I move from the corner of the cockpit. With the captain at the wheel, the mate went below to the fo'c'sle. From the wheelhouse, I looked below. The mate had lit the kerosene stove and put on the kettle. "Tea," he yelled up through the companionway. I didn't want tea. I wanted to go to sleep. I struggled to remain awake.

After tea, the mate fell asleep in the lower bunk. I couldn't tolerate the kerosene and gas smells below decks and returned to the open cockpit and curled out of the wind between the engine hatch and the bulwarks. In the noise and the dampness of the cold predawn, I fell asleep.

They reached the lobster traps as daylight broke. Both of them fished lobster all that first day. I just watched as they worked their traps. Neither gave any indication of having spent the night drinking and having gotten only two hours sleep. The work was repetitious. Locate a jig bouy, pull the ten traps, one at a time on the hauler, empty, clean and rebait each trap, reset the jig, and head off in search of the next set. Between the more distant hauls, the mate napped on the chest freezer in the open cockpit. I slept whenever I could while they worked through the morning and early afternoon. At two thirty, the captain opened the throttle and powered away from the ocean shelf, the course set for home. The mate took the wheel while the captain went below "to take a sleep."

Both men had worked together, each knowing what to do once they'd located the set lines. They joked continually in Acadian French while they hauled and cleaned traps. Once each jig was reset, the captain returned to the wheelhouse to search for the next marked bouy. They were too busy to pay much attention to their useless passenger. I didn't care. After watching them make the first few hauls, I'd seen all I wanted of lobstering. I'd once made a night trip with bait fishermen off the coast of California and had been a few days on a seiner in Mexico. The crews of these commercial boats work hard, but not nearly as hard as did these lobstermen. My many years on sportsfishing boats and sailing yachts had been a party compared to the day's work performed by the two Acadians.

Before we reached the narrow passage into the harbor, the mate woke the captain. The captain took the wheel while the mate busied himself on deck. I'd slept enough and was anxious to get ashore and away from the island. I joined the captain in the wheelhouse for the final leg to the wharf.

I didn't ask questions. Why? Once we got back to the captain's house, I had plans to instantly head for the mainland. The rest of the summer was ahead of me and whether they wanted me or not, I was gone. Just get off the island, shower, have a good meal, and then a long sleep.

In the calm of the bay, the captain talked while I tried to hear above the noise of the engine. He talked about the boat, a new vessel built along traditional lobsterman lines at a shipyard in Halifax. The Ford marine engine was also new, but he complained, reaching behind to grab the tech manual from a bulkhead compartment. "Look for the rpm's. Look for the rpm's at full throttle." Without my glasses, I couldn't read the spec sheet. "Thirty-five hundred rpm's at full throttle." He rammed the throttle forward and I watched as the tach crept to 2,700 rpm and held, going no higher. Other, older boats were passing us as we cut through the calm waters of the harbor. "I changed propellers two times to make more speed. We go too slow. Something is bad—no good."

Before tying up to the buyer's dock, I told the captain that I'd take a look at the engine. He sold the lobster and secured the vessel, and the three of us returned to his house. We drank a few 5.6 Alpine beers. I had to give the engine time to cool off. I'd burned myself too many times crawling around the hot manifolds and water jackets of marine engines.

Alone, with the keys to the boat, I drove to the wharf and, with my own tools, worked on the engine for over an hour. All I did was clean and regap the plugs, set the points, and adjust the carburetor and timing. Running in neutral, the eight cylinders sounded better than they had before I began. The proof was to be determined by how the boat ran in the water, not how the engine sounded tied up to the dock. I returned to the cottage, got the captain, and drove both of us back to the boat.

"Let's go!" This was just another of his impetuous command-invitations.

I cast off the dock lines, and he powered out into the harbor. Once into the open bay, without giving the engine time to warm up, he opened the throttle. The tach reached 3,900 rpm and the boat was planing over the smooth water. The captain screamed in excitement while the engine whined in perfect tune. "You made more rpm's than the book!"

"We go home and take a gin!" Of course we would. I had the Beefeater.

"O.K., captain, we'll have a drink and then I have to be going."

"Going where? You stay. Tomorrow you come fishing and make sure the engine works."

I didn't go fishing the next day. That evening, after dinner, after two more bottles of my gin with the mate and his fishing friends, the captain told the other captains that I was an expert marine mechanic. He lent me out for the next day to work on his friend's engine.

In my same clothes, without a shower, I slept on the couch for a second night. I did manage to find my shaving kit from among the pile of gear in the back of the car and scrubbed my teeth before going to bed. At two in the morning, before he left for his lobster traps, the captain woke me. "You sleep. Later my friend will take you to his boat. Make his engine work."

Welcome to the island! Welcome to the impulsive, impetuous, unpredictable world of the Acadian lobstermen!

I spent the next day tuning up the old, greasy, rusted engine on another boat. Then I fished lobster for the remainder of the season. For the summer, working their schedule six days a week—there's no fishing on Sunday—I slept two hours each night on the small couch and made up the rest of my sleep at sea. On Sunday the village meets in the community center for dancing, drinking, and, more often than not, brawling. Occasionally there's a wedding, but that too is a time for dancing and drinking. There was no time for research, except for the data I could collect on the captain, his family, and the mate.

For the next five years, during my time off from teaching duties, I returned to the island whenever I could. After lobster season, they fish tuna. Other boats, with proper licenses, fish mackerel. I became accepted as a mechanic and fisherman, not as an anthropologist. The work left me little time for research. During the second year, arriving early to learn of preparations for lobstering, the captain welcomed me with, "Philip, I usually hire another fisherman for the summer, but I knew you were coming to help me fish. Did you bring the gin?"

There was a time when I needed to spend long hours with a 95-year-old resident recording oral history, but my unpaid duties as a fisherman and mechanic left little time for sleep, much less time for ethnographic endeavors. Neither the captain, the mate, nor any of the other fisherfolk understood that my purpose in their community was for reasons other than catching lobster or fishing or fixing someone's engines. This, indeed, was participant-observation of a severely demanding nature.

I haven't returned to the island for almost nine years. The research will never be written up. In the course of my visits with these Acadian islanders, I became accepted to the point that I learned of all of their illegal activities, even participating in some. The socioeconomic advantages derived from poaching, bootlegging, ripping off the federal and provincial bureaucracies such as unemployment, social assistance, and the fisherman's loan board, can never be reported.

We exchange Christmas cards, and I keep promising to return for a visit. But I am getting too old to work lobster, and I've never been partial to gin.

NOTE

1. The name of the island and those of my hosts and friends have been intentionally deleted. These are unique people, friendly, loving and caring people, who live life with exceptional vigor. That they accepted me and eventually told me of their illegal activities—games that they play against a system which overlegislates and exercises constraints upon their traditional ways of life—ethically prohibits me from writing about them. To all of my friends on the island, I offer thanks for some very personal lessons as to what it means to fully live life in a harsh environment.

REFERENCES

BERREMAN, GERALD D.
1962   Behind Many Masks: Ethnography and Impression Management in a Himalayan Village. Society for Applied Anthropology, Monograph 4.

BRIGGS, JEAN L.
1970   Never in Anger: Portrait of an Eskimo Family. Cambridge, MA: Harvard University Press.

EIGHTEEN

Of Softball Bats and Fishnets: A Summer in the Alaskan Bush

GEORGE GMELCH
Union College

I was in Yakutat, the only settlement along a three-hundred-mile stretch of remote coastline in southeastern Alaska. I planned to spend a week there to get acquainted with some of the Tlingit Indians before traveling fifty miles down the coast to begin a study of Indian and white salmon fishermen. And, I was to meet with village leaders to explain my research and to obtain their approval.

But even before I met with the leaders, I noticed that people were decidedly cool toward me. My greetings to passersby, for example, were often not returned. One morning, while I was walking along the dirt road from the village to the pier, a man came into view walking toward me. We were the only people on the road, yet when he came to within thirty yards of me he swung over to the other side of the road and as we passed he turned his head and looked off into the distance. Each time I entered Flo's, the small village café, the patrons lowered their voices. And when new customers came in, they routinely took the tables furthest from mine—or so it seemed.

Damn, I thought, what have I done to bring this on? Mentally I reviewed my first few days in the village, searching for anything that might explain the cool reception I was getting. I remembered having jotted down some notes to myself in the café a couple of days before, mainly a list of things I needed to do. Perhaps that had aroused suspicion? I thought about how writing notes might have been perceived—an unknown man walking around the village at all times of day, then taking notes in the café.

I was no stranger to this situation; I had been the object of suspicion before. As a graduate student I had lived for a summer in a village in the Mexican highlands taking part in an anthropology field training program. My wife, Sharon, and I had arrived in the village of San Antonio Acuamanala in the middle of a fiesta, and I remember how the crowd watched curiously as we unloaded our gear. Over the next few days, we were asked many questions about our religion. It seemed to take a long time before the people of San Antonio began to warm up and

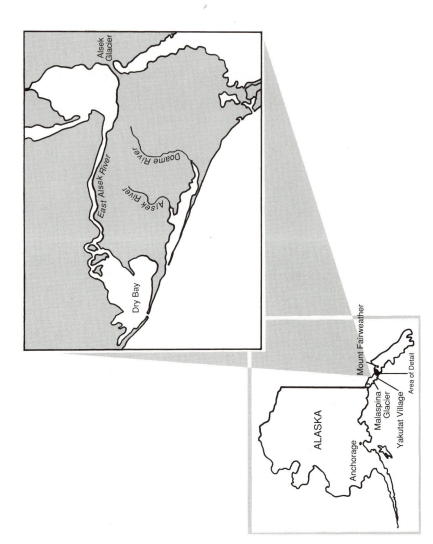

Dry Bay area, southeastern Alaska

talk to us willingly. Later, Celia Sanchez, the village paramedic who became our friend, revealed to us that the week before our arrival a light plane had flown over the village dropping leaflets promoting Seventh-Day Adventism. In this Catholic village, we had been mistaken for Protestant missionaries.

Were the people of Yakutat mistaking me for someone else? The next morning I went to the U.S. Forest Service office to ask about some aerial photographs of Dry Bay. As soon as I explained who I was and what I wanted, the woman at the desk burst into laughter. "Everyone in town," she said, "thinks you're with the IRS. They think you're here looking for unreported income."

When the village council meeting took place, John Chapman, head of Glacier Bay National Park, was with me. Park Service officials had already had one meeting with the council, but he explained again that the Park Service was being required by the U.S. Congress to do this study. In 1980 the Dry Bay area had been designated a "preserve" and added to Glacier Bay National Park. Park planners anticipated problems in trying to oversee the activities of commercial fishermen, trappers, and big-game hunters, particularly given the tensions that existed between the Tlingits and the non-natives who competed for the same resources. They had even tried to trade the Dry Bay area to the State of Alaska for another parcel of land, but the deal had fallen through.

I explained to the council how I would go about doing the research: that like most anthropologists I would live in Dry Bay among the people and observe and participate in the activities which took place there and that I would write up my observations and the things people told me in field notes which would later be used to write my "report." A Tlingit elder spoke, implying that native fishermen might be less than eager to participate in the study. I knew of the interethnic tension, and I could imagine his skepticism about an outsider really understanding the Tlingit point of view. Nevertheless, I remained enthusiastic. I was excited about the prospect of working in the Alaskan wilderness and of comparing how different peoples—Tlingits and whites—fished and used resources.

I chartered a small plane to take me to Dry Bay. Sitting in the copilot's seat I got a good look at the terrain, which directly below us was a flat coastal foreland latticed with rivers and small streams flowing to the ocean through muskeg and spruce forest. From their milky appearance, I could tell which rivers were fed by runoff from the glaciers. I counted three brown bears and four moose. In no hurry to return to Yakutat, and proud of the dazzling scenery, the young pilot turned inland toward the mountains. Within a few minutes we were over the snow-covered peaks of the Brabazon Range. Glaciers descended from U-shaped valleys, the ice and snow streaked black, dirtied with stone and rock debris.

We landed in a clearing near the small cabin where Clarence, the ranger in Yakutat, had recommended I stay. Within minutes I had unloaded my gear and stood watching as the plane disappeared over the horizon. The only sound was the distant hum of its engine. It was a lonely feeling. As I lugged my gear toward the cabin, I noticed bear tracks in the sandy soil, then claw marks on the cabin door and window frame. I got out my shotgun. I had been warned to carry it whenever I left camp and to put it near my sleeping bag at night. "Put the buckshot in first and then the slugs," explained one Park Service official, "because if you have a bear inside your tent at night, you won't be able to see him well and you'll want a wider pattern of shot to make sure you hit something." I was also counseled to "wear bells, carry a whistle, and make lots of noise" when hiking, and *never run* should I encounter a bear, for that could trigger their chase instinct. I thought of Clarence, who had told me how important it is in Alaska to be cautious and prepared. "Small mistakes," he had said, "that are inconsequential in the Lower 48 can be fatal in the north." I had dutifully recorded all of their advice in my notebook, but privately I thought they were overdoing it. Now I wasn't so sure.

The next morning I set out downriver, shotgun over my shoulder, to meet some of the local fishermen. I walked several miles before reaching the first camp, the next camp was another mile away. It was immediately apparent that the Yakutat ranger who had recommended that I live at the cabin didn't understand my research, that anthropologists like to live *among* the people they study rather than commute. Or perhaps it had been a perverse joke, as I now faced the prospect of having to move all of my gear by foot six miles to the only suitable location for my research—a small fish-processing station where the fishermen gathered to sell their fish. It was here that the salmon were gutted and iced before being flown out to Yakutat in an old DC-3, and fishermen spent some time relaxing and socializing.

In Dry Bay, unlike Yakutat, there was no confusion about who I was or what I was going to do. Again, however, I was to meet with hostility of a different sort. The Park Service had sent all of the fishermen a letter explaining the nature of my research and who I was—an anthropology professor from New York. In this case, I might have gotten a better reception if I had been an IRS inspector. The fishermen had been almost unanimously opposed to the Dry Bay area becoming part of the national park system. The land had previously been under the jurisdiction of the U.S. Forest Service, which in large measure had left the fishermen alone. Now they feared there would be new regulations restricting their activities. And they did not want anyone, least of all the federal government, telling them what they could or could not do. As one fisherman put it, "I came here to get *away* from Big Brother."

My job was to document the very activities—hunting and fishing— they feared might be restricted. Worse still, from their perspective, I was a college professor "from back East," New York no less. "A pointy-headed intellectual," I overheard one man say. Maybe if I had been from the University of Wyoming or Idaho I would have been more acceptable.

One day during my first week, a young, grizzled fisherman, high on pot, alcohol, or both, came into my camp on his three-wheeler, pistol visibly at his side. "Keep your nose out of my business or there'll be trouble," he threatened. I tried to explain calmly what anthropologists do and why the Park Service had to do this study, but he sped off before I could finish.

The other white fishermen were not overtly threatening, but they, too, made it clear that they were opposed to the research. It was "unnecessary," they said, and "a waste of taxpayers' money." They also said I could not possibly learn enough in one summer to make it worthwhile.

At first I had little contact with the Tlingit fishermen because few came to fish in the area until July, when the sockeye arrived. Unlike the non-natives, who fish in the Dry Bay area all summer long, the Tlingit move between a number of rivers and fish according to when the different species of salmon (king, sockeye, silver, pink, and chum) begin their spawning migrations.

Competition between the Tlingits and whites over fishing sites in the Dry Bay area had strained relations between the two peoples with some nasty results. Over the previous four years, Tlingit fishermen were fired at several times in an attempt to drive them away. One Tlingit fish camp had been set on fire, and the helicopter used to haul the Indians' catch to the fish processor had been shot and disabled.

Although each group was distrustful of the other, my study required that I develop rapport and gather information from both. I tried to divide my time between them, but some individuals always viewed me with suspicion whenever they saw me interacting with members of the other group.

During the first week or two, I noticed that when I approached a group of white fishermen, one by one they walked off, only to regroup somewhere else. After the summer was over I learned more about what the fishermen had thought of me from the backcountry ranger based at Dry Bay who heard much of the gossip. They joked about my appearance—I wore tennis shoes instead of rubber boots—and they said that my speech, like my clothes, was too clean. The rumor was that I lived near the safety of the fish processor because I was afraid of bears. The ranger also told me what he had observed in my interactions with the fishermen: "Your body language just didn't fit with theirs. . . . You stood too erect while they tend to slouch with their thumbs cocked in their pockets. And you made too much eye contact while they prefer to look away and fidget."

Though the Tlingits never walked away from me when I approached them, they didn't make me feel welcome either. My early attempts at conversation were often met with the most minimal responses, and sometimes with silence. The Tlingits are a reserved and private people, unaccustomed to asking or being asked questions. And in the beginning I didn't have enough knowledge of Alaska, the region, or the issues that concerned the Tlingits to have an informal conversation without asking questions. When I arrived at one of their tents I always had the sinking feeling that I was intruding, that they were busy and didn't have the time to chat.

Nevertheless, my rapport with members of both groups gradually improved. At the fish processor, after each fisherman unloaded his catch, he usually hung around to talk and learn how the other fishermen were doing before returning to the solitary life of the fish camp. In addition to the little things that any stranger in a new setting does to develop good relations with local people, I drew the younger men into playing frisbee, pitching horseshoes, or shooting baskets on a makeshift backboard. The games often ended up in a relaxed conversation, sometimes over beer.

I tried to demonstrate to both Tlingit and white fishermen alike that I respected their knowledge and capabilities: the way in which they dealt with the hazards of bears and of fishing in small boats in the swift, frigid waters of the Alsek where floating logs and chunks of ice from calving glaciers upriver could destroy a person's nets and where falling overboard could easily mean death. I listened attentively to what they said, like a conscientious schoolboy. They were, indeed, my teachers. I told each fisherman that everything I learned from them was confidential and that even in my own field notes I was not using their real names. I promised to let each of them read and comment on the first draft of my report and that if they disagreed with some point I had made but could not convince me that I was wrong, that I would include their objections in the report.

The fishermen, Tlingits and non-natives, gradually came to accept that I had an open mind about them and their activities, that I had not come with fixed ideas about the appropriateness of fishing and hunting or of building cabins and airstrips in a protected wilderness area. Ultimately, a few fishermen invited me to their fish camps for a meal.

My wife Sharon's arrival in Dry Bay several weeks into the fieldwork also seemed to help. While the wives of most fishermen did not come to Dry Bay, mine had and she was seven months pregnant. She hiked with me to visit distant fish camps and took an unexpectedly severe pounding in a boat while ascending swift water miles up the Alsek River. Some thought she was foolish to come to Dry Bay in her "condition," where storms can ground airplanes for days putting medical attention out of reach. But whatever the wisdom of her being there, her presence seemed to make it easier for people to accept me. Perhaps because with a wife and a child on the way I was seen as a family man, something to which the fishermen could relate.

But the turning point in my rapport with local fishermen happened on the Fourth of July. All of the non-native fishermen gathered at the fish processor to celebrate; the height of the festivities was a softball game played on a bluff above the river. I had once played baseball for a living and still enjoyed the game. In my first two at bats I hit the ball hard and far, making two home runs. In the sixth inning, when our only bat broke nearly in half, I helped one of the fishermen repair it with screws and plenty of tape, and with choked grips we resumed play. In the field, with the enthusiasm of play and forgetting for the moment my low status among the fishermen, I gave the other fielders directions on which cut-off man to throw to. When a debate broke out over a quirky play, I knew the rule that resolved the disagreement. Being able to play ball was the accidental key to acceptance. Following the game there was some good-natured joking about my play, and the fishermen seemed decidedly friendlier. During the game, the ranger, without my knowing, had told some of the fishermen that I had once played professionally.

In earlier research I had often played sports with the people I was living among as a way of getting to know them better, but also for fun and exercise. It always seemed to me to make a difference in their attitudes toward me, but I had never really known for certain. This time, at the end of the summer when I was at the Park Service headquarters in Glacier Bay reviewing the summer's fieldwork, I had a long chat about my fieldwork with Richard Steele, the back-country ranger. "The ice breaker," he said, "was the softball game. When they saw how hard you hit the ball and that you really knew how to play the game, you became a regular guy. . . . You were no longer just a weirdo professor from back East who wore tennis shoes and clean clothes and had good posture."

What the ranger's observations also revealed to me was that I had failed to realize how differences in *class* can be as big an obstacle to developing rapport as differences in *culture*. When arriving in Dry Bay I had unconsciously assumed that I would have little difficulty making friends among the white fishermen, who ostensibly were from the same mainstream American culture as I. It would take more understanding and effort, I thought, to get to know the Tlingits. But the differences in class between me—white-collar academic—and the largely blue-collar fishermen were no less tractable.

While I received confirmation from the ranger that I had been accepted by the whites, I wasn't totally sure what the Tlingits thought of me and my research until several years later when I got a phone call from an Alaskan attorney who was representing twelve Yakutat fishermen in a suit against the State of Alaska over fishing rights. The Tlingit fishermen wanted to know if I would come to Alaska and help them. They wanted to know if I would testify in court as an "expert witness" on the history of their fishing in the Dry Bay area. The Alaska Department of Fish and Game had banned "surf fishing," that is, fishing the ocean waters outside the mouths of the Alsek and East rivers. Since only the natives fished in the surf, they believed the banning of the fishing there was discriminatory. The department justified its actions, in part, by claiming that surf fishing was not "traditional" among the Tlingits. The Indians knew it was and hoped that I knew enough about the history of their fishery to back them up.

In November 1987 I testified for the Tlingits in the Alaska Superior Court. It was the final irony—a complete reversal of roles. There I sat in the witness stand giving "expert" testimony on various aspects of Tlingit fishing and culture while in the gallery sat the real experts, the Tlingit fishermen who had taught me virtually everything I knew about them and their fishery. Later, outside the courtroom, after two hours of testimony and cross-examination by the State's attorney, they informed me that I had gotten it *right*.

ACKNOWLEDGMENTS

I wish to thank Anna Allen, Phil DeVita, Sharon Gmelch, Chase Henzel, Miriam Lee Kaprow, Phyllis Morrow, Trecie Melnick, Richard Nelson, and Richard Steele for their excellent comments on earlier drafts of this paper.

NINETEEN

On Jogging with Fascists and Strolling with Reds: Ethnoethnography and Political Polarization in an Andalusian Town

MICHAEL DEAN MURPHY
University of Alabama

In a witty and insightful keynote address, Melford Spiro (1986) recently likened one task of the ethnographer to T. S. Eliot's conception of the poet's special talent: They both seek to make the strange, familiar.[1] That is, by their methods of description and analysis ethnographers attempt to render intelligible the alien customs of other people. The traditional mission of the ethnographer has been to perform this procedure by breaking through the preconceptions and stereotypes that establish the strangeness of other societies. In part this has been accomplished by attempting to represent other people in scientific terms that are not only more customary, and therefore more familiarizing, but hopefully more discerning than the exoticizing rhetoric of the adventurer, the missionary, and the colonial administrator.

That this is no easy undertaking is revealed in the numberless accounts of the often humorous, sometimes dramatic, and occasionally bumbling efforts of ethnographers to understand the strange (to them) behavior of the people with whom they live and about whom they hope to write with some authority. Much of this genre of "tales of the field" (Van Maanen 1988) is part of anthropology's oral tradition, but a few written memoirs, such as Richard B. Lee's (1969) account of fieldwork among the !Kung San of southern Africa, have come to exemplify the difficulty of penetrating the mysteries of "otherness" so that it might be understood in familiar terms.

Of course, anthropologists have not failed to notice that the subjects of ethnographic investigation themselves may invest considerable thought to figuring out what that most curious character of all, the anthropologist, is doing in their midst (e.g., Murphy 1985). This effort of the host to understand the anthropologist and to deduce something about his or her culture from their encounter, has been referred to by

Robert Lawless (1986) as "ethnoethnography." A rather famous example of this activity is reported in Laura Bohannan's (1966) frequently reprinted article, "Shakespeare in the Bush," in which she describes the keen, but surprising, sense that the Tiv of West Africa made of the story of Hamlet.

In their evocative accounts of memorable, albeit humbling, field experiences, both Bohannan and Lee confront the problem of intercultural communication in the classic circumstance of the Western anthropologist engaging the people of an exotic society located beyond the margins of our own civilization. The !Kung San and the Tiv had to rely almost entirely on their own cultures to make sense both of the anthropologists among them and of the distant and largely incomprehensible societies that they represented. Yet the people I chose to learn from, the Andalusians of southern Spain, not only are fully in the mainstream of Western civilization, but they also have had a great deal of direct and indirect contact with Americans, and their understanding of American culture is correspondingly rather elaborate. As a consequence, my Andalusian friends had two well-developed models of behavior to draw upon in order to make sense of me, my discourse, and my doings: a model of the familiar (in which behavior is judged according to criteria applied to the conduct of local people) and a model of the strange (in which behavior is evaluated according to culturally constructed stereotypes of outsiders, in this case Americans). The interaction of these two models, I was to learn, may simultaneously advance and hinder cross-cultural communication.

In what follows, I will describe not only the efforts of some of the Andalusian townsmen I lived with for fifteen months to understand my presence among them but also the effects this process had on my work and my own complicated feelings about it. While most townsmen seemed to accept at face value that I was there to study a fiesta and various devotions associated with the supernatural patroness of their community, they very much wondered which of several politically inspired perspectives I would ultimately take. In being sensitive, perhaps at times oversensitive, to their attempts to figure me out, I not only gained insight into the culture of political polarization in Andalusia, but I also worked through a personal conundrum in a manner that is not uncommon in ethnographic research.

I chose to work and live in Almonte, a town of 15,000 people located in western Andalusia, because it is the site of a magnificent pilgrimage that honors its supernatural patroness, a lovely Gothic statue of the Virgin Mary known as *La Virgen del Rocio* (the Virgin of the Dew). Rocio is housed in a basilica situated at the very edge of the great marshes of the Guadalquivir River about fifteen kilometers from the town itself but still within its administrative boundaries. Like most marianist devotions in Andalusia, the Rocio cultus is structured around lay religious brother-

hoods (*hermandades*), which link the popular, and occasionally un-
orthodox, fervor for the Virgin Mary to the ecclesiastical hierarchy that
seeks to exert some control over it.[2] Rocio differs from most other
marianist devotions in Spain because her first and principal brotherhood
in Almonte (known as the *Hermandad Matriz*) presides over seventy-
eight auxiliary brotherhoods (*Hermandades Filiales*) scattered throughout Andalusia and the rest of Spain.

Although the statue has been a revered object of devotion for
Almonteños and others in the area for seven centuries, her popularity
has increased enormously during the twentieth century; attendance at
her annual pilgrimage in the spring has skyrocketed from about five
thousand at the turn of the century to a million and a half at present.
Rocio has so captivated Andalusians that she is widely regarded as the
patroness of the whole region, not just the town itself. Both socialist/
secular and conservative/ecclesiastical authorities, in rare agreement, have
proclaimed her to be the Queen and Patroness of Andalusia.

While outsiders are universally impressed by the united front that
the Almonteños present in defense of their traditional primacy in the
festivities that honor their Virgin, viewed from the inside it quickly
becomes obvious that the town, as is true of many Andalusian communities, is very much politically polarized. Until recently Almonte's
social structure reflected a very lopsided distribution of the resources
of the community. With the collaboration of their conservative allies
from the agricultural and urban middle classes of Almonte, a few wealthy
landowners dominated the economy, the politics, and the religious life
of the town. Most Almonteño men, however, were *jornaleros*, or agricultural day workers, who either possessed no land at all or owned a plot
insufficient to support a family. Severely constrained by a labor market
that often did not provide them with adequate employment or wages,
many Almonteños lived in abject poverty. The systematic and pervasive
economic inequities that favored a few, and disadvantaged the many,
fueled profound class antagonism and political polarization along the
usual lines: The wealthy and their minions supported the parties of the
right, the workers favored the politics of the left.

During the Second Republic (1931–36) Almonte's leftists briefly
presided over the town government leaving the conservatives with
only Rocio's Principal Brotherhood to wield influence over popular
sentiments. But democracy was crushed by the Nationalist rebellion,
and during the nearly four decades of the Franco regime the rightists
regained their domination of both the secular and the religious life of
the town. While Almonte's brotherhood is closely identified with the
rightists who make up its board of directors, this fact has not dissuaded
the working-class people of the town from enthusiastic participation in the Rocio cultus, although many are quick to point out that the
statue belongs to the *pueblo* (the town and its people) and not to the

brotherhood, which merely handles the administrative details associated with it.

When the Franco era ended, and democracy was restored to Almonte, the Socialist party won the overwhelming majority of votes in the elections that followed, and they are now firmly ensconced in the town government. But the socialist town council has been very careful to limit itself to a purely logistical role in Rocio's huge pilgrimage, leaving the actual administration of the rituals and other religious matters to the *Hermandad Matriz*, which continues to be run by the conservatives who used to wield political power in the town prior to democratization.

Periodically the leftist town government and the rightist brotherhood have clashed over matters concerning Rocio, but for the most part these political adversaries have proceeded very cautiously in their necessary dealings with one another, each seeking to avoid the appearance of using Rocio to further political ends. Both factions fear reprisals from their fellow townsmen for unseemly manipulation of the beloved patroness of the town. The vox populi of Almonte, when it speaks to issues concerning Rocio, is a potent force to be reckoned with in local politics.

Such reticence to take strong public positions on the matter of Rocio is not shared by outsiders, however. Particularly since the reestablishment of democracy, the pilgrimage has become increasingly controversial, with rightists and leftists each seeking to explain Rocio in a manner that best suits their respective ideologies. Is Rocio a manifestation of the strength of Catholic (and, therefore, conservative) sentiment in Andalusia? Is Rocio a glorious expression of Andalusian folklore and popular culture that has little to do with the institutions of the church or the values of conservatives? Or is Rocio an example of cultural mystification in which the material basis of profound class conflict is covered up by illusory displays of community solidarity?

The anthropological literature on popular religion in Andalusia alerted me to the fact that marianism has long been a battleground in which the right and the left conduct ideological combat.[3] Yet, when I arrived in Almonte in 1984 to begin my work there, I only abstractly understood the complicated political significance of devotion to its Virgin. Indeed, at first I only dimly perceived the vigorous, but often subtle, struggle being waged by leftists and rightists in the town (and outside of it as well) to define the public meaning of the pilgrimage to Rocio and all of the activities, both religious and secular, organized around it. Nevertheless, I very quickly was made aware of the intense interest that some Almonteños displayed in trying to figure out what my political intentions were in studying their Virgin. Which of the two most extreme genres of writing about Rocio that they knew of did I intend to advance: the saccharine devotional tract or the venomous atheist diatribe?

Although somewhat reassured by the fact that I am an American—and thus, according to their understanding of us, probably quite anti-communist—some of the politically conservative leaders of the brother-hood entertained suspicions that I was a red herring whose true purpose was to gain as much inside information as possible to spice up an indictment against them. In fact, a few years before my arrival on the scene, a documentary film crew showed up in the town and, as it was subsequently reported to me by indignant rightists, rather shamelessly misrepresented their motives in producing a film about Rocio. When their documentary was released for theatrical distribution, many towns-men, including some leftists, were outraged at the virulence and vul-garity of the attack against the cultus of Rocio. Indeed, the film was so unremittingly hostile in its depiction of some of the town's personalities that it led to court proceedings which ultimately resulted in its censor-ship, an astonishing and (to my knowledge) unique event in post-Franco Spain.[4] In short, although the rightists viewed me as a representative of an admired nation, at least some of them were wary of me and alert to any trickery on my part. Their suspicion was reflected in the fact that I never did gain access to the archives of the brotherhood.

On the other hand, many of the town's leftists considered me to be a "typical rightist American" until otherwise proven to be something else. Their preconceptions included the likelihood that I would be a capitalist apologist, an ardent supporter of Reagan, and an exemplifica-tion of the cowboyism that they take to be at the center of American national character. I found it particularly trying when popular TV per-sonalities from American melodramas—such as J. R. Ewing and Kojak—were invoked as somehow being decisive keys to understanding Ameri-can character. I sometimes suspected that "Dallas," "Dynasty," and "Knots Landing" were regarded as rather more typical of American domestic life than I devoutly hope to be the case. Spaniards, so often lampooned in the images of Don Juan, Carmen, and the like, are not themselves entirely immune from the temptations of the caricature.

In retrospect I now realize that I was equally discomfited by the stereo-types of both the right and the left, and only partly because of what I judged to be their respective inaccuracies. More than once I felt the unhappy sting of recognition in summary judgments of American cul-ture. In any event, in retrospect I am struck by how fundamentally similar were the characterizations of Americans offered by leftists and rightists in the town; our presumed cultural and characterological traits were merely evaluated differently. From some townsmen (the rightists) I lis-tened to America being praised for all the wrong reasons; from others (the leftists) I heard sweeping condemnations, not just of the American government but also of the diverse people that it represents.

Lest I give the impression that the townsmen were difficult, un-friendly, or obstructionist, I am happy to declare that nothing could be further from the truth. Hospitality is not just a theoretical virtue with Andalusians; kindness to strangers is not merely extolled, it is extended gracefully and automatically. Nevertheless, rightists and leftists alike scrutinized my behavior for any telltale signs that might reveal my true intentions. In so doing they drew upon their observations of American tourists and servicemen and their beliefs about what Americans are like, some of which are derived from their interpretations of the endless depictions of American life on television, in films, and in the Spanish print media. But they also sought to understand my behavior in their own terms and with particular reference to the decidedly Andalusian symbolism of political affiliation. While many townsmen were clearly very interested in discerning my political ideology, they did not, with rare exception, directly inquire about it. At first I was bothered by this indirection, but eventually I concluded that many Almonteños simply believed that their observations and inferences were likely to be more trustworthy guides to my politics than any claims I might make.

Seeing is believing to be sure, but it can also be mighty perplexing. To some degree at least, my behavior as an ethnographer confounded both the Almonteño model of Americans and the complex of symbols and understandings that sustains and reinforces political polarization in the town. In part this was due to my desire to gain some measure of rapport with both camps by avoiding undue identification with either one. But it is equally true that simply carrying on the task of ethnography was a source of confusion for them, at least at first.

This confusion was vividly driven home to me by the following incident. After arriving in Almonte, I quickly adopted the custom of jogging every morning with "Pepe," a townsman who is closely associated with the conservative elite of the community. Early each morning we would jog down and back a well-traveled road leading to a neighboring town. News of this confirmed the suspicions of some that I was an American rightist of the standard stereotype. At about the same time, I also took to strolling through the town occasionally in the afternoons with "Enrique," a prominent communist intellectual of the community. This pleasant habit led to some pointed questioning of me by a few rightists who warned me of the dangers of improper associations. Undeterred, I continued my association with both not only because Pepe and Enrique were first-rate consultants whose experiences and points of view rarely overlapped but also because they are excellent companions whom I came to regard as valued friends.

My friendship with these two Almonteños, socially situated at the extremes of the ideological factions of the town, produced consternation in some observers and hilarity in at least one, who recounted the following story. Two friends, deep in their cups in a local tavern, argued at length about "who" I was (leftist or rightist) because their respective work schedules allowed each to observe only some of my daily activities. The man who saw me jogging each morning with Pepe was quite sure that I was a *facha* (a fascist), while his friend, who saw me in conversation with Enrique many afternoons, was equally convinced that I was a *rojo* (a red, or leftist). Thus, the venerable Spanish saying, "Tell me with whom you walk and I will tell you who you are," was applied to my case with exquisite literalness.

Eventually, and with some measure of dismay, I could not avoid recognizing that for most Almonteños I was obviously a rightist despite my close friendships with a number of leftists. The combination of being an American and my decision to learn as much as possible from the officials of the brotherhood doomed me to identification with the rightists of the town, the presumptive champions of an anachronistic *franquismo*. Especially at first, I associated with many knowledgeable *rocieros* (devotees of Rocio) who also happened to be members of, or associated with, the traditional rightist elite of the town. As my work with them developed, I became very good friends with some people whose political views were considerably to the right of my own. Although I talked with a wide range of Almonteños about Rocio, trying to acquire as comprehensive an understanding of the cultus as possible, it was my association and friendship with some rightists that defined my politics for many townsmen, partly, I believe, because that was what was expected of an American. While my presence in the town stretched the stereotype of Americans entertained by some of my Andalusian friends, particularly those who know me well, it did not substantially alter it for many others.

By the time that full realization of my dilemma sunk in, it appeared to me that there was not much I could do to change the situation. I found this to be very disturbing even after I concluded that it did not substantially affect the work that I was trying to do. My personal relationships with families of the right theoretically may have interfered with building rapport with some leftists, but in fact I never found it difficult to talk with anyone about Rocio and her ardent devotees, the people of Almonte. My problem with being labeled a rightist was not methodological, it was psychological. As someone whose own political beliefs are moderately left of center, I simply did not like the fact that people identified me with the right. Yet my friendship with people of the right was genuine, and I certainly was not prepared to reject it in order to make some sort of political statement. Moreover, it seemed unlikely that such an apparent about-face would be believed anyway. Since circumstances conspired to identify me with the right and since there was little that I could to about it without risking hurting the feelings of some of my friends, I determined that I should just try to make the best of a nettlesome situation. My solution to the dilemma, although I only slowly came to recognize it as a solution, was to make my personal problem a part of the research that I was conducting.

The attention that I paid to the efforts of the townsmen to figure me out proved to be quite illuminating. For example, it alerted me to some of the subtleties and nuances of the symbolism of political polarization in a community long divided by class antagonism. Among other things, it helped me understand the class and ideological coding of various kinds of participation in the religious and ceremonial life of the town. I learned that some of my ordinary ethnographic activities, such as observing and participating in the many processional rituals that punctuate the Almonteño calendar, pegged me as a rightist. To the leftists of the town it is perfectly acceptable to observe non-Rocio processions (such as occur during Holy Week or Corpus Christi), even changing one's position or vantage point during the processional route. It is quite a different matter, however, to actually join in the processional entourage as I frequently did, for that suggests identification with the rightists associated with the brotherhood, not mere bemused observation of them from the sidelines.

Similarly, I learned that it is much more acceptable for a leftist to enter a church if it is located outside of his own community. One insightful leftist friend of mine commented once that when he visited churches and shrines outside of Almonte with me his presence communicated curiosity, not commitment. To him that made all the difference in the world. To be seen entering Almonte's church by his fellow townsmen would have symbolically aligned him with the wrong end of the political spectrum, the *fachas*. For my friend, and for many others of his political convictions, the mere act of entering a church, then, is not inherently distasteful, but because of the nature of the symbolism of political polarization, being observed by significant others entering the church of one's own community most definitely is.

In short, since I was motivated for both personal and professional reasons to ameliorate, if possible, my overidentification with the right, I became attentive to the symbolism of political identification in the town, particularly as it related to popular religion. One result of this sensitivity was a refocus of my inquiry, or better, a widening of it to include the symbolism of political polarization in general. I suspect that when a fieldwork problem such as mine becomes so personalized that it strikes a nerve in the ethnographer's identity, it is not at all unusual for the dilemma itself to be externalized by being placed on the research agenda, whether or not its relevance was anticipated in the original fieldwork plan. In other words, being typified as a rightist led me to focus on the issue of political polarization in the town, thus objectifying the source of my subjective discomfort.

Both the preconceptions that Almonteños entertain about Americans, their model of our "strange" ways, and the local meaning of certain aspects of my behavior as an ethnographer, combined to produce a widespread assessment of my politics that did not exactly enthuse me. When I began to understand the processes at work in typifying me, even though I was unwilling to take any dramatic measures to counter them, I did seek to renegotiate my reputation closer to something more compatible with my actual beliefs.

I was not certain what effect, if any, my efforts to moderate my reputation were having, until one day a particularly skeptical leftist of the town, after observing me field some tough questions about what conclusions I had arrived at concerning Rocío, remarked that he enjoyed watching me "bullfighting" with the people of the town. The image that immediately came to my mind was that of the elegant figure of the bullfighter artfully executing the cape passes that allow him to evade the furious charges of the bull. As often happens with such compliments, however, the more I thought about it the less sure I was of whether to be proud or chastened; certainly I was rather more cheered by the imputation to me of the quality of artfulness than that of evasiveness.

When I mentioned my concern to a friend of mine (who happened to be leftist himself), he laughed and said that if I was truly learning to *torear* with the people, then I was simply acquiring proficiency in another local art, and, he allowed, a vital one at that. He explained that I was not alone in feeling that I was being socially located closer to one or another political extreme than truly corresponded to my beliefs, nor was I unique in trying to do something about it. In talking to others in the town about this, it soon became apparent that being politically labeled in a manner that made me feel uncomfortable was not merely a result of a flawed stab at ethnoethnography but rather part and parcel of the town's political culture. My experience with political polarization simply personalized a process of apparently great salience for Spanish society: the pronounced tendency toward hyperbole in the characterization of the political positions of others. Of course, there can be little doubt that the bifurcation of political sentiment in Spain has a clear-cut historical basis in the economic and political inequities that have benefited a handful at the expense of the multitudes. Although Spain has made dramatic progress in political and economic arenas in recent years, memories still burn bright in Almonte of the grinding poverty of the *jornaleros*, of the brutality of the civil war, and of the political repression that followed its conclusion.

While the sources of political polarization seemed clear enough to me even before I went to Almonte, my own encounter with it vividly revealed one of its smaller consequences: the feeling of many Almonteños that their political views are often misrepresented by their fellow townsmen, that they are not as leftist or as rightist as others portray them to be. The bullfighting metaphor used by an Almonteño observer of my behavior suggests that any effort to shift one's collective assignment of political identity is likely to be viewed as a studied maneuver intended to beguile the community with false suggestions of moderation. In such an environment there seems to be as little escape from polarization for the familiar local as for the strange ethnographer. My own experience suggests that learning from the juxtaposition of the strange and the familiar works in both directions simultaneously, as observer and observed regularly exchange hats. Both the ethnographer and the host grapple, consciously or not, with models of familiarity and strangeness. Yet the burden of not confounding the two falls only to the anthropologist.

NOTES

1. Spiro, following Eliot's lead, argues that ethnographers, like poets, also seek to make the familiar strange by placing the customs of their own society in comparative perspective, thus stripping them of their aura of inevitability.

2. A "marianist" devotion is one that centers around the Virgin Mary, mother of Jesus Christ. Andalusia is one of the most important centers of marianism in the world; not for nothing do many Andalusians refer to their region as *la tierra de Maria Santisima*, "The Land of Mary, the Most Holy." "Cultus" is a technical term for a system of religious devotion or worship that avoids the negative connotations its synonym, "cult," has acquired through popular and journalistic usage.

3. Especially important is the essential body of work of anthropologists Isidoro Moreno (1982, 1985), Salvador Rodriguez (1985), Stanley Brandes (1980), and David Gilmore (1975).

4. The film, however, was not censored because of its highly hostile approach to Andalusian popular religion. Rather, specific charges were made against a prominent, rightist Almonteño personality of the past that could not be substantiated in court proceedings initiated by members of his family.

REFERENCES

BOHANNAN, LAURA
1966   Shakespeare in the Bush. Natural History 75(7):28–33.

BRANDES, STANLEY
1980   Metaphors of Masculinity: Sex and Status in Andalusian Folklore. Philadelphia: University of Pennsylvania Press.

GILMORE, DAVID D.
1975   Carnaval in Fuenmayor: Class Conflict and Social Cohesion in an Andalusian Town. Journal of Anthropological Research 31:331–348.

LAWLESS, ROBERT
1986   Ethnoethnographers and the Anthropologist. Anthropology 10:55–74.

LEE, RICHARD B.
1969   Eating Christmas in the Kalahari. Natural History 78(10):14–27, 60–63.

MORENO NAVARRO, ISIDORO

1982 La Semana Santa de Sevilla: conformación, mixtificación, y significaciones. Seville: Biblioteca de Temas Sevillanas.

1985 Cofradias y hermandadades andaluzas. Seville: Editoriales Andaluzas Unidas. Biblioteca de la Cultura Andaluza.

MURPHY, MICHAEL D.

1985 Rumors of Identity: Gossip and Rapport in Ethnographic Research. Human Organization 44:132–137.

RODRIGUEZ BECERRA, SALVADOR

1985 Las fiestas de Andalucia. Seville: Editoriales Andaluzas Unidas. Biblioteca de la Cultura Andaluza.

SPIRO, MELFORD E.

1986 On the Strange and the Familiar. Keynote Address of the First Annual Chicago Symposium on Culture and Human Development. October 23–25.

VAN MAANEN, JOHN

1988 Tales of the Field: On Writing Ethnography. Chicago: University of Chicago Press.

Navigating Nigerian Bureaucracies; or, "Why Can't You Beg?" She Demanded[1]

ELIZABETH A. EAMES
Bates College

Americans have a saying: "It's not what you know, it's who you know." This aphorism captures the—usually subtle—use of old-boy networks for personal advancement in this country. But what happens when this principle becomes the primary dynamic of an entire social system? The period of three years I spent pursuing anthropological field research in a small Nigerian city was one of continual adjustment and reordering of expectations. This essay discusses a single case—how I discovered the importance personal ties have for Nigerian bureaucrats—but also illustrates the general process by which any open-minded visitor to a foreign land might decipher the rules of proper behavior. I was already familiar with Max Weber's work on bureaucracy and patrimony, yet its tremendous significance and explanatory power became clear to me only following the incidents discussed below.

I heard the same comment from every expatriate I met during my three years in Nigeria—U.S. foreign service officers, U.N. "experts," and visiting business consultants alike: "If you survive a stint in Nigeria, you can survive anywhere." The negative implications of this statement stem from outsiders' futile attempts to apply, in a new social setting, home-grown notions of how bureaucratic organizations function. This is indeed a natural inclination and all the more tempting where organizational structure appears bureaucratic. Yet in Nigeria, the officeholders behaved according to different rules; their attitudes and sentiments reflected a different moral code. A bureaucratic organizational structure coexisted with an incompatible set of moral imperatives. The resulting unwieldy, inflexible structure may be singled out as one of British colonialism's most devastating legacies.

Please bear in mind the problem of understanding that another culture works both ways. Any Nigerian student reading for the first time the following passage by a prominent American sociologist would probably howl with laughter:

The chief merit of a bureaucracy is its technical efficiency, with a premium placed on precision, speed, expert control, continuity, discretion and optimal returns on input. The structure is one which approaches the complete elimination of personalized relationships and nonrational considerations (hostility, anxiety, affectual involvements, etc.). (Merton 1968:250)

Even those well-educated administrative Nigerian officers who had once been required to incorporate such notions into their papers and exams do not live by them.

To many foreigners who have spent time in Nigeria, "the system" remains a mystery. What motivating principles explain the behavior of Nigerian administrative officers? How do local people understand the behavior of their fellow workers? Why do some people successfully maneuver their way through the system while others founder?

Recently I attended a party. As often happens at a gathering of anthropologists, we started swapping fieldwork stories and meandered onto the topic of our most unpleasant sensation or unsettling experience. That night, I heard tales of surviving strange diseases, eating repulsive foods, losing one's way in the rain forest, being caught between hostile rebel factions or kidnapped by guerrilla fighters. As for me? All that came to mind were exasperating encounters with intransigent clerks and secretaries. I began to ponder why these interactions had proved so unsettling.

My discipline—social anthropology—hinges on the practice of "participant-observation." To a fledgling anthropologist, the "fieldwork" research experience takes on all of the connotations of initiation into full membership. For some, a vision-quest; for others, perhaps, a trial-by-ordeal: The goal is to experience another way of life from the inside and to internalize, as does a growing child, the accumulating lessons of daily life. But the anthropologist is not a child; therefore, she or he experiences not conversion but self-revelation.

I came to understand my American-ness during the period spent coming to terms with Nigerian-ness. I found that I believed in my right to fair treatment and justice simply because I was a human being. I believed in equal protection under the law. But my Nigerian friends did not. What I found was a social system where status, relationships, and rights were fundamentally negotiable and justice was never impartial. In the United States, impersonalized bureaucracies are the norm: We do not question them, our behavior automatically adjusts to them. But imagine spending a year working in a corporation where none of these rules applied.

You see, a Nigerian immigration officer will sign your form only if doing so will perpetuate some mutually beneficial relationship or if she or he wishes to initiate a relationship by putting you in her or his debt.

For those unlucky enough to be without connections (this must necessarily include most foreigners), the only other option is bribery—where the supplicant initiates a personal relationship of sorts and the ensuing favor evens matters up.

Hence, Nigeria becomes labeled "inefficient," "tribalistic," and "corrupt." And so it is. Yet this system exists and persists for a profound reason: Whereas in Europe and Asia power and authority always derived from ownership of landed property, in West Africa the key ingredient was a large number of loyal dependents. Because land was plentiful and agriculture was of the extensive slash-and-burn variety, discontented subordinates could simply move on. The trick was to maintain power over subordinates through ostentatious displays of generosity. This meant more than simply putting on a lavish feast: You must demonstrate a willingness to use your influence to support others in times of need. Even now, all Nigerians participate in such patron-client relationships. In fact, all legitimate authority derives from being in a position to grant favors and not the other way around.

Actually, only a miniscule portion of my time in the field was spent dealing with Nigeria's "formal sector." My research entailed living within an extended family household (approximately a dozen adults and two dozen children), chatting with friends, visiting women in their market stalls, even at times conducting formal or informal interviews. And during the years spent researching women's economic resources and domestic responsibilities, I came to understand—indeed, to deeply admire—their sense of moral responsibility to a wide-ranging network of kin, colleagues, neighbors, friends, and acquaintances. Even now, I often take the time to recall someone's overwhelming hospitality, a friendly greeting, the sharing and eating together. Such warm interpersonal relations more than made up for the lack of amenities.

The longer I stayed, however, the clearer it became that what I loved most and what I found most distressing about life in Nigeria were two sides of the same coin, inextricably related.

The first few months in a new place can be instructive for those with an open mind:

LESSON ONE: THE STRENGTH OF WEAK TIES

My first exposure to Nigerian civil servants occurred when, after waiting several months prior to departure from the United States, I realized my visa application was stalled somewhere in the New York Consulate. Letter writing and telephoning proved futile, and as my departure date approached, panic made me plan a personal visit.

The waiting room was populated by sullen, miserable people—a roomful of hostile eyes fixed on the uniformed man guarding the office door. They had been waiting for hours on end. Any passing official was simultaneously accosted by half a dozen supplicants, much as a political celebrity is accosted by the news media. Everyone's immediate goal was to enter through that door to the inner sanctum; so far, they had failed. But I was lucky: I had the name of an acquaintance's wife's schoolmate currently employed at the consulate. After some discussion, the guard allowed me to telephone her.

Mrs. Ojo greeted me cordially, then—quickly, quietly—she coaxed my application forms through the maze of cubicles. It was a miracle!

"What a wonderful woman," I thought to myself. "She understands." I thought she had taken pity on me and acted out of disgust for her colleagues' mishandling of my application. I now realize that by helping me she was reinforcing a relationship with her schoolmate. Needless to say, my gratitude extended to her schoolmate's husband, my acquaintance. As I later came to understand it, this natural emotional reaction— gratitude for favors granted—is the currency fueling the system. Even we Americans have an appropriate saying: "What goes around comes around." But at this point, I had merely learned that, here as elsewhere, connections open doors.

LESSON TWO: NO IMPERSONAL TRANSACTIONS ALLOWED

Once on Nigerian soil I confronted the mayhem of Muritala Muhammad airport. Joining the crowd surrounding one officer's station, jostled slowly forward, I finally confronted her face-to-face. Apparently I was missing the requisite currency form. No, sorry, there were none available that day. "Stand back," she declared. "You can't pass here today." I waited squeamishly. If I could only catch her eye once more! But then what? After some time, a fellow passenger asked me what the problem was. At this point, the officer, stealing a glance at me while processing someone else, inquired: "Why can't you beg?" The person being processed proclaimed: "She doesn't know how to beg! Please, O! Let her go." And I was waved on.

A young post office clerk soon reinforced my conclusion that being employed in a given capacity did not in and of itself mean one performed it. Additional incentive was required. Again, I was confronted with a mass of people crowded round a window. Everyone was trying to catch the clerk's attention, but the young man was adept at avoiding eye contact. Clients were calling him by name, invoking the name of mutual friends, and so on. After some time, he noticed me, and I grabbed the opportunity to ask for stamps. In a voice full of recrimination, yet tinged with regret, he announced more to the crowd than to me: "Why can't you greet?" and proceeded to ignore me. This proved my tip-off to the elaborate and complex cultural code of greetings so central to Nigerian social life. In other words, a personal relationship is like a "jump start" for business transactions.

LESSON THREE: EVERY CASE IS UNIQUE

Mrs. Ojo had succeeded in obtaining for me a three-month visa, but I planned to stay for over two years. Prerequisite for a "regularized" visa was university affiliation. This sounded deceptively simple. The following two months spent registering as an "occasional postgraduate student" took a terrible toll on my nervous stomach. The worst feeling was of an ever-receding target, an ever-thickening tangle of convoluted mazeways. No one could tell me what it took to register, for in fact, no one could possibly predict what I would confront farther down the road. Nothing was routinized, everything was personalized, and no two cases could possibly be alike.

This very unpredictability of the process forms a cybernetic system with the strength of personal ties, however initiated. "Dash" and "Long-leg" are the locally recognized means for cutting through red tape or confronting noncooperative personnel. "Dash" is local parlance for gift or bribe. "Long-leg" (sometimes called "L-L" or "L-squared") refers to petitioning a powerful person to help hack your way through the tangled overgrowth. To me, it evokes the image of something swooping down from on high to stomp on the petty bureaucrat causing the problem.

During my drawn-out tussle with the registrar's office, I recounted my problem to anyone who would listen. A friend's grown son, upon hearing of my difficulties, wrote a note on his business card to a Mr. Ade in the Exams Section. Amused by his attempt to act important, I thanked Ayo politely. When I next saw him at his mother's home, he took the offensive and accused me of shunning him. It came out that I had not seen Mr. Ade. But, I protested, I did not know the man. Moreover, he worked in exams, not the registry. That, I learned, was not the point. I was supposed to assume that Mr. Ade would have known someone in the registry. Not only had I denied Ayo the chance to further his link to Mr. Ade, but ignoring his help was tantamount to denying any connection to him or—more important for me—his mother.

This revelation was reinforced when I ran into a colleague. He accused me of not greeting him very well. I had greeted him adequately but apologized nonetheless. As the conversation progressed, he told me that he had heard I had had "some difficulty." He lamented the fact that I had not called on him, since as Assistant Dean of Social Science he could have helped me. His feelings were truly hurt, provoking his accusation of a lackluster greeting. Indeed, things were never the same between us again, for I had betrayed—or denied—our relationship.

LESSON FOUR: YOUR FRIENDS HAVE ENEMIES

Well, I did eventually obtain a regularized visa, and it came through "long-leg." But the problems inherent in its use derive from the highly politicized and factionalized nature of Nigerian organizations, where personal loyalty is everything.

Early on, I became friendly with a certain social scientist and his family. Thereby, I had unwittingly become his ally in a long drawn-out war between himself and his female colleagues. The disagreement had its origins ten years before in accusations of sex discrimination but had long since spilled over into every aspect of departmental functioning. Even the office workers had chosen sides. More significant, though, was the fact that my friend's chief antagonist and I had similar theoretical interests. Though in retrospect I regret the missed opportunity, I realize that I was in the thick of things before I could have known what was happening. Given the original complaint, my sympathies could have been with the other camp. But ambiguous loyalty is equivalent to none.

Once I had learned my lessons well, life became more pleasant. True, every case was unique and personal relationships were everything. But, as my friends and allies multiplied, I could more easily make "the system" work for me.

Most Nigerians develop finely honed interpersonal skills, which stand them in good stead when they arrive in the United States. They easily make friends with whomever they run across, and naturally, friends will grant them the benefit of the doubt if there is room to maneuver. The psychological need remains, even in our seemingly formalized, structured world, for a friendly, personable encounter.

On the other hand, as I was soon to learn for myself, anyone adept at working this way suffers tremendous pain and anxiety from the impersonal enforcement of seemingly arbitrary rules. For instance, a friend took it as a personal affront when his insurance agent refused to pay a claim because a renewal was past due.

As a result of my Nigerian experience, I am very sensitive to inflexible and impersonal treatment, the flip side of efficiency:

Leaving Nigeria to return to Boston after two and a half years, I stopped for a week in London. I arrived only to find that my old college friend, with whom I intended to stay, had recently moved. Playing detective, I tried neighbors, the superintendent, directory assistance. Tired and bedraggled, I thought of inquiring whether a forwarding address had been left with the post office. Acknowledging me from inside his cage, the small, graying man reached for his large, gray ledger, peered in, slapped it shut, and answered:

"Yes."

"But . . . what is it?" I asked, caught off guard.

He peered down at me and replied: "I cannot tell you. We are not allowed. We must protect him from creditors."

I was aghast. In no way did I resemble a creditor.

Noticing my reaction, he conceded: "But, if you send him a letter, I will forward it."

Bursting into tears of frustration, in my thickest American accent, displaying my luggage and my air ticket, I begged and cajoled him, to no avail. I spent my entire London week in a bed 'n breakfast, cursing petty bureaucrats as my bill piled up. *"That,"* I thought, *"could never happen in Nigeria!"*

NOTE

1. The theoretical analysis from a lengthier essay has been deleted from this presentation. In the original version, great pains were taken to avoid any possible evolutionary interpretation of the relationship between patrimonial and bureaucratic authority. Over the millenia, bureaucracies have been invented and reinvented in Africa, Asia, and Europe. Moreover, patrimonial relationships exist everywhere bureaucracies exist.

   The suggested readings (below) provide the bases for most of my original analysis of aspects of interactional and bureaucratic organization discovered in my Nigerian fieldwork. For those interested, a more thorough analysis can be found in my original essay of the same title in L. Perman (ed.), *Work in Modern Society* (Dubuque, IA: Kendall/Hunt Publishing Company, 1986).

   I am grateful to Oladele Akinla, Paul Brodwin, Anne Hornsby, Dorinne Kondo, Anne Sweetser, and Jeong-Ro Yoon for helpful comments on an earlier version of this essay.

REFERENCE

MERTON, ROBERT K.

1968   Social Theory and Social Structure. New York: Free Press. Chapter VIII: Bureaucratic Structure and Personality.

SUGGESTED READINGS

BENDIX, REINHARD

1977   Max Weber: An Intellectual Portrait. Berkeley and Los Angeles: University of California Press (first publ. 1960).

BRITAN, GERALD M., AND RONALD COHEN, EDS.

1980   Heirarchy and Society: Anthropological Perspectives on Bureaucracy. Philadelphia: ISHI Publications.

FAGE, J. D., AND ROLAND OLIVER, EDS.

1982   The Cambridge History of Africa from the Earliest Times to c. 500 B.C. Cambridge: Cambridge University Press.

FAIRBANK, JOHN K., EDWIN O. REISCHAUER, AND ALBERT M. CRAIG

1973   East Asia: Tradition and Transformation. Boston: Houghton Mifflin.

FALLERS, LLOYD A.

1956   Bantu Bureaucracy: A Century of Political Evolution among the Basoga of Uganda. Chicago: University of Chicago Press.

GRANOVETTER, MARK S.

1973   The Strength of Weak Ties. American Journal of Sociology 78:1360–1380.

LLOYDD, P. C.

1974   Power and Independence: Urban Africans' Perception of Social Inequality. London: Routledge & Kegan Paul.

SMITH, M. G.

1960   Government in Zazzau 1800–1950. London: Oxford.
1974   Corporations & Society. London: Duckworth.

WEBER, MAX

1978   Economy and Society. Berkeley and Los Angeles: University of California Press.

 # Munju

TRECIE MELNICK
University of Alaska, Fairbanks

The Hamats mean the most to me on the bad days. Those are the days of market ladies pointing to my purse and jacking up the prices, and small children tugging at my braids and running, yelling at me *"munju, munju,"* the young Central African men on the streets of Bangassou grabbing at my ass as I ride by on my bicycle. I try to look undisturbed and calm, but my front tire weaves in the sand, hands gripping handle bars, legs pumping, pumping. The vocal assaults slap my cheeks like locusts in the wind. Those faces blur in my sight. They become monstrous, exaggerated masks that follow me, moving in like spirits in an African novel. All bastards. I want to see the kinder side of Central Africa, to get away from the dueling hostility and the mutual racism. My own ethnocentrism has emerged again like a winged termite from its mound. I head toward the neighborhood where the Hamats live.

The dirt glares red in the early afternoon. From a distance, only a long image shows under the canopy shade. As I move closer, Mahamat's figure shifts, growing stronger as does his tall face with the bad right eye. He is the father of the Hamat household, tilting his chin up, straining to see through the harsh light. Stretched out on his side like a tired vine, one hand drips over the edge of the reclining chair—his chair—as he finishes a bowl of cassava sauce. He recognizes me and smiles with the good eye as I duck under the grass roof to shake his hand. *"Baramo"* ["How are you?"] I greet him.

"I'm fine. You haven't come to see Awa and Zeneba for days."

"I know. I've been busy with school. Are they here now?"

"Everyone's here. Go on in."

Awa's laugh leaps on the other side of the tall woven fence surrounding the Hamat compound. She calls in Sango, "Patrice? Finally, you've come." As I enter through the gap in the fence, she takes the bike and leans it against the house. She seems tall for a fourteen-year-old. Squeezing my hand she scolds, "We're very angry at you. You haven't come for a week. We thought you had forgotten us." She always says that. "Sit here," she commands, still squeezing. She arranges the triangle of cooking stones with her free hand, and finally she lets go of my fingers. Standing up, she pulls a handful of straw out of the roof of the cooking shelter.

I wonder how long it will last, a low grass roof just high enough to sit under while someone boils up a pot of peanut sauce. Some days, Awa and her sisters sit under the charcoaled roof, with friends, painting crimson lines of henna on each other's palms and feet. Year after year the underside of the grass cover grows blacker, as black as Awa's arms, and feathers of grass fall down in her hair. With each new fire the smoky scent becomes stronger, and the roof thins. Awa reaches over and yanks out another clump of roof. She crams the handful into the center of the smoking logs, and blows. The flames reach out and she places the beaten, blackened little teapot in the middle of the three stones.

It's a relief to be here with the Hamat women, who have become understanding and protective of me in the year and a half I've known them. It's here that Awa asks me, "What do white people eat?" and I ask, "Have you met the fiancé your father has chosen for you? Do you like him?" Here I can speak and gesture without checking myself because within the Hamat's grass encirclement we don't regret our differences but savor them.

Awa doesn't care one way or the other about her fiancé. She answers my questions with "I've met him. His name is Omar. I've met him twice." I prod her: "But what do you think of him?" She shrugs her shoulders. She knows she may not be married off for several years. She doesn't seem eager, unlike her sister Zeneba, who grins every time I ask her those questions.

Awa has two sisters, Zeneba and Dana. Today, both of them are up to their elbows in bright orange palm oil. Zeneba, who is the oldest of the three, dips her hands to the bottom of the pot pulling out the larger shucks of palm nuts while Dana strains the sediment with a basket. When I ask to help, Zeneba laughs, the contours of her broad face shining in the harsh light. Skinny Dana cocks her head to one side, orange running down her forearms as she pipes, "You don't need to help. You just rest and talk to us. Did you go to the market today?" Dana is just a couple of years younger than Awa. Her smiles don't burst out like Zeneba's. Her good-natured laughs are controlled, and the lips return easily to a serene pose. Mariam, Awa's mother, sweeps up discarded palm nuts, telling me, "You can't work yet. Have some tea first." Awa hands me the glass of tea, very sweet with cloves and a handful of sugar cubes. As I drink, Mariam puts her broom down and pulls a stool up next to me. She asks me how my week is going, how my classes are, and whether I've heard from my family. Then, scooting her stool closer to mine, she asks about each sister by name and also about my mother, father, and grandmother.

She questions me further, remembering what I'd told her about each family member. "Is Vikki still playing music?" "How is your sister who sells houses?" "Why isn't she married yet?" Changing the subject, I complain about being charged higher prices at the market. Zeneba snaps her orange-coated fingers once for emphasis and says, "They do that to

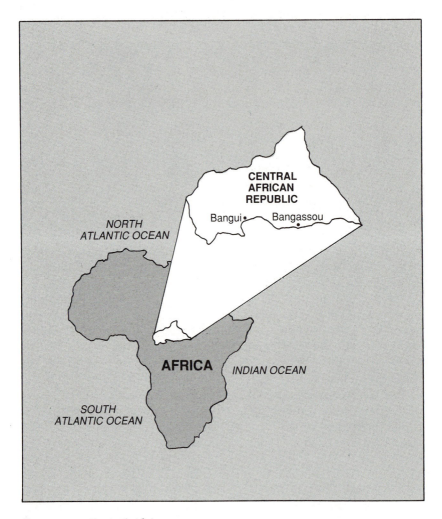

Bangassou, Central Africa

you because you're white. It's not fair. They raise the prices on us too. They say to me, 'You're Muslim. You have lots of money so you can afford to pay more—Muslim woman.' It makes me so mad." Mariam adds, "Next time you go to the market, go with Awa. She'll get you good prices."

I drink the tea down fast, eager to get my hands in the orange slime. This is the first time they've let me help make palm oil. Mariam first takes me aside and wraps an old piece of cloth around my skirt to protect it and pulls my stool over to the big pot. I swish my hands in warm oil, thick as honey. Then, following Zeneba's example, I reach to the bottom to pull out the palm shucks and set them aside in another pot.

With our hands deep in the oil, every now and then when Zeneba's eyes half close and she gazes down into the vat of orange, I snatch at her hand like a fish. Her eyes flash open as she chuckles and calls me a *"bandit"* (troublemaker). She snatches back at my hands. While we swim our hands in the oil, Mariam goes on about her brother, Isouf, whose second wife has just had a baby. It's a boy and the naming party will be next week. Will I come? Of course I'll come.

When I moved to Bangassou I knew that I couldn't expect popularity and that any kind of acceptance in the community would take a long time. But I had hoped to be able to find a few people I could count on. I first met Awa during my Saturday walks through Tokoy, the Muslim neighborhood. She brought me into her family's compound. There I met her sisters, her mother; eventually, Awa's father became less aloof and friendlier to me. I liked the Hamats from the start because they called me by name. And I made a point of writing down each of theirs to memorize them between the first meeting and the next. Zeneba's sounded the most unusual to me and was the hardest for me to learn.

Strangers call me "Melnique" if they know me as a teacher. The Central Africans use last names as Americans use first. If someone doesn't know my name and wants to get my attention, he may call out, *"Wali"* ("Woman"). When I first heard this I was insulted. I wasn't used to being called by a label. But this is also customary. If someone wants to get a stranger's attention, he calls them by what they are: Child. Woman. Man. Calling someone *"koli"* ("man") is like calling your waiter "sir." Frequently I'm called *"munju,"* which means "white person." Depending on the tone and context, *munju* has many connotations, sometimes neutral, often not: white person, foreigner, whitey, honky. I never get used to being a *munju.*

Munju used to refer only to French people. In colonial days, when the Central Africans heard the French saying "Bonjour" to each other all of the time, they came to call them that. The label "Bonjour" evolved into "Mungu" and came to refer to all whites. At its mildest, *munju* describes or identifies a white to distinguish her from a black person. "A *munju* who I have never seen before was downtown today."

From there the meanings become more derogatory. The implications go from "white person" to "white thing." For example, as I pass through a neighborhood, sometimes mothers hold their infants and say in Sango, "Look, look at the *munju.*" But in another context a mother might say to her baby, "See the *munju*? If you're not good, that *munju* will eat you." In fact, there is a local legend of a white woman with long hair who lives in the river and at night pulls fishermen from their canoes to drown them. She is called the *"mamywhata,"* and for some children a *munju* and *mamywhata* are the same. No wonder when I walk through some parts of town, young children sometimes freeze, staring at my white skin and long braids, and then run off screeching for their mothers. After having four or five children flee in terror of my face in one afternoon, I become self-conscious. The adults usually just laugh and tease the child with, "Are you afraid of that *munju*? She's coming. She's going to eat you."

Children use the word *munju* a little differently than adults do. Some kids say "*munju*" innocently, trying it out as a word they have heard their parents use to refer to whites. Curious, they peek around their doors softly repeating "*munju, munju*." If brave enough, they might come running out to shake my hand and stare at me.

It's cute at first, but soon the timid chiming of "*munju, munju*" becomes a clamoring like crows cawing from the trees. Bigger children with bones sticking out at all angles run after my bike, mouths opening like puppets, "*munju, munju*." Skinny children with legs dry as firewood, come running out of their houses. Then the tall boys follow, with the long legs blotched with never-healing sores. The older ones don't run behind but stride beside me, hauling their houselike shoulders from side to side, hardening their consonants as they call out "*munju wali*" ("white woman"). Volume increases as I imagine the voices gathering behind me, closing in, jumping in front of my path and then away at the last minute. "*Munju*" seems to fall from the trees as I look to escape, glaring at the children. I am unable to distinguish between the innocent *munju* of little girls and the "honky-go-home" *munju*'s darting at my eyes. Those are the days when I walk, looking straight ahead rather than meandering. I clutch my market bag close to me and brush by the kids with their arms extended to shake hands. People recognize my mood and laugh. I can no longer differentiate between "*wali*, Melnique, *munju, munju wali, mamywhata, munjumunjumunjumunju*—Patrice!" Only people who know me well call me Patrice.

When I'm feeling defensive, Awa has to call out "Patrice" a couple of times to get my attention because I'm blocking everyone out. She assures me that she doesn't think I'm a *mamywhata* as we walk together through the Muslim section of the market and the name-calling dissipates. She tells me that when I was gone to Bangui, the capital, for two weeks her friends in the market would ask her, "Where's your *munju*?" Coming from Awa, the word means "white friend."

The Muslim community is less hostile to me because they know I'm friends with the Hamats. And the Hamats know what it's like to be in the minority. In the Central African Republic the Muslims are a small part of the population. Many of them are recent immigrants from Chad and Sudan. Mariam's parents came from Chad. As a Jew I am more comfortable with them. Our histories overlap. Unlike a few of my encounters with zealous first-generation Christians, the Muslims don't try to convert me. I've had Central African children conclude that if I wasn't Christian, I must be with the devil—a detail they'd learned in church. As a

Jew from Dallas, I'm often asked why I killed Jesus and why I killed Kennedy. The Muslims are as unfamiliar with Judaism as are other Central Africans. But like them, I'm not a Christian. This gives us something to talk about. I know a few Hebrew words, and sometimes we've compared Hebrew and Arabic to note the similarities. They are surprised to learn that Jewish law, like Islam, forbids the eating of pork. Although I don't practice, I discuss these details with the Hamats for a source of commonality.

When I was just getting to know the Hamats, they kept me at a polite distance. They expected me to sit in a straight-backed chair, at a little table inside the house, while family and friends sat outside together on mats and *barambo* [a type of wood] stools. They ate off the same plate digging their hands into the cassava mash and peanut sauce laughing and talking in rapid Sango while I sat inside, alone with my own plate. But eventually I was allowed to sit outside at a table fairly close to the others, though I was still given my own bowls of food. Sometimes Mariam gave me food different from what the others were eating. There is a stereotype that whites don't eat cassava root (*gozo*), so when I arrived Mariam would put some money into Dana's palm and send her off to the market to buy bread for me. I'd be given my own piece. I wanted to be down on the mats and *barambos* with the others, and eventually I was allowed to sit on the mat next to Mariam. But even then, I was given my own plates though I had graduated to being served *gozo*. And finally, I was allowed to share, eating off the same plates with the others. But Mariam kept a close eye on how much I ate, and when I didn't eat as much meat as she thought I should, she pushed some over to one side and designated it as mine. It was the end of Ramadan holiday, and they must have forgotten that I had ever been a "special guest." So there I sat, down on the mats with my hands in the same bowls, tugging at the same lumps of *gozo* and elephant meat.

Over time we developed a dialogue centered around photos and maps. I show Mariam my photo album, pointing out my high school friends, family, my house in Texas. "Where's Texas?" Mariam asks, staring keenly at a picture of my sister. She takes my map out of the back of the album and stretches it wide. "Texas is here."

"Where's Mecca?" she asks. I show her and she traces the path from Bangassou all the way to Mecca.

"Mmmecca," she sounds out. She taught herself to read. "We're going to Mecca someday."

"When?"

"When we have the money. That's the holy city. Here's Bangassou. Where's Dallas?"

"Here."

"Aiiiyyyooo! That's far."

The Hamats help me through the days when *"munju, munju"* stings my cheek, the days of curses under my breath. Safe inside the Hamat compound I forget the shouts of the young men on the streets. I forget as I help Zeneba dig shucks out of the palm oil, as I watch Awa and Dana paint crimson lines across our soles. Mariam takes her family pictures and mine, lays them across the map, and together we decide it isn't so far.

TWENTY-TWO

Research in the Celtic Twilight: Spiritual Aid in the Field

JOHN MESSENGER
Ohio State University

We named him "Brendan" for a literary figure who occasionally visits Inis Beag and is renowned among the islanders for his love of "spirits" and his practical jokes. Our friends thought it strange for us to name a *leipreachán*, since it is not an Irish custom to do so. The folk peoples of the west country avoid the fairies, seldom talk about them publicly, and refer to them respectfully as the "gentry" or the "good people" if the need arises. But during our stay on the island, we came to feel the immaterial presence of this creature so intensely and to anticipate his pranks with such enthusiasm that we eventually came to view him as a third member of our family, well deserving an affectionate and suitable name.

Initially, Brendan's particular mode of expression was to open our door or one of our windows during the night when we were asleep, a practice that continued intermittently month after month, no matter how carefully we checked bolted door and locked windows before retiring. At first we suspected an actual or potential thief, but nothing was ever stolen; besides, crime of any nature is virtually unknown on the island. Then we considered a practical joker, but no one ever admitted "coddling" us in this manner, and local pranksters eventually call attention to their deeds. Finally, after examining and discarding in turn other possible explanations, we were forced to conclude that a *leipreachán* had taken up residence in our apartment and was calling attention to his presence in this way.

Our neighbor, an elderly, unmarried nurse who lived in the adjoining apartment of our ancient building, complained of hearing violin music emanating from beneath the eaves outside her bedroom window late at night. Her door and windows were never opened, and we never heard violin music, but Brendan may have been responsible for both. We don't know if the music continues, but we suspect not, for it has become obvious that Brendan returned home with us.

My wife and I spent last year on Inis Beag, off the west coast of Éire, as anthropologists documenting recent history and the contemporary way of life of the people living there. Because of an interest arising out of a previous research experience, when we studied the effects of Christianity on a Nigerian tribe, we spent a good deal of time describing the religious beliefs of the islanders. These consist of both Roman Catholic elements and pagan Celtic survivals which coexist or are syncretized, much to the dismay of the more sophisticated curates who have lived on Inis Beag. The pagan array of spiritual beings includes shades, changelings, mermaids, *púca*, witches, *bean sidhe*, water spirits, workers of good and evil magic, those with the evil eye, and, of course, Brendan and his ilk. The youth overtly disallow the existence of other than Church approved supernatural entities, but the elders cling to traditional pagan beliefs, about which they are extremely secretive for fear of being ridiculed. After we were well known and accepted by the islanders, we talked with many old people who admitted having seen shades, mermaids, *púca*, and the like in corporeal form, but try as we might we met only Brendan, and then indirectly through his nocturnal escapades rather than face to face.

The fairies of Ireland are divided into two camps: the trooping fairies and the solitary ones. Of the latter, the most notorious is the leipreachán, who is noted for his shoe-making and treasure-burying proclivities, although his versatility extends beyond mere cobbling and hoarding. Hardly two Irish writers are in agreement as to whether the leipreachán, the *clúracán*, and the *fear dearg* are three different spirits or are one spirit, the leipreachán, in different moods and shapes. The islanders prefer the former interpretation, but we prefer the latter in light of Brendan's singular behavior. The *clúracán* is best known for making himself drunk in cellars, while the *fear dearg* limits his activities to practical joking of a bizarre nature. Since joining our present household, Brendan has displayed both tendencies, as well as others I will describe presently. So we have decided that, contrary to island opinion, he is a *leipreachán* of rather remarkable talents. I must admit, however, that to the best of our knowledge he has thus far produced neither shoes nor shillings. This fact led us to suspect he was a *sprid i dteach* after we had become accustomed to his presence in our domicile on Inis Beag; but this spirit, although inhabiting many cottages in nearby Clare and Connemara, appears never to have ventured out to the Western Isles. Perhaps he is less of a seaman than the *leipreachán*, or thinks Inis Beag is Tir na nÓg and, being more of a recluse than his solitary mates, does not wish to mingle with the good people who are said to abide there.

W. B. Yeats describes Brendan's multifarious companions as ". . . withered, old, and solitary, in every way unlike the sociable [trooping fairies]. . . . They dress with all unfairy homeliness, and are, indeed, most sluttish, slouching, jeering, mischievous phantoms." We heartily dislike the thought of Brendan possessing such unwholesome qualities, but who are we to challenge ancient tradition? It may be that since we have departed from island standards in classifying him as a *leipreachán*, it is also permissible for us to deviate in portraying his character and be much kinder than Yeats. We cannot vouch for Brendan's appearance and thus will have to depend upon the eyewitness accounts of our island informants and those fortunate individuals who advised Yeats. *Leipreachán* will not reveal themselves in any manner to most human beings, will make their presence known to some by various deeds, and will appear to only a very few whom they especially favor. By firmness of belief in their existence, services rendered, and disservices shunned does one win their favor. Evidently our conviction of belief left something to be desired, for we offered Brendan every material comfort the island had to offer, including access to our Tullamore Dew, and were very cautious so as not to offend him in word or deed. All to no avail. Even today he refuses to materialize despite every inducement.

Our last few days on Inis Beag were hectic ones, filled as they were with packing, finishing a written report to our sponsors, and bidding farewell to dear friends. Realizing that we were experiencing severe emotional stress, Brendan quite obligingly chose not to distract us during the last week. This revealed a strength of character that I am sure would have surprised Yeats. As soon as we boarded the ship in Galway, all thoughts of Brendan disappeared from mind until a morning early in September, only two weeks after we had settled again in a duplex near the university campus. The first indication of the fact that we had been followed across the Atlantic and halfway across the continent came with my discovery of an open front door, when I made my initial sally downstairs at dawn to bring in the newspaper and put on the water to boil. I thought little of the incident at the time and may not even have mentioned it to my wife, because I remembered that I had failed to try the doors before going to bed. It was an oversight which has prompted me to check them conscientiously each night since that fateful event. But the front door continued from time to time to gape open, in spite of all precautionary measures, and was soon joined by the back door. After three such episodes, the truth at last dawned upon us: Brendan was here. We were very pleased, for his presence, insubstantial though it was, served as a link between ourselves and Ireland, whose people and beauty we missed so much during those first weeks at home. With the passing of time and the increase in Brendan's versatility, we have come to accept his presence with deep satisfaction and more than a touch of pride. Let me tell you of his ever-growing repertoire of pranks, which reveal those typically Irish traits of resourcefulness, humor, and imagination.

Brendan has always shown a predilection for opening doors and windows, but after settling down here he soon took to switching on the basement lights and manipulating the thermostat. When the weather first became uncomfortably cold in late October, we turned on the furnace and kept the thermostat at sixty-eight degrees during the day and six degrees cooler at night. The outdoor temperature suddenly rose one night, and we were awakened by the discomfort of being bathed in perspiration. Our warm room was being fed even warmer air from the vent. I hurried downstairs to find the thermostat set at seventy-four degrees. My immediate reaction was to sit down then and there in the living room and check through my memory my final movements before retiring: They most certainly did not include pushing *up* the thermostat control! Conversely, a week later, when the thermometer plunged to the lower regions for the first time, we were once again aroused from sleep, but rather from the discomfort of an icy bed. The cause of this condition was an upper window opened wide in the front bedroom, which had been locked since late August. Brendan's great strength was attested by the fact that locking and relocking the window almost proved too much of an effort for me.

As well as possessing heroic thews for one so diminutive, Brendan is telepathic. One evening I went to bed suffering from a severe headache and, once comfortably settled under the covers, recalled that I had neglected to take an aspirin. So I swung out of bed muffling curses, but as my feet touched the floor I heard the sound of running water from the bathroom. Both my wife and I were startled into a quick exchange of baffled exclamations, following which I stumbled into the bathroom to find the cold water faucet fully opened. Brendan had anticipated my desire. It took us more than an hour to recover from this experience and compose ourselves for sleep. Had the aspirin bottle with cover removed been standing on the ledge above the cooperative tap, we would never have slept that night. However, Brendan is seldom too obvious. Another example of his psychic powers is his ability to awaken one of us a few minutes before the alarm clock is due to sound, so that we can discover that he has depressed the alarm button sometime during the night. Pulling out the button marks the final stage of an almost compulsive retirement ritual we follow.

Early on election day, while standing in a cold schoolroom at the end of a long, slow moving line that led to two polling booths, my wife and I had occasion to chat for several minutes with our landlady. She introduced the subject of cold weather and storm windows, which gave rise to a train of thoughts in my mind leading, as you might guess, to Brendan. I very cautiously broached the subject of self-opening doors and windows in her half of the duplex, but found that her doors and windows opened only at her own bidding. Soon her curiosity was aroused by my further, rather clumsy probing into the allied matter of self-regulating basement light switches and thermostat controls, and I was at last put into the position of revealing all. Rather than describing the uncommon happenings either in a light manner, punctuating my conversation with gay laughter, or in a serious mode consonant with my genuine sentiments, I unfortunately tried to do both. This left her bewildered, to say the least, not knowing whether or not to believe me and possibly a little uncertain as to the wisdom of renting to us. I have not mentioned the matter again in her presence, nor has she in mine. This is an unfortunate state of affairs, for I forgot to ask her about hearing violin music. The Inis Beag nurse refuses to answer our questions concerning her island virtuoso, and we are curious to know if Brendan has a penchant for entertaining elderly widows and spinsters with lively jigs.

In Éire we could never induce Brendan to drink our whiskey; thus we were forced to conclude that he was either a deviant or a member of the Pioneer Total Abstinence Society. Early in December, surprisingly, he began to imbibe. I became aware of it when twice the cork was pushed only part way into the neck of the bottle, a practice that my wife and I assiduously try to avoid. So we began to mark the liquid level by penciling a line on the label each time that we put the bottle away. Frequent inspections of the fifth revealed that at least once each week the level dropped an eighth of an inch. Does such pilfering reflect Brendan's size, or is he an inexperienced drinker, polite, or of the opinion that he is outwitting us? More important, however, is the question: Why did he choose to reveal his *clúracán* tendencies here rather than on Inis Beag? Possibly he disliked the Tullamore Dew that we ordered monthly from a shop on the mainland, as did some of the islanders, but finds the Powers that we brought back with us (duty free) more to his taste. On the other hand, he may be reading our magazines and has been taken in by those clever Whiskey Distillers of Ireland advertisements.

None of Brendan's doings are malicious, you must understand. The fairies most often harm those who have maltreated them, and many fairy pranks are gestures of amicability. A careful examination of the circumstances surrounding Brendan's many deeds reveals that each is committed shortly before our attention is drawn to it, as in the case of the impotent alarm clock. The purloined whiskey is, of course, another story, but Brendan knows that we can well afford a thimbleful of Irish each week. We do wish, however, that he would switch his allegiance to the cheap Scotch or bourbon we keep on hand to serve guests who insist upon mixed drinks. Irish whiskey is never cheap in this state.

Brendan has affected our lives beyond merely furnishing us with unexpected and amusing diversions and a sense of Gaelic camaraderie. He has, for instance, provided a stable marriage with even greater stability; for when either of us is forgetful so as to irk the other, Brendan serves as a convenient scapegoat. If appointments are missed, letters are mailed unstamped, or the car is left unlocked overnight, and it is obvious that Brendan cannot be blamed, Brendan is blamed. Doing so channels discharged emotions in a most effective way and restores an atmosphere of affability within minutes.

I have made a point of giving my students at the university a weekly rundown on Brendan's doings ever since delivering a well-received lecture on comparative religions some weeks ago. I have found that these reports work quite as effectively as a boisterous joke, mention of "Charlie Brown," or questioning a football player in drawing them away from their school newspapers, opening their sleepy lids early on a Monday morning, or revitalizing lectures that tend to be boring because of my mood or the topic under discussion. I suspect that I have converted several students to a belief in fairies by sheer enthusiasm and by the obvious honesty of my own convictions. If only Brendan could observe me in the classroom, he would surely become convinced of my sincerity and appear.

The proselytizing efforts of my wife, on the other hand, have met with far less success among small schoolchildren. They are disbelievers one and all and brand as "tall tale tellers" the folklorists whose stories about the Irish fairies they have heard. To these youngsters Brendan represents nothing more than coincidence coupled with forgetfulness, naive enthusiasm, and possibly even deception on my wife's part. This has been a bitter pill for us to swallow, we who were nurtured on Andersen and the Grimms and who looked for ghosts beneath our beds before the lights were turned out.

Needless to say, my colleagues have been even more reluctant to accept the reality of Brendan. Anthropologists are a tough-minded lot who espouse cultural relativism, naturalism, and the other "isms" that humanists and theologians find so repugnant. The customary attitude of the fieldworker toward what his subjects interpret as supernatural events is one of extreme skepticism or active disbelief. There are some anthropologists, however, who at least maintain an open mind where these phenomena are concerned. I am reminded of a friend and his wife, both members of the secret society of anthropologists, who are the parents of several obstreperous children and, as a result, take great care to prevent an African fertility figurine from crossing the threshold of their bedroom. My wife and I have witnessed events, both in Nigeria and in Éire, whose causes could be explained by recourse to either the sacred or the profane. Having been unable to determine to our own satisfaction the naturalistic causes of these occurrences, we have always been willing to consider the reality of the supernatural, but with something less than open minds. This tender-minded attitude is regarded as poison oak in the more scientific groves of academe.

Twice tongue in cheek colleagues have suggested that my wife and I take steps to rid our apartment of Brendan. I have both times met the suggestion by reaffirming our strong devotion to Brendan and his ways, but the exchanges have set me to thinking of what we might do were he to become unruly. We have a friend in Nigeria, a particularly competent worker of magic, who would be able to compel Brendan to return to Inis Beag if the need arose, but utilizing his services would be out of the question. We brought back with us from Africa several indigenous icons that once would have accomplished the desired end, but I am afraid that lack of use and storage in damp basements for several years have reduced their potency. I am sure that local Catholic priests, unlike their Irish brethren, would regard exorcism as out of the question, even though we were of their faith. Quite frankly, we are at a loss as to how we might cope with a *leipreachán* Jekyll turned Hyde.

Which brings me to the present. At Christmas we visited relatives in a nearby city and there had occasion one evening to show colored slides and talk about the island with seldom seen friends. One of them, of obvious Irish descent, was considerably stimulated by the pictures and the conversation, and he questioned us at great length about the varieties of fairies and their activities and about our experiences with Brendan. It seems that as a youth, at his grandfather's knee, he had heard tales of the good people in the old country and had retained a vivid impression of their reality. If today he entertains doubts as to their existence, he at least has the will to believe, which he expressed with fervor as the evening wore on. Early the next morning we were awakened by the insistent ringing of the telephone to find that it was our Irish friend, who excitedly told us of discovering his front door wide open just ten minutes earlier and of being unable to draw water from any faucet in the house. It was apparent from his almost inarticulate utterances that he hoped it might be Brendan's handiwork, and we were crestfallen to think it might. Had Brendan followed us once again; was he attracted to this charming and sympathetic Gael; and would he choose to remain behind?

For a week after returning home we were restless and impatient, awaiting some sign of Brendan's continuing presence. At last we were rewarded by finding the turntable and preamplifier of our phonograph system turned on several hours after it had been dusted and nothing found amiss. Then the following morning the level of spirits in the Powers bottle had lowered perceptibly, and we were jubilant! Manipulation of the phonograph was a new achievement for Brendan, one he had mastered during our absence, no doubt to demonstrate his joy at our return. There may be another motive underlying the accomplishment, however, for we discovered upon our arrival home several misplaced records, of unaccompanied Irish fiddling, in one of the album racks; the implications of this are intriguing to contemplate. We have no idea what the future will bring, but we will welcome each new manifestation of Brendan's virtuosity and hope that he will remain a member of our household, at least until we return once again to the Western Isles.

Some will think that I have written this piece to arouse consternation or envy in my fellow professors. Nothing could be further from the truth. When it is published, I will sign a copy with our favorite island toast—"*Seo dhuit; gob fliuch, sláinte an bhradáin, grásta Dé, agus bás in Éirinn*" ("May you always have a wet mouth, the health of a salmon, the grace of God, and die in Éire")—and stand it against a newly opened fifth of Powers. If this doesn't induce Brendan to materialize, nothing will.

TWENTY-THREE

The Matter of the Chickens[1]

ANONYMOUS

> The state should confine itself to establishing rules applying to general types of situations and should allow the individuals freedom in everything which depends on the circumstances of time and place, because only the individuals concerned in each instance can fully know these circumstances and adapt their actions to them.
>
> *Hayek*

As a research site, I had selected a remote, traditional village located in an area little known to the outside world. Whatever information and understanding I might gain through ethnographic research would substantially expand current knowledge of the area. I was the first foreigner to take up residence in this kinship-based agricultural settlement. All of the villagers are genealogically related to each other, through either bonds of marriage or ancestry. Because numerous individuals were already related to each other before they married, a large number of the inhabitants were linked by multiple ties of kinship. In addition, the local value system specified that only persons related to each other should reside in the village; nonrelatives should not live there. I was obviously a nonrelative, but because I had all my official "bona fides" in order, I was allowed to move in.

The people are shy and reserved. They do not readily open up to complete strangers, especially strangers to whom they are not related. I was to learn many months later from one of the schoolteachers, a few years my junior, why I was allowed to move into this village at all. I was still a student, not yet fully trained and able to assume a responsible adult role in my own society. Consequently I was perceived as a person not unlike the children of the village itself, still in the process of preparing for adult life but not yet having achieved this status. Establishing rapport was a slow process, requiring much patience and tact, but gradually I began to gain some measure of acceptance and get on with my work.

The village is located in the upper reaches of a short river near the junction of the coastal plain and the first foothills leading to the mountainous interior. The climate is hot and humid, with extremely high annual rainfall. Rains fall throughout the year with a barely noticeable dry season in which rain falls at least once every few days. Normally, rains are frequent, very heavy, and accompanied by high winds and tumultuous thunder and lightning. At certain times of the year the rains are regular, almost to the point of one being able to set a watch by their arrival. It is an eerie feeling to hear the heavy rains approaching the village from afar. The first faint sounds of the heavy droplets striking the forest canopy in the distance quickly give way to a deafening roar as the storm rushes through the village.

After only three months into my first experience at field work I began, at last, to feel comfortable and more in control of the seemingly endless bombardment of data. I had even begun to make some sense out of the new information and to feel that my skills were being sharpened. Some positive signs were evident that the years of training would pay off; perhaps I would indeed someday find success as an anthropologist.

And then I learned about the government's chicken program!

As best as I could make out, the government had proposed to give free chickens to rural villagers throughout the country! This struck me as an imaginative idea demonstrating a positive concern for the progress of poor rural farmers. Before I first heard of the plan, I had been preoccupied with trying to learn the nuances of the local dialect and with getting a handle on the basic subsistence pattern and rhythms of daily social life. The news of the "free chicken" program was unanticipated and did not fit any of my data categories. Obviously I needed to collect more information.

My ethnographic work continued. I slowly began to more clearly comprehend the rationale and motivations for the chicken scheme. Ongoing discussions with villagers brought the general picture into sharper focus. The government had devised a plan to encourage farmers to raise chickens. The farmers were already raising their own chickens. These people had been doing so for a long time, but their chickens had always been free-ranging chickens, raised in the traditional way.

Village chickens are allowed to roam free during the daylight hours. During the day they wander about yards and occasionally stray into the nearby scrub vegetation surrounding the houses. They fend for themselves, chasing down and snapping up whatever tasty morsels they happen upon. Their diets consist of food scraps tossed out from houses, wandering unwary insects, toads, frogs, lizards, and small snakes. These chickens will attack virtually anything they consider remotely edible. In their ravenous quest for food they can easily outdistance any creature that attempts to approach them by running and flying short distances.

One day while chatting with friends, we spied a chicken halfway across the soccer field in front of the village school. It was struggling to swallow an eel it had probably caught in one of the drainage ditches that wind through the village. The eel was half swallowed, with at least six inches of its body still protruding from the chicken's beak. I judged its diameter to be about an inch and a half. One of my friends jumped up and dashed off after the chicken, calling to a small boy some distance away to try to catch the bird and extract the eel before the chicken choked. The chicken, however, was not about to give up such a prize feast. Off it ran, dodging its pursuers and avoiding all attempts at capture. The bird was not caught; evidently it survived.

Throughout the day these chickens congregate and raid the rice drying on mats that women set out in the bright sunshine. Women and children shoo them away periodically, but within a few minutes the birds simply resume their attempts to peck off more of the grain. At the end of the day the women toss out a few handfuls of rice to the chickens. As dusk rapidly overtakes the daylight, women and children take up long poles and begin to force their roosting chickens out of the branches of trees surrounding the houses. To protect the chickens from predators, the villagers drive them into the crude coops that are built close to the houses. Owls, weasels, and civets, along with the odd wild forest cat, are all astir at night and would certainly delight in capturing a chicken if the chance permitted.

People seem to keep chickens primarily to have a ready source of eggs for making special cakes and other confections that are prepared for special occasions and holidays. A chicken or two can be slaughtered for a meal if unexpected guests arrive. Local custom dictates that strangers and guests should be fed and treated hospitably, and chickens serve as the basis for preparing an instant supper on these unexpected occasions. As will be seen, however, chicken is never a dish of choice.

I continued to discuss chickens and the chicken program with a number of friends from the village and slowly began to develop some understanding of the government's scheme. The plan was for each farmer to receive fifty free chicks plus a three-month supply of chicken feed. The farmer, at his own expense, was required to build a coop of specified size and type. Since the coop could be constructed out of materials that were readily available in the surrounding forest, this part of the project would cost a farmer only his time and labor. The only condition imposed upon the farmer was that he had to agree to cover the inside floor of the coop with rice straw and, after the straw became saturated with droppings, shovel it out and deposit it as fertilizer around the vegetables planted in backyard gardens. New straw then would be laid on the floor and the process repeated, thus generating a never-ending supply of organic fertilizer for the farmer's gardens.

The whole plan sounded to me realistic and solid. Further, a certain amount of responsibility was placed upon the individual farmer. What could be a better plan! It not only coaxed and persuaded but also rewarded. It gave the farmers free chickens and their feed for three months and required them to purchase feed for an additional three months, after which the hens would begin laying. In checking I discovered that not one village member had participated in the program. They all seemed to know about it, but no one had any intention of taking advantage of the plan.

Clearly there was something I didn't understand. If the chicks and three-month supply of their feed were given away free of charge, and the farmers did not have to lay out any cash for materials to be used in constructing the coop, there must have been, from their point of view, something wrong with the chicken scheme. I knew that they certainly were not averse to hard work. I had seen them work long hours in the blazing sun and pouring rain. At times they work throughout the night oblivious to our Western diurnal schedule. But I had no idea why the farmers were so reluctant to join the chicken scheme. A considerable amount of time passed before I was able to collect enough information to be able to account for something that, at first, seemed inexplicable: that no one was taking advantage of a giveway program!

As my data collection continued, one fact became apparent: There was a catch to the government's scheme. The fifty chicks were free, and their feed was free for the first three months; however, the hens would not begin to lay eggs until they were about six months old. This meant that any farmer who joined the program would have to pay for the feed for the final three months before the hens began producing eggs.

I asked why feed would have to be purchased for these chicks. After all, no one purchased any feed for the chickens they presently owned. As soon as they could run about their traditional village, chickens began to fend for themselves, scratching for food around the yard.

Ah, yes, someone told me, that was true, but these were a different kind of chicken. The chickens that villagers had always kept were free-ranging chickens—chickens fully capable of foraging for their own food, scratching for scraps, catching insects and small animals. The bite of grain given them provided variety, kept them healthy, and prevented them from wandering off. The chickens the government wanted them to accept were not free-ranging chickens. They were battery chickens— chickens utterly incapable of foraging for their own food. Battery chickens were completely dependent on human beings for food; and what's more, they couldn't be fed scraps but had to eat specially purchased chicken feed, which would require a steady outlay of scarce cash.

Once I had understood these new twists and turns, I knew that the government's scheme indeed contained a serious flaw, perhaps not fatal, but serious nonetheless. From all that I had learned to this point, I knew that it was exceedingly unlikely that people who were largely subsistence producers would willingly purchase food for their chickens when they didn't purchase food for themselves. They grow all of their staple food (rice); catch a large proportion of their fish and shrimp; and snare, trap, and hunt several kinds of wild birds, three kinds of deer, and even the occasional porcupine for the pot. Wild fruits and vegetables abound in the forest. These are regularly harvested in quantities sufficient for domestic consumption and, occasionally, for sale.

In addition, the surrounding forests provide the villagers with free construction materials needed for the manufacture of houses, sheds, granaries, dugout canoes, larger boats, the wooden parts of tools, mats, and baskets of all varieties and sizes. What had to be purchased—from their point of view—were such things as iron blades, nails, monofilament for fishing lines and nets, paint, and other products from the industrial world that made life a bit easier than it was when they used more traditional items. The point, I think, was not whether farmers had sufficient cash to purchase the chicken feed; some probably did, and some clearly did not. The point was that to spend money on food for a relatively insignificant animal—that is, relatively insignificant by their own standards—when they did not spend money on a daily basis for their own food did not make much sense within their system of values. Indeed, if the environmental and social conditions were comparable to those under discussion, I think it would make little sense in the value system held by virtually any group of people anywhere in the world.

I again left the matter of the chickens and continued with the main tasks of fieldwork interviewing, participating in as many events as I could, traveling to the forest, going fishing, accompanying men tending their snare lines, clearing trees and brush for swiddens, going along on the burn, planting and harvesting rice, and a myriad of other tasks of daily life all aimed at gathering data from which to write my dissertation. I didn't much concern myself with the chicken scheme, thinking that I now completely understood why no one in the village was interested in the program. But I was wrong. There actually was much more to the matter of the chickens than I had imagined.

At this point I began to learn one of the most important lessons of my first fieldwork. Comprehension does not emerge automatically out of the data collected by an ethnographer. In one respect, attaining understanding is a bit like hand-forging steel: Most of the work—and it is work—comes after the material is already assembled. While additional factual information is always welcome, more data alone are not sufficient for the success of an ethnographic enterprise. The information has to be balanced by a rational reconstruction that is sensitive to the culturally relative factors of place, circumstance, and purpose. Only then can the data later be worked into understanding and eventual presentation. The anthropologist must eventually disclose his or her results, to the public and to the anthropological and scientific community. Otherwise, no social purpose is served in going to the field.

My new insight into the matter of the chickens came about quite serendipitously. On a trip away from my field site, I had the opportunity to discuss this and other matters with some volunteer friends. One fellow worked in a statistical department of the government and was familiar with matters involving the country's trade. After some discussion, he sketched out the following scenario.

One day a government worker who had been examining import-export figures noticed what he thought to be an alarmingly large number of eggs being imported into the country. After discussing the matter with other officials, they evidently concluded that there was no good reason why sufficient eggs for the domestic economy could not be locally produced. If domestic egg production could be increased, then a healthier balance of trade would result, and any actual or imagined net national deficit might in significant ways ameliorated. What could be simpler than producing eggs? Thus, the idea for the government's chicken program was born and led to the creation of the scheme. Fifty free chicks and a three-month supply of feed were to be given to each farmer who would build the specified coop and utilize the droppings as directed.

Armed with additional information and new insight I once again returned to the question of the chickens. The more I pursued the matter, the more interesting it became. However, before this puzzle could be solved—before a satisfactory understanding of the matter achieved—a number of missing pieces had to be found.

I next began to inquire into the villagers' food preferences. I had discovered that a meal was not considered to be a real meal unless rice was included. However, rice was not the central issue. The important question was: What did people prefer to eat *with* their rice? By this time I had a fairly comprehensive understanding of the range of the foodstuffs regularly consumed in the village, as well as considerable knowledge of local preferences for seasonally available fruits and vegetables. I began to ask people about the most salient sources of protein: beef or water buffalo, fish, shrimp, shellfish, wild birds, deer, and chicken and eggs. What I had previously learned—but not sufficiently understood— quickly became obvious. When they had the choice, villagers preferred to eat fish, shrimp (or prawns), and shellfish over any other animal protein. This generalization, of course, applied primarily to daily plain fare. For special ceremonial meals and feasts, beef, buffalo, and forest game were traditionally the appropriate fleshy foods. My friends indicated that they would always prefer the flesh of fish and shrimp taken from the river and the sea over beef, or indeed over any animal or bird of the land. They were most insistent in proclaiming that they really didn't like to eat chicken at all. They would rather eat just about anything else!

At that point, I asked about eggs. No, they really did not like eggs. Eggs, of course, were very useful; they were used as one among many ingredients in cakes and other confections made on special occasions, but they were not eaten as a special dish. I then recalled that in all of the meals I had eaten in houses throughout the village, I had never seen anyone serve a cooked egg.

The story continued, becoming more intricate and variegated as it developed. Ever more features and characteristics of local life, behavior, and attitudes were becoming part of the plot. Nevertheless, there was still more to this rather complex matter. If large numbers of farmers all over the country decided to join the chicken scheme, what would be done with all of the eggs and the chickens that would be produced? I never did learn whether there was to be a government quota on the number of participants in the plan. This issue never came up in discussion.

The progressive part of the government's economic development scheme was to improve the standard of living in rural villages. This is where the chicken droppings enter the picture. The idea was to create a usable byproduct as a result of raising chickens and producing eggs. In theory, a virtually inexhaustible supply of organic fertilizer would be created by all of those cooped-up chickens. The dung and straw mixture could then be spread around vegetable plants growing in backyard gardens to increase their productivity.

On the face of it, the idea was imaginative and creative. But there was a problem with this part of the scheme: Most people in the village did not have backyard vegetable gardens; if they did, they were quite paltry and only planted occasionally, not even every year. Yet, people were eating vegetables every day. On special occasions they served numerous vegetable dishes, and many of the flesh dishes contained vegetables as well. Thus, a question arose: Where were the villagers getting these vegetables if they didn't plant backyard gardens?

Once again we must consider the socioecological nature of this remote village in an isolated part of the country. The village is the terminus of all other settlements and can be reached only by river. Because all other neighboring villages are downriver, this village is left to exploit the very large areas of surrounding forest for itself. All of the present and previous populations that have resided in this area have been practicing swidden cultivation for centuries. As a result of this pattern of periodically shifting the locations of houses associated with this subsistence technique, the surrounding forest contains numerous stands of fruit trees in ancient overgrown house yards. These trees continue to seed themselves long after the people who planted them have moved on. They yield bounteous harvests of fresh fruit nearly every year. Further, this practice of planting fruit trees in backyards continues today, and the yields of the villagers' own trees, plus those of the forest, are far greater than anyone can possibly consume.

In addition to these fruits, wild vegetables such as mushrooms, bamboo shoots, sour fruits, and palm inflorescences are found scattered in great abundance throughout the forest. These too are regularly harvested. Women and children make expeditions to the forest to collect mushrooms. Men or women bring back supplies of fresh bamboo shoots from the forest whenever they have a taste for them. Men will search out a wild palm and extract the inflorescence for a special feast. Small children can often be seen wandering along the village paths late in the afternoon, collecting large armfuls of young wild fern shoots for a tasty evening meal. Other types of edible ferns grow in profusion along the river bank and are easily plucked from a dugout canoe. Thus the food supply available to this village is a very rich one indeed. The settlement is located in an environment that abounds in both wild plants and perennial domesticated varieties that have gone wild. These foods are continually harvested by villagers and made important contributions to their daily meals and nutrition.

Consequently one of the reasons why the farmers in this village do not plant backyard vegetable gardens is the existence of a readily available supply of wild fruits and vegetables in the surrounding forest. The abundance of these foods ensures that villagers have a more than adequate food supply and a highly varied diet. The simple question thus becomes: What could motivate people to plant vegetables when all of these naturally occurring plant foods are available? The answer seems clear and obvious.

To proceed further unwinding this complex tale takes us out of the setting of the village and into a larger context: that of the regional systems of economics and transportation. The area of the field site I had selected has a very low population density and is heavily forested in all directions. The closest village is downriver, about three miles away. The next closest village is about two more miles away. To reach the third closest village, one would have to travel an additional ten miles. There are no other villages in any direction in this part of the country. The settlement in which I lived can be reached only by boat, a trip of roughly an hour and a half from the district seat. In a different direction, a trip of two hours or more by outboard is required to reach the national capital. When I began my research, there was no road communication in the area. During the period of fieldwork, construction began on an extensive system of road links throughout the district, but this village could not be connected to the rest of the system due to engineering problems. The village remained accessible only by boat. It was no doubt because other parts of the country are less forested, have a higher population density, and have better communication and transportation facilities, that a number of farmers in these areas did opt to join the government's scheme.

In the general region of the village, no town is large enough to have shops in which people can purchase goods or food for their daily needs. Thus their pattern of subsistence results partly from choice and tradition, and partly from necessity. The village has two very small stores, neither of which will ever make their owners wealthy. Only the barest essentials are regularly stocked: cooking oil, sugar, flashlight batteries, pressure lamp mantles, cigarettes, condiments and sweets, matches, and kerosene. Occasionally one can find a few cooking pots or the glass chimneys for kerosene lamps. For purchases other than these most basic necessities, one has to travel some thirty miles by boat to the capital. In this river valley there are only two other villages of equivalent size (150–200 persons). All of these villages are ten or more miles upstream from the mouth of the river. The other villages of the district are all located fifteen or more miles away. Thus there is no appreciable concentration of population closer than the capital, some thirty miles distant, by boat.

Occasionally inhabitants of these remote locations get a chance for a change from their regular diet. Every few months a fishmonger from another part of the country wends his boat upstream to the village, hawking his stocks of freshly caught saltwater fish. Villagers invariably purchase some of his wares, which are highly prized as a change from the routine fare of freshwater fish. Without the visits of these fishmongers, there is no way for villagers to purchase saltwater fish unless someone makes the long journey to the capital and brings some fresh seafood from the local market.

Some of the villagers have their own means of transportation. In this village of approximately two hundred inhabitants, there are about a half dozen outboard engines and boats. Many people, of course, have their own dugout canoes, but these are of no use in traveling dozens of miles away to larger population centers. In the past, before the age of outboards, all travel was by dugout canoe and involved many long hours of difficult paddling under the broiling sun. Presently, no one would even consider making such an onerous journey.

Consequently the village itself has no way of carrying goods to larger population centers on a regular basis. Thus, if farmers were to produce large numbers of eggs and chickens for sale, they themselves would have to create the system necessary for transporting the goods to market. Because of the food preferences of the inhabitants throughout the whole region, there was no village or local market for eggs and chickens, and there never would be such a market. The largest potential market for eggs is in the large urban centers at the other end of the country, at least two days travel.

One reason that so many eggs had to be imported for these centers is that there are fewer rural villages in the surrounding countryside. In addition, the dietary preferences of the urbanites differ from those of rural villagers. Thus, the eggs needed by these urban populations were imported from a neighboring country.

The essential point is this: If the people of the village where I lived were to participate in the government's chicken program, they would have to make a long trip by boat and then another trek, again twice as long, by road, in order to get the eggs they produced to market. Besides the lack of a system of transportation to move the eggs, there also was no marketing infrastructure to absorb any of the eggs that might be produced. Had the farmers participated in the chicken-and-egg scheme, they also would have had to create their own marketing plan. It seems that it had never occurred to any of the planners to ask what the farmers of the village would possibly do with all of those eggs once they had been laid!

Anthropologists long have known that very strong kinship sentiments and obligations can act as impediments to the development of successful entrepreneurial activity. The villagers I knew had virtually no experience with markets, pricing, credit, or calculating profits. Their general attitude toward novel undertakings, conditioned by centuries of experience with swidden agriculture, fishing, hunting, and gathering—in other words, an orientation primarily toward understanding the natural environment—is very conservative. Their farming system is finely tuned to local climatic, topographic, and edaphic conditions with which they are thoroughly familiar. They rarely make a mistake in what we would call "calculating the odds" on any part of their lives in which they obtain their basic sustenance. The system of market capitalism with which we are all so familliar is far from what these villagers know and understand. Consequently it is no wonder that they are leery of uncertain ventures, risk taking, and especially the kind of thinking that views money as "capital," as a kind of economic resource.

Finally, as one man pointed out to me, some farmers living in villages located in an adjoining river valley had taken the government up on the offer of free chicks. My friends surmised that these few participants could easily fulfill the minimal egg needs of the inhabitants of this district. This would then leave the capital and the urban areas at the other end of the country, all many hours away, as the closest possible places to sell eggs. And then, of course, there would be the costly gasoline to buy for the outboard engine and the land travel in order to transport the eggs and make the return trip to the village. The return trip would most likely have to be made empty because the village could barely support its two small shops. To try to open up additional shops, to be stocked by these return trips, would certainly have resulted in losses for all concerned.

"The Matter of the Chickens" now becomes understandable. The villagers did not join the government's chicken scheme because, from their perspective, to do so would have been not only unwise but financially disastrous as well. After all, they had plenty of food and didn't like to eat either chicken or eggs. They lived in a sparsely populated area that would be unable to absorb all of the eggs and chickens which would be produced if the plan were successful. There was neither a transportation system nor a marketing system in place to receive the products. The villagers themselves had neither the capital nor the experience necessary to create these infrastructural systems. Joining the scheme would have been a poor choice from any imaginable perspective.

Some months later, the agriculture department, which was sponsoring the scheme, paid one of its irregular visits to the village. Officials, assistants, outboard drivers, and other functionaries were along on the expedition. Tables and chairs were set up, and the village turned out for the meeting. One of the topics raised by the officials was the chicken scheme. A letter had been sent to the village outlining and explaining the plan; however, the department had never received a reply from this village. What had happened? The officials were somewhat mystified, as numbers of farmers from other villages throughout the country had joined the plan. "Letter?" "What letter?" "We never got a letter."

To have to explain what was wrong with the chicken scheme to the officials administering the plan would have required the patience of Job and the diplomatic tact of Gladstone. What self-respecting bureaucrat could admit the inutility of his program? It was much easier for all concerned, and in keeping with local ideas about social style, to simply have not received the letter announcing the program.

POSTSCRIPT

One of the tests of any anthropological study is the interpretation of events. To interpret any event, one must decide how and what meaning is to be assigned to an event. D'Andrade (1986) has argued that if we are unable to determine the assignment of conventional meanings, we will have little chance of succeeding in the assignment and interpretation of nonconventional meanings. This has been a journey into the understanding of conventional meanings. The interpretations presented here are of everyday and mundane events, not of arcane, exotic, or esoteric matters. The problems faced by these villagers are no different than those faced by villagers anywhere else in the world. The plans of officials are the same the world over, only the details differ.

Whenever I work with informants I make two assumptions: People are not stupid and they are rational. One important implication of making these assumptions is that if it appears that people are behaving stupidly or irrationally (or nonrationally), then I have failed to understand (1) why people are doing what they do, (2) what they are trying to accomplish, (3) what constraints they are operating under, or (4) all of the above. It is important for me to push my understanding as far as possible and not to give up the search for new and previously unknown information. I never know what my informant knows that I don't know.

One of the important obligations I assume in becoming an anthropologist is to never give up the search for new interpretations and meanings of events. I feel comfortable with Sir Karl Popper's obiter dictum that no knowledge is certain (1972:74–78). Any understanding is subject to question and further scientific scrutiny. Any understanding is subject to being overturned by new evidence and reasoning. While I cannot be certain that my understanding and interpretation of "The Matter of the Chickens" is correct, I can at least provide a reasonable challenge to one who might question otherwise.

ACKNOWLEDGMENT

I would like to thank all of my friends, informants, understanding officials, and colleagues, who had a hand in making this essay possible.

NOTE

1. The name and affiliation of the author have been intentionally omitted to preserve the anonymity of the research site, informants, and government officials, as well as to mitigate possible difficulties for future research in the area.

REFERENCES

D'ANDRADE, ROY
1986   Three Scientific World Views and the Covering Law Model. *In* Metatheory in Social Science, Pluralisms, and Subjectivities. Donald W. Fiske and Richard A. Shweder, eds. Pp. 19–41. Chicago: University of Chicago Press.

POPPER, KARL R.
1972   Two Faces of Common Sense: An Argument for Commonsense Realism and Against the Commonsense Theory of Knowledge. *In* Objective Knowledge, An Evolutionary Approach. Karl R. Popper, ed. Pp. 32–105. Oxford: Oxford University Press.

TWENTY-FOUR

Celebrating Impermanence: Gypsies in a Spanish City

MIRIAM LEE KAPROW

John Jay College, City University of New York

[Anthropological libraries are] stocked with descriptions . . . of tribes . . . whose lives revolve around dominant themes: rationalized, highly structured institutions; metaphysical metaphors; and central ideas. But what of those tribes . . . who do not appear to be of a metaphysical bent; who show little concern about conforming to a unified, coherent philosophy or social system, who live . . . with as little fuss . . . as possible; who appear . . . [to be] without the constraints or esthetics of a systematic, ordering structure? (P. J. Wilson [1977:26], writing on the Tsimihety of Madagascar)

Throughout the twenty-three months I was doing fieldwork among Gypsies in Saragossa, a city in northeastern Spain, I was terrified. It was not the Gypsies who intimidated me, nor the quarter I lived in, a working-class barrio of 30,000 people. Nor was it Saragossa, a service and communications city with light industry of some 600,000 people. I was fond of all of these and was truly glad to be in Spain. The national political situation did not frighten me either, for I considered myself too unimportant to be threatened by Spain's then-aging dictator, Franco (who died just before I left in early 1976).

The source of my anxiety was the sure conviction that I would never get a doctorate and therefore would never become an anthropologist. I was certain I was going to fail because, unlike my role models of ethnographic fame, I could not locate anything among the Gypsies I had come to study resembling a genuine group. I could find no sets of people mobilized around the same activities, let alone any system of such groups. My efforts to analyze the ideology were equally distressing. These gypsies obviously had ideas and values; after all, they were living, breathing people. But their ideas were fluid and changing, even mercurial, and were not neatly patterned. What would other anthropologists say, I agonized, when I would come home *without data*—without evidence of a whole culture with its internally coherent systems of religion and symbols?

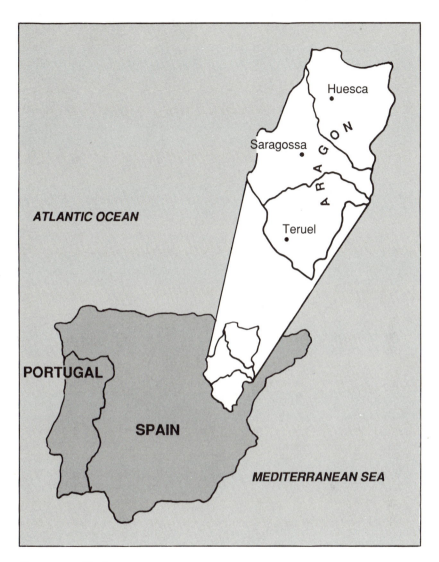

Saragossa, Spain

As a student at Columbia I had read ethnographies in which anthropologists drew elegant genealogies, elaborated ideologies, and described moieties, clubs, age-sets, and secret societies, as well as intricate economic and political structures. Yet here in Saragossa (*Zaragoza*, pronounced TharaGOtha in Iberian Spanish) after two years in the same neighborhood, I had never seen examples of the kinds of organization so commonly found in the anthropological literature. To recognize a group, for example, one must observe people in repetitive, patterned interaction over time. I never saw the same Gypsies even *doing* anything together for an extended period, much less over the two years I was doing fieldwork among them. There were a few exceptions where they congregated for several hours or more. Baptisms, weddings, and funerals could convene some twenty to fifty people. Fighting could convene people too, though on a smaller scale; there were also a few small clusters of kin-related nuclear families. Otherwise, though, I rarely saw any significant number of these 185 Gypsies coming together for any other reason. I was desperate, wanted to extend my time in Spain, and went home mainly because my family wanted me back and because my dissertation director, Conrad Arensberg, wrote to suggest that two years was sufficient for doctoral fieldwork.

THE BACKGROUND: STYLE, WORK, AND KINSHIP

Like most peoples loosely categorized under the term *Gypsy* who have been studied by anthropologists and other social scientists, these gitanos did not fit common romantic stereotypes about Gypsies. Although stigmatized, they were not pariah, for they lived among non-Gypsies in this working-class barrio, shopped at the same stores, and went to the same hospital clinics, films, and cafés as did their non-Gypsy neighbors. They were not physically distinguishable, were monolingual Spanish speakers, and were sedentary, not nomadic. (Almost all gitanos are sedentary today. Some were already sedentary by the early seventeenth century, if not before.) Their economic class ranged from low to middle income. They had cars, TVs, tape recorders, and other accoutrements of urban life.

The one stereotype about Gypsies that did apply had to do with style. The vitality, the zest—the sheer energy with which they embarked on anything, gossiped about anyone, ate, cleaned the house, met at the cafés—was remarkable. There was a dash, a vividness, a gusto, that has made me, along with others who have worked with Gypsies, miss them terribly when we are away. Their flair, their élan, intensified everything; "Every day is a drama," I used to write home.

Another stereotype about Gypsies—their supposed love of "freedom"—also reflected a certain truth, though the reality was far more interesting than the romantic fiction. These Gypsies, like so many other Gypsies studied by anthropologists, were not proletarianized: They controlled the organization, schedules, and products of their own work. If avoiding proletarianization means being "free," then these Gypsies enjoyed freedom, for three-quarters of them managed their own enterprises in this way. In this regard they were strikingly different from most of their non-Gypsy neighbors, who were employed in salaried jobs (and were therefore more vulnerable to Spain's rising unemployment rate). These women and men worked as scrap metal collectors, in the discount clothing and ceramic trades in the municipal markets, as whitewashers and painters (these last, men only), and in a medley of other occupations. Several families worked very briefly in short-term harvests, a brief, profitable, labor-intensive activity in which workers can control their own time while making a decent salary.

They were not proper capitalists, either, for their work was not capital intensive. Again, like Gypsies studied elsewhere by other anthropologists, these Gypsies, too, did not invest their profits to enlarge their businesses. On the contrary, when any of these businesses began to grow large enough to require the hiring of nonfamilial labor, they reduced the volume of trade or, more frequently, spent the "extra" money more freely than usual. Such noncapitalist organization has been the continuing despair of social workers and other members of aid-to-Gypsy organizations, who keep trying to bring Gypsies into wage labor and to introduce capital-intensive methods among those who are self-employed.

I got to know some 47 households of approximately 185 people (the total number shifted a bit as some got married or moved), mostly in this one quarter, or barrio, but also several households in other quarters. The Gypsies whom I knew constituted about half of the Gypsies throughout the barrio of 30,000 people and, furthermore, were only a small proportion of the entire Gypsy population of Saragossa.

Among these forty-seven households I knew well (those families whose houses I could enter whenever people were awake and stay as long as I wished), there was little evidence of kin groups beyond the nuclear family. Since the absence of unilineal corporate descent groups is characteristic of western Europe, this was not disturbing. There was even some evidence of nonlineal organization: three clusters of grandparents and one or two of their married children together with their spouses and young grandchildren. It is possible that these three family aggregates lay somewhere between nuclear family and stem family, but I should emphasize that these nuclear families lived separately even though they often worked together. Furthermore, these familial clusters were not very different from the so-called extended families of their non-Gypsy neighbors of the same and varying economic classes. Among the Gypsies at least, these family clusters could easily be fractured by quarrels.

WHAT I DID NOT LEARN AT GRADUATE SCHOOL

In graduate school I had been trained to look for structures—the component units, or building blocks, that together make up a society. These component units, the different statuses and roles that people enact, are usually related to class, property, power, religious practices, age, and gender. Though all these units collectively constitute a larger social system, an essential point about them is that they divide and separate people.

Now, one of the arguments I came across repeatedly in the anthropological literature was that, because society by definition is made up of structures and because we are social animals, none of us can ever escape the constraints of our various social statuses—our age, gender, social class, and so forth—except under very special conditions. These conditions, one read, are to be found only in religious rituals, pilgrimages, rebellions, mob actions, and similar kinds of conjoined, passionate drama. Such performances, according to the literature, connect people intimately, for they temporarily erase the separations made by hierarchy and status. The key word is "temporarily," for these brief moments of egalitarian intimacy, called *communitas*, were always presented as evanescent, fleeting escapes from the ordinary constraints of daily social life.

All this seemed entirely sensible, for it was brilliantly demonstrated in the persuasive writings of Victor Turner and others—that is, until I met the Gypsies in Saragossa who turned everything around. These gypsies, whose social life was organized around *avoiding* structure, taught me that communitas—the escape from structure—could be an ongoing process. They taught me, furthermore, that communitas could be embedded in ordinary, not sacred or unusual, activities. Again and again I would see how communitas was encoded in daily fights, rather than in ideal cooperation played out in, say, religious rites or pilgrimages.

It was fighting more than anything else that brought these Gypsies into intimate, face-to-face relations where ordinary statuses were erased. In fact, these fights actually ensured that there would be no permanent divisions. Thus there were no feuds, for the personnel involved in fights was always fluctuating. Although the same types of fights were repeatedly reenacted, the players shifted and rotated as friends and enemies changed places. Fights were like commuter trains with a life of their own, continually moving back and forth along well-known routes, continually admitting and disgorging new passengers. Feuds would have been impossible. Structuring the fights into allies and foes would have ground this society to a halt.

The pattern of economic activities was also one of avoiding structure. Here again, there was little evidence of organization beyond the adhesions of a few elementary families. Most of these Gypsies did not assemble in the same work places nor cooperate at the same work tasks. There were a few exceptions: one instance of three brothers who worked with a brother-in-law in the whitewashing business and did form a continuing work group, one instance of very short-term work on seasonal harvests that required large numbers of workers, both Gypsy and non-Gypsy, and two instances of a few kin-related nuclear families going to a huge car dump to extract the lead from car batteries. Aside from these occasions, the Gypsies did not work together over the two years I was there. In fact, even the work of harvesting and lead extraction was restricted to short periods among small clusters of very close kin—

temporary working associations comprising two to four households of grandparents and their married children.

Political activities were even more evanescent: in fact, there were no group-wide political activities. There was no structure of statuses or offices endowing anyone with authority (these Gypsies were supremely egalitarian). But more important, the Gypsies simply did not do "politics" together. They did not mobilize around issues of Gypsiness or around any other issue. Indeed, almost all the people involved in so-called Gypsy politics were non-Gypsies—members of aid-to-Gypsy organizations principally concerned with bringing adult Gypsies into wage labor, registering their children in the schools, and providing low-cost housing.

If I could not find *the* group or *a* group, neither could I find any structure of "traditions" (a word I now enclose in quotation marks when I write about the Gypsies). Where was custom? I wondered. What was custom? I wondered. Why do they get married one way this week and another the following week? I was eager to accept any ideology or artifact, for that is what anthropologists collected, I thought. Why, then, was there no Gypsy law, sacred system, or even cuisine? Where were the stories, if not around the campfire (since this was a city), around the kitchen table, or in front of the television?

ADMINISTERING PSYCHOLOGICAL TESTS

I had to interrupt fieldwork for several months to come home so I expounded the problem of not being able to locate a proper group—a set of people organized around a common activity or ideology—to Professor Margaret Mead. Dr. Mead suggested that I administer a systematic set of stimuli in order to elicit patterns. I was to discover that the patterns these stimuli would elicit would again be what I now began to notice as the Gypsies' resistance to structure.

Dr. Mead had me trained in administering Rorschach, Thematic Apperception Tests, and a host of other psychodynamic and cognitive tests. Once back in Saragossa, though, I found that I could not administer these tests according to the methods I was taught. Giving the tests was a variant of Laura Bohannan's "Shakespeare in the Bush," for it was the Gypsies who ended up teaching me what the tests were about. For example:

> "What are these blots for?" asked several Gypsies (none of whom could read) looking at Rorschach. "I've heard of these, they're for crazy people. What do you want them for, Mimi?"
>
> "I need them to get my *título* [degree]," I answered, finally admitting everything, because I realized now that I had no idea what I was doing. "My teacher wants me to give them to you."
>
> "Ay, sí, bueno," they said, "in that case, of course we'll help you."

They did not add "*pobrecita* [poor you, you're really in a mess]," but it was implied.

I learned to give the tests to the men first. If I gave them to the women first the men would still be curious, and the test would become a collective endeavor of whichever men were around advising the women how to respond. "Don't tell Rosa what to say," I would alternately plead and argue, "I'll do yours later. This is supposed to be for one person only!" Response: "Rosa, you tell Mimi it's not a pot, it's a hat."

The women were far too busy to come to my house for the nonsense of test taking; they came for serious matters, such as coffee and chat. But the children, I thought, would be easier to corral alone, and I had with me a battery of tests specially designed for children. I must have been working on the curious assumption that children were acultural when I thought I could administer these tests quietly to individual children as I would have done at home or in a school. My assumptions about the children were proved to be wrong, of course. The children did not prize being alone any more than their parents did, and they came to my apartment with at least one sibling or cousin and usually in clumps of three and more. (Their sociability and that of their parents was not really a Gypsy or Spanish "custom," I suspect, but rather a kind of sophistication at public life that anthropologists of northwestern European and North American descent are unused to and frequently remark on. Indeed, I found this same sociability among my academic colleagues in Spain. When we climbed small mountains and I would wander to a solitary place to stare contentedly at the scenery, they would inquire solicitously, "*¿Estás triste? ¿Estás aburrida?* [Are you sad? Are you bored?]") Thus, when I gave the tests to the children inside my apartment the adult scenario was repeated. All of the other children would chime in to give suggestions to the test taker. And like the adults, the children came to do what they wanted, not to take tests but to enjoy themselves.

The timing of tests, I had been told at the Postgraduate Center for Psychotherapy in New York (where Dr. Mead had me trained), was crucial, so I had invested in an expensive stopwatch. "What is this?" I would ask, pointing to a blot or picture. I pressed the stopwatch to Start. "Mimi, do you have a *Danone* [yogurt]? Do you have chocolate or cherry today?" "Me too, give me one, too; me too, me too," the other children would cry. "Mimi, LISTEN to me! Where are your red earrings? May I wear them? Where are the crayons? I want to draw now!" I would scribble "2 min 35 sec have passed; answer not given." "Okay, Carmen (trying again), what is this?" "Ayy, Mimi, that stuff's not worth anything, it's ridiculous, it's not worth a damn [*no vale eso, es una porquería*]; besides, I told you [she had not], it's a picture of a girl. Give me the next card. Where are the crayons?" Eventually we would go into the kitchen for yogurt, after I had collected some partial responses.

When I showed the test protocols to psychologists at home, they were struck by how minimal the responses were. Both Rorschach and Thematic Apperception Tests (TATs), ambiguously constructed pictures that may be interpreted many ways, have been given cross-culturally and usually evoke responses of at least two hundred words. With the Gypsies, TATs were typically: "That's a man with a violin. Give me the next card." Rorschachs were similar: "That's a bloodstain. Give me the next card." Such minimal responses are usually thought to be signs of mental retardation, childlike personality, or extreme anxiety. It was clear, though, that these categories could not apply to the Gypsies, who were managing their lives successfully and without any more apparent anxiety than their non-Gypsy neighbors had. All the tests seemed to do was to confuse matters more.

CLUES: HOW THE GYPSIES USE MATERIAL GOODS

The way these Gypsies treated material goods (the same items that their non-Gypsy neighbors had, contrary to the stereotype that all Gypsies are extremely poor), eventually revealed a pattern about the way they also avoid permanence and structure in general. (I must emphasize that "eventually" meant about five years later, for I hadn't a glimmering of an understanding until I had achieved sufficient distance from the original fieldwork.)

As these Gypsies avoid the continuity of organized groups, as they do not conserve custom, so they do not conserve goods. With the exception of the television, the washing machine, and a few other artifacts, they consume and repurchase costly and ordinary possessions much more rapidly than other Spaniards do. The Gypsies' lavish dissipation of their material inventory—no more profligate than the Kwakiutl potlatch, though with a very different significance—included throwing away large amounts of food at most meals and speedily consuming or depleting such valuable items as cars, furniture, new clothing, and money.

Clothing

I was sitting with Roya in her house watching television a few days before Christmas when she showed me three pairs of trousers she had bought for her three eldest boys to wear Christmas Eve. Roya and her husband were in the discount retail-clothing business. They bought new clothing wholesale and sold it in large, open-air municipal markets at prices about twenty percent lower than those of the retail stores. I asked Roya why she had spent money on trousers bought in a retail store since similar ones from her very own stock would have cost her half the retail price.

Roya did not answer my question. I asked, I pestered her, again. Perhaps she could not articulate what I really wanted—which was no less than a full scholarly analysis of her culture, one that I was unable to construct myself. She repeated what was important to her: The trousers were too small, the waists needed to be let out. Then, with her teeth, Roya ripped the waist button off each pair of trousers, leaving a gaping hole in the material where the button had been. She did not use the scissors that were lying on the sofa between us.

How should I interpret this? I wondered. Why had Roya torn new clothes that she had bought at retail prices? Yes, there seemed to be a pattern, but I was more confused than ever. Why, for example, had Roya's daughter Porrina, a typical teenager who loved to borrow other people's clothes, borrowed my stockings, put them on over her shoes, and then walked around the house in them, thus tearing them immediately?

Sofas

Sofas were the occasions of many puzzles. Constancia had a new one, red vinyl and very popular at the time. The vinyl presented an attractive surface, and Constancia's grandchildren were drawing on it with indelible ball point pens. Aghast, I kept taking their pens away. "Stop it," I reprimanded them, unnerved by such lack of middle-class respect for property, "stop it! Constancia, look, *look* what the children are doing to the new sofa!" "Ayy, *estos niños,* what can you do with children?" she murmured placidly and turned back to her cooking. More on sofas: Constancia's neighbor had just gotten a secondhand maroon vinyl one with a smallish tear. It was summer and she (the neighbor) had moved her sofa outdoors. One day she was outdoors washing clothes in a basin and complained about the hot sun. To cool off she enlarged the small tear in the sofa with her knife, pulled out some foam-rubber stuffing, soaked it in the basin of water, and sponged her neck. I was convinced I would never get a degree.

The Suitcase

I would be scientific, I thought. I would record with photographs and notes the fate of a suitcase my grandmother had given me to take to Spain.

Roya, her five children, and I were going to join her husband, Jaime, in Castellón de la Plana, a coastal city 125 miles east of Saragossa. Jaime commuted between Castellón and Saragossa because he was in the discount clothing trade and Castellón had a big market and because one of his grown sons from his first marriage, now his sometime business partner, also lived there. Roya, the children, and I were going to Castellón to attend the wedding of one of Jaime's relatives, have a short vacation, and work in the market.

Roya and Jaime owned their small apartment in Saragossa, as well as their furniture and their clothing inventory. Jaime's son had a secondhand Mercedes in good condition in which he and his father traveled to the markets. Nevertheless, the family (like other Gypsy families) lacked a few conventional items, one of which was suitcases. When Roya asked to borrow mine for the trip, I gave her one that had belonged to my mother's mother. I thought this matrilineal suitcase would make a good gift because it seemed indestructible; it was an old-fashioned one made of tough leather on a steel frame, and nothing had ever cut or bent it. I told Roya the truth: I no longer wanted it—it weighed too much to take on planes and was a monster to lug around. I was to see that this apparently unbreakable suitcase that had lasted almost three generations in my own family was not rugged enough to last more than a week with the Gypsies.

When we got to Castellón, the suitcase was put in a back room of one of Jaime's son's house, where we stayed. The following day I noticed that it looked different: Its shape was odd, it no longer had a smooth, rectangular outline but was buckling in some places, ballooning in others. Sensing something momentous was occurring, I decided to take photographs—documents, I thought, for my dissertation. By the second day, the sewed-in lining was separating from the leather, and by the fourth day, frame, leather, and lining were bending in different directions. In the end, Roya and her family left it in Castellón and came home to Saragossa without it.

Magical suitcases? Although I saw the suitcase changing, I was never in the room when someone was using it or when the children may have been playing with it. When I told this to my friend who was a social worker in the principal clinic in Saragossa, she told me that drug prescription sheets given to outpatient Gypsies within the hospital to take to the pharmacy in the same building would often be handed in rumpled and practically illegible a half-hour later.[1] Now I had two rolls of film recording the natural history of one artifact's life, together with a sheaf of notes recording masses of probably irrelevant facts, including climate. A problem loomed: How to understand these data?

NO ROOT METAPHORS

[When an anthropologist] comes across an irreligious tribe, he redoubles the vigour and subtlety of his inquiries. He tries to squeeze his information harder to make it yield that overall superstructure of symbolism which his analysis can relate all throughout the book to the social substructure. . . . So thwarted in this exercise was Fredrik Barth when he studied a group of Persian nomads that he was finally driven to write a special appendix to clear himself of the possible charges of superficiality. . . . Good marks to Barth for so frankly recording his own surprise and professional frustration. (Mary Douglas [1973:37, 38], discussing Barth's *Nomads of South Persia*)

One of anthropology's well-known contributions is that it tries to explain the inner rationale of behavior or custom that outsiders might find strange or even disturbing. But in order to explain seemingly unusual behaviors and customs, the anthropologist has to find some underlying patterns, some consistency and continuity. How was I to explain consistent variation and avoidance of structure? Structure implies continuity, and continuity seemed to be absent here.

These Gypsies were not aficionados of history; they did not, as I have mentioned, preserve traditions any more than they preserved material items. If anything, they were anticonservative. Thus they had no ongoing economic groups, religious system, or cuisine. Thus their politics was based on *avoiding* commitment to mobilizing around group-wide issues. If they seemed so individualistic, if enemies and friends interchanged frequently, if fighting seemed to erupt and subside randomly, what remained predictable was the unpredictable.

Ideology followed suit. Here were people who refused to use things to stand for anything else—who did not construct symbolic systems and for whom a cigar was a cigar. Nor did they fashion folk tales or other stories. When I asked what a film was about, trying to be a conscientious fieldworker, they would answer, "It was so good, she was rich, what a good film." If I pressed for detail, they would change the subject. "Have some coffee, Mimi. Are you hungry, do you want anything to eat?"

I learned to extract data on the run—sometimes literally, dashing alongside someone in a hurry, sometimes sandwiched in at mealtimes. Whatever the environment, I had to restrict myself to a few questions: "Please pass the salt, Ernesto. How much did you make on the scrap metal sale? How much did it weigh?" It was not that these Gypsies were reluctant to share information, but they really preferred that I do fieldwork by observation. They handed out their bankbooks and funeral insurance policies freely. I went to the clothing wholesalers with them, to the markets, to the scrapyards for the weighing in, to the police chief's office as they arranged a bribe to free an errant nephew from jail, to visits and weddings and baptisms. Anyone living with them long enough could have found out, as I did, how much the Gypsies spent and earned and who was fighting with whom, and they could have watched all of these events. But data in action, not data in memory, was how the Gypsies organized their lives and, of course, my fieldwork.

So the psychological tests really did elicit a systematic configuration— a pattern of avoiding pattern, a design for resisting continuity and neat structures. It was a pattern, in fact, of ebullience, zest, and vigor (who could be bored among Gypsies?), and it was a privilege to be admitted into this scenario. But it was not the stuff of which life histories are made. I cannot imagine any Gypsy I know sitting down to deconstruct his or her culture or even bothering to engage in such dialogue with an ethnographer. It would be impossible to do the kind of postmodernist anthropology currently popular, in which informant and ethnologist together devote themselves to sessions of analyzing text. And yet . . .

The very content of this essay has been determined by the Gypsies themselves. There was no single, dramatic event available to analyze, no superb refabricating of the meaning of *Hamlet*, no enormous joke played on the Christmas gift of a cow. These anticonservative Gypsies simply did not maintain their activities long enough for the ethnographer's convenience. Indeed, it is their own avoidance of structure that led to my writing this essay by listing a series of acts, instead of relating a spectacular event or root metaphor.

It is precisely such resistance to structure, I believe, that is the contribution that the study of Gypsies and others like them[2] can make to social research in general. These Gypsies from an obscure barrio in a lesser-known Spanish city remind us that the range of variation in human societies and social groups extends from the maximally to the minimally organized. Perhaps what has been called the "constraint[s] of having to provide a coherent and systematic account [and] . . . the esthetic necessity of basing a monograph upon a central theme or problem" (Wilson 1977:32) has led writers of ethnographies to underreport those social situations in which intricate organization is lacking. If we anthropologists have succeeded splendidly in discovering underlying structures, we also have experienced some frustration, or at least deflation, when we stumble across social groups in which it hardly exists. But after all, abstaining from structure does not have to be restricted to ephemeral[3] states. Avoiding continuity—that is, celebrating the moment—can also be institutionalized.

ACKNOWLEDGMENTS

Two people have helped me understand what I was seeing but could make little sense of. Conrad Arensberg, who often taught in metaphors, once suggested that the opposite of a Gypsy was an Alpine peasant who inherited a bed three hundred years old. He also taught me about the similarity of people in the upper and lower rinds of society—those who have nothing to gain and those who have nothing to lose—as regards indifference to public opinion and the preservation of material goods. Anita Volland, with whom I have had long discussions through the years about impermanence and who has studied the relation of culture and art forms among the Gypsy flamenco artists of Seville, also has been very helpful. Her article on the existential underpinning of eighteenth- and nineteenth-century Gypsy flamenco song (1989) addresses some of the issues I have lightly touched on in this essay. George Gmelch, Sharon Gmelch, Laura Kenny, Serena Nanda, and Mary Elizabeth Perry all pointed out flaws in the argument of this essay and generously made suggestions to improve it, as did the editor, Phil DeVita. I thank them all.

NOTES

1. I am grateful to María del Pilar de Cobián, the medical social worker at Cáritas Diocesana in Saragossa, for identifying Gypsies in the hospital records. She was able to do this because she had worked with the Gypsies in Saragossa professionally for many years. Without her help, I could not have identified them, apart from the Gypsies I knew personally, because neither appearance nor speech or last name are reliable markers.

   On a more general note regarding these Gypsies' treatment of material goods, George Gmelch reports the same treatment of material goods among the Irish Travellers, a people historically unrelated to, but very similar to, the Gypsies discussed here (personal communication September 1989). So does Mulcahy for the Rom, another Gypsy people different from these gitano Gypsies (Mulcahy 1989).

2. For examples of similar involvement in the present and avoidance of structure among Irish Travellers, see S. B. Gmelch 1986b. For another kind of Gypsy people, the Rom in Spain, a bilingual Indic- and Spanish-speaking people (called *húngaros* in Spain; Rom is their self-designation), see Mulcahy 1989. For the Rom in Canada, see Salo and Salo 1977. For an overview of similar avoidance of structure among "Gypsy-like" peoples in general, see Gmelch 1986a.

3. The classic statement about the ephemeral phases (called *liminality*, or *liminal stages*), when ordinary statuses are stripped away and people come into intimate, face-to-face contact—called *communitas*—is, of course, that of Victor Turner (1974), especially Chapter Seven.

REFERENCES

DOUGLAS, MARY
1973   Away from Ritual. *In* Natural Symbols: Explorations in Cosmology. 2d rev. ed. Mary Douglas, ed. Pp. 19–39. London: Barrie & Jenkins.

GMELCH, SHARON B.
1986a   Groups That Don't Want In: Gypsies and Other Artisan, Trader, and Entertainer Minorities. Annual Review of Anthropology. Pp. 307–330. Berkeley, CA: Annual Reviews.
1986b   Nan: The Life of an Irish Travelling Woman. New York: Norton.

MULCAHY, F. DAVID
1989   Material and Nonmaterial Resources, or Why the Gypsies Have No Vises. Technology In Society 10:457–467.

SALO, MATT, AND SHEILA SALO
1977   The Kalderash in Eastern Canada. Ottawa: Canadian Centre for Folk Culture Studies, Paper 21, National Museum of Canada.

TURNER, VICTOR
1974   Dramas, Fields, and Metaphors: Symbolic Action in Human Society. Ithaca: Cornell University Press.

VOLLAND, ANITA

1989　*Carceleras*: Gitano Prison Songs in the 18th Century. *In* Papers from the Centennial Meeting of the Gypsy Lore Society. Matt Salo, ed. Washington, DC: GLS.

WILSON, PETER J.

1977　The Problem with Simple Folk. Natural History 86 (December):26–28, 30–32.

SUGGESTED READINGS

KAPROW, MIRIAM LEE

1982　Resisting Respectability: Gypsies in Saragossa. Urban Anthropology 11 (3–4); 399–431.

1984a　Reply to Bolton. Current Anthropology 25 (1):34–35.

1984b　The Ultimate Anarchists. The Sciences 24 (4):38–41.

1985　*Review of* Gitanos de Palencia, by Cuadernos de Trabajo Social. Newsletter of the Gypsy Lore Society, North American Chapter 8 (4):1, 3, 6, 8.

1990　Taming the Gypsies and Other Dangerous Classes. Iberian Studies. Forthcoming.

SCHNEIDER, PETER

1969　Honor and Conflict in a Sicilian Town. Anthropological Quarterly 42:130–155.

TWENTY-FIVE

Innocence in the Cooking Pot; or, Getting Stuck in the Mud in Hopiland

ARMIN GEERTZ
University of Aarhus

It is probably an occupational disease that moves anthropologists to tell anecdotes "from the field," but sometimes, in the higher interest of academic reflection, the old story of the innocent-anthropologist-in-the-cooking-pot can add perspective to complicated issues and perhaps liven things up a bit. The following story reflects the contradictions of a complex problem that has afflicted the Hopis for many centuries and with accelerated intensity during the last hundred years.

The temperature was in the high eighties and the sky was overcast on that day in October 1978. As I turned off the highway, I wondered whether I would be needing the air-conditioning that day. My family and I were on our way to pick up a new acquaintance we had made who wanted to drive with us to Flagstaff. The trip over the plateaus and through the desert valleys of the Hopi and Navajo reservations usually took two and a half to three hours over the Tuba City route.

The rain of the last few days had turned the dirt road to Hotevilla on Third Mesa into a clay morass filled with holes that made cars slide and sometimes sink into the mud right up to the drive shaft. In the short period of time I had been on the reservation, I had become quite familiar with getting stuck in the mud and sliding into cliffs of clay. I had also learned how to twist a car through dried and eroded washes and sail over flooded roads. Some of the roads and trails on the reservation made my Dodge pickup cry for mercy.

Not today, I thought to myself, just an ordinary spin to town on civilized highways (without a flat, thank you) and then a comfortable motel where you can bathe away the grit and grime, followed by a beer and pizza, a film or two—the usual needs in the cause of cross-cultural work.

We made it to the sandy streets of Hotevilla without mishap. The village was alive with the signs of harvest: Gaudy bunches of corn were hanging on the gables, adding color contrasts to the desert brown sandstone walls. White sheets lay on the ground and were covered with blue corn kernels laid out to dry. There was a festive mood in the air.

The sandy streets meandered between the blocks of houses and finally led to the home of Mr. David Monongya. Stepping out of the car, I caught a breathtaking glimpse of a far, blue mountain lording over the desert landscape. The recurrent excitement that such visions always aroused in me was intensified by the thought of the enormous distances involved.

I knocked on the doorpost and was invited in by the old Indian who was waiting for me. We greeted each other and then, carrying a plastic bag filled with his things, I guided him out of the house. He was old and blind, but I marveled at his agility as I watched him climb up into the truck. He was probably in his eighties at the time—even though all of the old codgers love to tell impressionable Anglos that they are 110.

I had just started the engine when his wife came hobbling out. I rolled my window down and she said, "Oh, there's just one thing: You must be sure to stop down at the bridge around one o'clock. He is supposed to meet some people there!"

I didn't really understand what she was referring to, nor did I know where "the bridge" was. But I figured that there probably was a group of people somewhere on the road to Flagstaff. The rumor usually spread whenever someone with a car would show up, and suddenly a crowd of men, women, and children would materialize out of nowhere, all with errands to do in town. My wife, Monongya, and I sat on the front seat, and our two kids sat in the back under the camper shell, so I figured resignedly that there was room for a few more. Little did I know what was in store for us!

After a brief shower, the sun broke suddenly through just as we reached the edge of the mesa on our way down to Dinnebitto Wash. A majestic panorama stretched out before us: an impressive interplay of red and blue mesas, volcanoes, and mountains rising above the deserts where the brown plains were broken by green blotches and the harvested corn plants stood like armies of scarecrows.

As we drove into the shadow of the mesa lip, I thought about Monongya. He is a short, wiry old man with a lighthearted and talkative way of being. His charm and intelligence made an impression on me during the few days since I had met him. He told us many humorous stories in fluent English and yet, for all of his lightheartedness, we quickly discovered a seriousness that found its resources in the cosmological as well as the political implications of his role as a leader.

I approached David Monongya on the nineteenth of October in order to enlist his assistance in my field project, which had nothing particularly to do with Hopi prophecy. But I thought that if our association proved to be workable, I could pursue a firsthand study of the role of a prophet that might in turn throw light on prophets and prophecy in general. After Monongya had told me that he would consider my proposition, he asked me if I would drive him to Flagstaff, to which I happily agreed. It was obvious that he was in need of someone to care for him during his travels, and if I could assist him, I would have a good chance of observing his role not only as the prophetic leader of the traditionalist movement in Hotevilla but also as a well-known international figure considered by most enthusiasts and Indian groups to be a great religious leader.

I woke out of my reverie fifteen miles later and remembered that we were supposed to meet some people. We hadn't passed anybody, and there would be no bridge for the next thirty miles, so I asked Monongya if we weren't supposed to meet some people.

"Ya, we should have been there by now," he answered. Him not being able to see and me not knowing where we were going was truly an example of the blind leading the blind. Perhaps there was a bridge further on that I had never noticed before, I thought, but after a few more miles I figured that Monongya's friends were waiting back at the bridge over Dinnebitto Wash, a good ten miles back up the valley.

I began to think unkindly that if they didn't have the sense to show up for a free ride then there was no reason to turn back after them. But Monongya explained that we were supposed to meet up with a group of Navajos who were marching from the area near Zihi-Dush-Jhini Peak (Big Mountain) all the way to Flagstaff (a journey of about 150 miles!) in order to protest the relocation operations that were and still are required of the Navajos by an act of Congress concerning the Hopi-Navajo land dispute. A substantial number of Navajos are required to leave the Hopi side of the new partitioned lands.

This information scared me. I didn't want to become involved in any protest demonstration against police, dogs, and tear gas, nor could I understand why Monongya was involved with the hereditary enemies of the Hopi people. Everyone knows the chilling stories of blood and violence spread by Apache and Navajo raiders among Pueblos and whites alike. There were still incidents of armed violence where lonely Hopi farmers are found murdered in their distant fields. My family and I had actually arrived the day after the son of our host at Hotevilla was found shot dead in their clan fields. I couldn't stop the images passing through my mind of a group of Navajo raiders thundering out of the desert in their souped-up Cherokee Wagon FWDs, throwing my wife and kids in the back seat and leaving the old man and me bound to the frame posts of our gutted pickup—which goes to show what TV can do to American mythology.

But to my surprise, Monongya told us that the Navajo protesters wanted him to lead them in prayer before they started on the highway to Tuba City! Stranger bedfellows have been witnessed elsewhere in world history.

I remembered that a blue sedan was parked about ten yards away from the road near the Dinnebitto Wash. We all agreed that we would turn back and see if the owner of the car knew where the meeting was supposed to take place.

I stopped near the junction of the road to Dinnebitto about thirty yards from the blue sedan. As I walked toward the car, I hesitated. I couldn't see any details from where I stood, but it sure looked deserted. I wondered why someone would drive through all of that mud just to wait for a protest march. I didn't notice until afterwards that there were no tracks in the wet clay. Even though I had no interest in wading out to the car without galoshes, I couldn't see any marchers throughout the valley as far as the eye could see. So I figured that a little mud could be scraped off.

But it was worse than I thought. My shoes gathered more and more mud like two growing amoebas. Not without irritation, I considered this peaceful ride to Flag to be wanting a bit. The clay sticking to my shoes didn't help my mood either.

Of course, no one was in the car, and by that time my only interest was to get back onto the road so that I could scrape off all of the mud. I was so intent on looking for a stick out there in the mud that I didn't notice the white car until it pulled up to the roadside several yards from where I was standing. I hadn't gotten as far as the road, so I stood anchored in mud as the driver rolled his window down and his partner, who was wearing sunglasses, jumped out of the car on the passenger side. As I stood there, foolishly hoping that they wouldn't notice the mess I was in, I noticed that they were Hopis in their middle twenties and that they did not look very friendly.

I asked them, "Do you guys know if the march will be starting from here?"

The driver hesitated at first, and then answered, "No, it's at the junction."

"Are you going along?" I asked.

"No, we're just checking things out."

The young man who had gotten out of the car gave me an unmistakably menacing look through his black lenses and quipped, "It's called 'policing things out'!"

The driver nodded toward the blue sedan and asked in an unfriendly tone, "Who's your friend over there?"

I answered, "I don't know; he's not my friend. I went over to ask him about his march, but there's no one there."

"What does he look like?"

I felt increasingly uncomfortable. I could sense their rising hostility toward me. They began throwing questions at me: "What's your name? Where are you from? Who's the owner of that car? Come on, be specific! Who are you working for? Who's paying you? You're lying! What the hell are you really doing here? You're just ripping the Hopi people off! How much money do you have?" and on and on.

The guy with the glasses started closing in on me. But I was indignant. This was a damned interrogation, and even though I wasn't strapped under a lamp, I was literally stuck beneath the merciless sun. They took turns interrogating and accusing in rapid and aggressive succession, which hardly left room for sensible answers. There was only a rising sense of alarm: I forgot about who I was, where I was, and what I was doing there. In truth, I didn't really know why I was standing there at all. My whole being was focused on my tormentors. In the growing mental haze, I saw that they were interested in my money and that sooner or later they would find out that it was all in the pickup.

What a contrast I experienced at that moment: from stupid fears of violent Navajos to a confrontation with real life Hopi bullies! I was a perfect victim—an old man and my family in need of protection, and I couldn't even move my feet, which had sunk a few inches more, by the way.

But just at that moment the interrogation changed direction. The questions were now concerning David Monongya and his clique and why I was helping him cheat the Hopi people. They told me to stay away from him. I felt relieved; if that's all they were interested in, then they could waste their time on me all they wanted!

The younger one said quite suddenly, "Why don't you associate with us and get the whole story, man? We are the Progressives. We are the synthesis between the old and the new! That old stuff is a lot of bullshit. This is our land, all of it!" He made a dramatic sweep with his arms.

The fact that I had joined the Hotevilla volleyball team didn't impress them, but just as they were about to start in again, I heard a car coming. The younger one cried, "We'll get you!" as he jumped into the car, which was already squealing on its way.

Feeling suddenly ill, I tried to move out of the mud to safety but stopped short at the frightening sound of shoes sucking their way toward me! I almost jumped out of my skin when I turned and saw a well-dressed Anglo fellow in a two-piece suit and mud halfway up his shins not more than five feet away from me. He had risen either from the mud or from the blue sedan! Then I remembered that a car had driven up which had stopped the interrogation. Just then the rain began pouring down with a vengeance. I wondered at myself and the nut who was on his way out to get me. Even those Hopi bullies stopped short of the mud, which is probably what really saved me anyway. Whatever this guy wanted, it must have been important.

He introduced himself as a freelance journalist working for the *Navajo Times*. He told me that he was writing a book about the land dispute and had noticed that I had David Monongya in my car. By then I was beginning to have serious doubts about pursuing this prophet business. It seemed that associating with Monongya had its drawbacks.

And then the journalist began his interrogation right out there in the rain and the mud: who was I, what was I doing there , where did I come from, and so on, all with that irritating objective air which journalists carry on their faces and that look of the inalienable right to interview strangers in the mud in the rain.

I broke in: "Say, look now, I don't feel like being interviewed at the moment. Those guys were threatening me, and I would just like to calm down a bit." By this time, the marchers could be heard and seen coming down the Dinnebitto Road, beating on a drum. I could see Monongya bouncing up and down in my car, gayly laughing and clapping his hands.

"What were they threatening you about?"

"Oh, I don't know, something about me ripping them off and David taking money off of them and using it for his own purposes."

"Do you think David is using money for his own purposes?"

That made me mad, "How the hell should I know? I just met the bugger two days ago!" And then I just walked away, making indignant sucking sounds in the mud.

David Monongya! Of course I knew about his international reputation as a prophet and political leader, but I was not prepared for the disgust and bitterness concerning him that I met among the villagers of Hotevilla. Nor was I prepared for the swift change of plans on this crazy October day just because some old guy was sitting in my vehicle.

I related my harrowing experiences to Monongya and my wife as I drove the truck up the road a bit. Monongya didn't seem to be impressed; he just told me to relax and forget about it. He was the type who is unmoved by the turmoil of the world, maybe enlightened by an inner calm or just plain ignorant of the evil lurking in his vicinity.

As we got out of the pickup, about fifteen young Navajo men and women came marching, followed by four pickups filled with people and supplies. They stopped in front of us and stared silently. I wondered what the powers-that-be had in store for me this time and whether they might be hiding a cooking pot or two in one of their trucks. We waited nervously a few minutes for their leader to make his way out of the lead truck. He was a big Navajo fellow in his late thirties by the name of Larry Anderson. He turned out to be the national treasurer of the American Indian movement.

He shook hands with Monongya and thanked him for coming. Anderson's wife, a Hopi woman in her forties, greeted him with a bear hug. Monongya held on to his leather pouch as if his life depended on it, and then he gave the following short speech: "I had hoped that I could bring some others with me, but everyone is busy with the harvesting, and so they don't have time to join you. But I have come to see you off. I will try to meet you when you get to Flagstaff."

While this meeting between leaders was going on, I gratefully remained in the background, trying to look inconspicuous while the journalist and a photographer who had miraculously appeared from somewhere took pictures of the whole scene and taped the speeches.

As I began to calm down a bit, I heard with renewed dismay that Monongya was talking about having friends along from Denmark! There followed a short silence, and then he asked out of the back of his mouth whether I was still there. He hadn't noticed that I had sneaked away.

Reluctantly, I came forward and said that I was there. He told me to introduce ourselves, and this I did. Anderson and the woman shook hands with me, and Anderson recited the following speech directly to me:

> We started up at Big Mountain. We are marching against the relocation program of the BIA [Bureau of Indian Affairs]. We feel that we are only test cases right now, and eventually all native Americans will end up being relocated. We are protecting our civil rights.
>
> We had hoped that the Hopis could join us, but as I understand from Grandfather David, harvesting is going on, and I hear there also are several ceremonies happening at the different villages.

I considered telling him the real reason why nobody was showing up, but I thought better of it. Anderson continued:

> I wish to emphasize that we are open to non-Indian participants as well. We are carrying at the front of our line, a spear decorated with eagle feathers. It is our emblem, it is not a symbol of war. This is a peaceful, non-violent demonstration. We are also carrying a pipe which was filled at Big Mountain and will be smoked when we arrive in Flagstaff.

I noticed that one of the young men cradled the pipe (which was wrapped in yellow buckskin) like a babe in his arms. It was obvious that even the younger ones knew that the pipe allowed direct access to the divine world and that the spear was a symbol of protection.

Anderson ended his speech by saying, "We are thankful that you brought our grandfather to meet us."

He was of course telling all of this to the journalist who was standing behind me, blitzing away, but it was an exhilarating experience to participate in this event. Even though I was not directly involved in these matters, considering the state of my nerves, the chain of events transformed me, as well as the others, into living symbols. This transformation increased my understanding of the situation as well as my understanding of my own role in it. The protesters stood before me as a group of concerned worshipers attempting to follow the divine commands concerning the proper and respectful use of this land and its sacred mountains. Monongya was the symbol of holiness, the aged wiseman who, enemy or not, was sacred. I became the symbol of the white world, specifically the European world, the understanding brother, servant to the prophet, and symbol of the white brother who played a major role in the mythology of the emergence of the human tribes from Earth Mother's womb. The fact that we were all more or less a group of charlatans each with our own personal ambitions did not reduce the truth of our symbolic transformation at that moment. Human frailty does not, in my opinion, detract from human greatness—on the contrary!

A silence followed. I was expected to say something symbolic, obviously, but I was trying to resist the almost drunken surge of feeling that this series of events was causing in me. I knew that I wasn't entirely in balance at the moment, and what could I tell these people that they would want to hear, anyway? I couldn't admit that I saw things a little differently than they did, could I now? So I jumped into it as I began losing my nerve: "I can say that there is growing concern among the Europeans about the Indian cause in all the Americas. As a representative of the European peoples, I wish you all the courage and the strength to continue your second long walk." This was, of course, in reference to their defeat by the cavalry a century ago, and as it turned out, the Navajos consider the relocation program in the same light.

I sensed a feeling of satisfaction among my fellow participants as they thanked me. Then Monongya was all business and said, "O.K., if it's all right with you, I want you all to line up behind me and then I will say a prayer and make a cornmeal path for you to protect you on your way."

Everyone lined up behind him, and after turning him in the right direction, I stepped back as he took the cornmeal from his pouch into his hand, raised it to his mouth, and breathed his prayer into it. Then he threw a little to each of the four directions and made a cornmeal path toward Flagstaff. Suddenly the rain stopped, and a break in the clouds allowed a brilliant ray of sunlight to fall on the old man as he performed his ritual. It made even the best of the cynics weak-kneed.

After that, he paused, stepped aside, and the marchers marched away without another word. As I was guiding him into the car, the journalist came over to interview him. Monongya replied to his questions, "I came here because I am under the Great Spirit, and I came to give my blessings. My prayer was to ask for protection for the marchers and all people. It is meant to bring blessings on everyone. And yes, I am against relocation."

Then we got into the car and drove away. Monongya laid his hands on my wife's and my thighs, "keeping the energy flowing," as he said, while we drove off to Flagstaff.

THE AFTERMATH

After years of study and reflection, I wrote an analysis of the experience recounted here which, among other things, criticized just about every idealized notion that we have about the Hopi Indians. The topic is obviously a controversial one, and my involvement in it brought me unwillingly into the limelight of controversy. I am not the type who seeks controversy. I have been called all manner of insulting names and am even labeled "iconoclast" by my supporters. But all I originally was trying to do was to mind my own business and write my analysis. I was not interested in becoming involved in the local politics on the reservation when I first visited the Hopis in 1978, nor was I interested in debating the issue with crazy whites who claim that the Hopis are beyond all expectations of sacredness, harmony, and peace, a people where women reign in true harmony with "Mother Earth" and where the men are "High Priests" of North America guarding the occultistic "spiritual" centers of the continent until the Great Spirit chooses to return. And, besides all of this wonderful stuff, they speak a timeless, spaceless, and obviously alien albeit admirable language.

But it was impossible for me to avoid any of this. The Hopis told me outright, after allowing me to see how they could frustrate the first three months of my fieldwork, that if I wanted to get any serious research done, then I would have to choose sides. Otherwise, I would never get beyond the stage of being a transient collector of arcane and questionable data. I was forced to promise to tell "Europeans" how things really are out on the reservation, and then I was free to conduct any amount of research I desired on any topic.

Needless to say, I accepted the conditions. The agreement did not entail too great a cost, because most of my research continued as it had along lines chosen by myself. The traditionalist faction was already suspicious of me anyway, and David Monongya told me no less than four days after our adventure to come back when the apocalypse was over. So there were not that many choices to make.

I was interested in ordinary Hopis—those who were neither politically progressive nor traditionalist, but who tried to live in the modern world to the best of their ability. Fortunately for me and for them, by the way, the best of their ability was deeply rooted in the traditional Hopi way of life. They put it bluntly to me: If it's a guru you want, then go to the traditionalists. I answered truthfully that it wasn't.

By the end of my stay, people were streaming to my house, many on their own initiative, in order to help me out with my project. This had its problems, too, but that was a luxury compared to no results at all. I managed to return home after 10 months of fieldwork with 160 hours of taped interviews, songs, discussions, and so on, 1,400 slides, and a 400-page diary.

I spent the next several years meticulously transcribing and translating my Hopi tapes. I was well on the way to producing traditionally solid ethnographic material on a little-known aspect of Hopi religion, namely, the ritual use of marionette and rod-type puppets.

But by 1981 the trouble began. A radical group of Danes, who supported the Hopi traditionalist movement, produced a political exhibition at a local museum in which the Hopis were portrayed in exactly the manner that the majority of the Hopis on the reservation abhor. I wrote a critical editorial in the local newspaper, which brought on a furor. I sent an English version of the editorial to the Hopi newspaper *Qua Töqti*, which was published in 1982, the same year my first ethnographic publication appeared in *Anthropos*. My intention in sending the editorial had been to let the Hopis know that I was keeping my side of the bargain even though I was pursuing my own academic interests. A short trip to the reservation that year confirmed this approach by the many positive responses from my Hopi consultants and colleagues.

However, angry reactions from white readers of the editorial continued coming in. Somehow I had challenged some dearly held myths that non-Hopis considered to be essential to their own existential well-being. The next year, I wrote a short article in *Anthropos* that was highly critical of Frank Waters's *Book of the Hopi*. I had come to the conclusion that many of the misconceptions about the Hopis that Americans and Europeans have, stem from Waters's book. The responses to that article have never stopped coming in! I have had quite a number of responses both positive and negative especially from Germany and the United States. But hardly any notice was made of my 1982 article on Hopi puppets, and it was by far the best of the two pieces, seen from an ethnographic point of view.

In 1986, when the deadline for the removal of recalcitrant Navajo families who resided on the wrong side of the Joint Use Area boundaries was scheduled, representatives of the American Indian movement staged lecture tours, demonstrations, and rock concerts throughout Europe and the United States in opposition to the relocation program, which they perceived as the genocide of the Navajo people by the U.S. government. I wrote a critical editorial in the local newspaper calling for a stop to the Navajo histrionics. Nobody had bothered to mention the fact that the relocation was requested by the Hopi tribe in order to remove the Navajos from Hopi lands. The Hopis were not interested in having the relocation plans stopped; they had already been avoided for several decades. After pointing this out, I was promptly labeled all manner of evil things and was accused of twisting the truth.

I knew of course that the exact opposite was true. So I wrote two essays in appeal to the international community that further explained my views on the matter: One was entitled "Hopi-Forschung und literarische Gattungen" for Hans Peter Duerr's book on anthropology and authenticity, and the other was entitled "Prophets and Fools," which was written for our new journal in Budapest, *European Review of Native American Studies*, the first half of which is reprinted in this essay.

These essays came on the eve of the publication of the Hopi texts that I had spent eight laborious years transcribing and translating. I had had enough of politics and was firmly committed to writing an analysis of my Hopi texts. In the meantime, and quite by accident, I discovered that the published drawings of a petroglyph near Oraibi, Arizona, which the traditionalists claimed tell of the end of the world, neither matched the original petroglyph that I had seen in 1979 nor did the drawings match each other! I presented this curious discovery at a conference in St. Andrews, Scotland, in 1987. The many American colleagues who attended were intrigued and encouraged me to continue pursuing the topic in an attempt to get to the bottom of the traditionalist controversy once and for all.

My analysis of Hopi puppets lies unfinished in my drawer, not only because I could not keep up with the schizophrenic pace of pursuing two major lines of research but also, and more importantly, because I could no longer continue my escape from the truth, which I had been trying to avoid from the very beginning. My own somewhat simplistic, or idealistic, if you will, conception of an objectively empirical search for scientific truth with no concern for problems of meaning or relevance was and is anachronistic seen in relation to the needs of the Hopi people and to the needs of our own culture.

My article was not actually criticizing the traditionalists per se. Rather, I was just allowing the other side of the issue to come out and, in the process, was criticizing our own culture and the romantic, nostalgic after-shocks of our own search for identity. The Hopis who have read the article recognized this immediately, and even though it does put the traditionalist movement in another light than it is used to being in, it is even more so a criticism of its white supporters who have uncritically and primitively been causing havoc out on the reservation.

My excuses notwithstanding, my essay raises some fundamental questions about the ethnographic pursuit and its literary expressions. It also raises questions about ideology and the pursuit of knowledge. Even though it is at times flippant, this essay nevertheless challenges all of us to reflect on what we are doing and why we are doing it, scientist and tourist alike. It is truly a question of whether there is any real difference between BIA officials, oilmen, tourists, scientists, and activitists.

At any rate, it is my firm conviction that since our own culture obviously uses the study of foreign peoples as one of its methods of self-reflection, and it will be done whether we like it or not, then it must be our duty to provide not only the most trustworthy data possible but also relevant and sensible interpretations. We must educate our own tribes about ourselves through the existential lenses of foreign peoples, and we must do it with integrity and talent.

ACKNOWLEDGMENTS

I wish to thank Christian F. Feest, editor-in-chief of the *European Review of Native American Studies,* for permission to reprint portions of my article "Prophets and Fools: The Rhetoric of Hopi Indian Eschatology."

My concluding remarks draw as well upon an article soon to appear in ERNAS entitled "A Container of Ashes: Hopi Prophecy in History." Following is a list of the publications mentioned in my concluding remarks.

REFERENCES

BORNEMANN, F.
1982   *Review of* Das Buch der Hopi. Anthropos 77:959–960.

GEERTZ, ARMIN W.
1982a   The Sa'lakwmanawyat Sacred Puppet Ceremonial among the Hopi Indians in Arizona: A Preliminary Investigation. Anthropos 77:163–190.
1982b   Adoration Is Not Appreciated. Quá Töqti, September 23, p. 4.
1982c   *Hotevilla Village and "Adoration Is Not Appreciated."* Aarhus: privately published.
1983   Book of the Hopi: The Hopi's Book? Anthropos 78:547–556.
1987   Hopi-Forschung, literarische Gattungen und Frank Waters' *Das Buch der Hopi. In* Authentizität und Betrug in der Ethnologie. Hans Peter Duerr, ed. Pp. 111–136. Frankfurt/Main: Suhrkamp Verlag.
1989   Reflections on the Study of Hopi Mythology. *In* Religion in Native North America. Christopher Vecsey, ed. Moscow: University of Idaho Press.

GEERTZ, ARMIN W., AND MICHAEL LOMATUWAY'MA
1987   Children of Cottonwood. Piety and Ceremonialism in Hopi Indian Puppetry. Lincoln: University of Nebraska Press.

GEHLEN, ROLF
1988   Propheten und Narren. Anmerkungen zu den Arbeiten von Armin W. Geertz. *In* Hopi und Kachina. Indianische Kultur im Wandel. Albert Kunze, ed. Pp. 137–143. München: Trickster Verlag.

KELLY, RICHARD S.
1988   Spiritueller Imperialismus oder die Vereinnahmung der Hopi. *In* Hopi und Kachina. Indianische Kultur im Wandel. Albert Kunze, ed. Pp. 132–136. München: Trickster Verlag.

WATERS, FRANK
1963   *Book of the Hopi.* New York: Viking Press.
1980   *Das Buch der Hopi.* Düsseldorf, Köln.

TWENTY-SIX

The Inseparability of Reason and Emotion in the Anthropological Perspective: Perceptions upon Leaving "The Field"[1]

KRIS HEGGENHOUGHEN
Harvard Medical School

Upon returning to New York City after a year with the Cakchiquel Indians in the mountains of Guatemala, it was most difficult for me to sit down directly and write in detail of my experiences in, and readings about, Guatemala. I was not quite the same person as before my field trip.

I glanced at the quotation pinned on my wall:

> The anthropologist has been the disengaged man par excellence, dissatisfied at home and questing abroad.

And at other passages that had caught my attention:

> The "professional" anthropologist is an alien. . . . He is estranged three times over: first in his own society, along with the generality of his fellow citizens; second, in the choice of his profession; and finally in relation to those whom he studies. . . . [but] . . . the authentic anthropologists will not make careers out of their alienation, but will understand it as a specific instance of a pathological condition, demanding political commitment and action; that is, they will reject the refined identity: "anthropologist." (Diamond 1974:94–95, 330–333)

In an effort to overcome this temporary sense of disequilibrium, I leafed through my notes in order to reflect on the total fieldwork experience and on the general purpose of anthropology. Before I could proceed I once again had to ask the questions: "What is fieldwork? Why do it?" in terms of the things I had just experienced. I felt a need to record my frustrations, hopes, and anxieties—almost as a type of confession.

I make *no apologies* for this *subjectivity*—this "presentation of self"—since I believe it is relevant for the reader to see the author

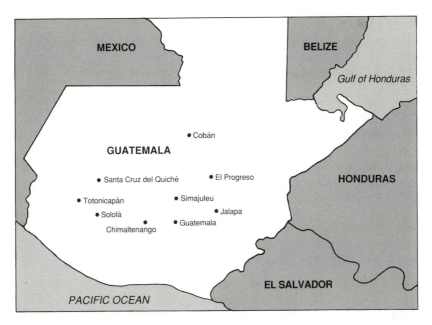

Guatemala Central Highlands

actually relating to people and situations. Through personal "intrusion" I hoped to achieve a complete, nonsterile, presentation of my experience as well as to increase the reader's ability to make an objective evaluation of what was being said. I wanted to present my feelings and my biases but deny that what was being said was therefore less "objective." In fact, I would argue the contrary.

The validity of the theory of knowledge that propounds the interdependence of reason and emotion, of subjectivity and objectivity, in the process of learning was particularly impressed upon me during my stay in Guatemala. In this essay I will attempt to discuss this realization. *The merger of the subjective and the objective is, in fact, one of the unique strengths of the anthropological approach.*

8 FEBRUARY 1974

Here I am in the village of Simajuleu. The radio is interminable next door. Here too! And the roosters, dogs, and pigs keep up a racket from four o'clock in the morning on. And I am tired. The altitude is only 6,000 feet, but combined with other things it's having an effect—and people wonder why I don't get out of my house before eight in the morning. But I'll get used to it, though life here is by no means all romantic. I keep having doubts about what I am doing. Am I wasting my time? Am

I getting at what I am here to find out? And what really is that? Who knows about "fieldwork methodology?" Am I doing the right things? Do I leave the village too often? Am I living in the right place? Am I reading and writing too much and not participating in the village life enough?

Serfarino, Francisco's twelve-year-old son, peeks in through the window. "What are you doing, Cristobalo?"

"Taking a bath." (I am not taking a bath. How can I take a bath in the dry season?) . . . "I am typing."

Arrogant me. Don't I know that is the way it is—just contact between people? "How do you do?" "How do you do?" "What are you doing?" "Walking." "Oh, you are walking." "What are you doing?" "I am cutting wheat." "Ja." "Take care then." "Yes, thank you. You take care also." "Oh, thank you." "Thank you." "*Tabana kwenta awi.*" "*Kwenta aka.*" "*Matiox.*" "*Matiox ok chawe.*"

Alejandra, Francisco's eleven-year-old niece, comes by, unexpectedly, with coffee.

13 FEBRUARY 1974

Cutting wheat. Cutting and binding, cutting and binding. On a yellow hillside among the brown and green of the pine trees with Inez and other men and boys. "Who taught you to cut wheat, Cristobalo? Let's cut your hair too, it's the same color." Talking, joking, working. Two boys rolling around goosing each other. Laughter. Far off on an opposite hill, one old man, all in white except for his red waist band, slowly, methodically, cuts his field. We, all in a group, spirited, cutting strips of cactus (*magay*) to tie the bundles of wheat. I carry more than a hundred pounds on my back for the first time with a tumpline across my forehead, up and down the *barrancas* (hillsides): aching neck muscles. The last few hundred yards, after about a two-kilometer walk, we make a race of it—and I keep up (Am I competitive? Am I into *machismo* things?)—falling down at the end, exhausted, gasping, sweating, and laughing. Lunch at Inez's house. Drinking *Kuxa* (homemade spirit). Oh yes, good *Kuxa* to make me feel mellow the whole afternoon. Tortillas and black beans.

8 APRIL 1974

What is all this "anthropology stuff"? Is what I learn worth anything? Would the people here want to buy it with a hundredweight of corn? Or, on a different scale, do we really have an influence over people in organizations that deal with human lives? Might it not be better to be a farmer, a carpenter, a physician, or even an artist—to make something concrete, to make a more definite contribution? It is impossible to keep from thinking this way when I live so close to these people who have, on the average, no more than five to ten *cuerdas* of land per family on which they might produce a total of fifty hundredweights of corn (at five dollars a hundredweight). One comes to think of the luxury of it all. In this juxtaposition, anthropology seems so parasitic. Who pays for the luxury? Do anthropologists return something? Not "anthropologists," but I—shall I be able to return anything? Will it matter?

13 APRIL 1974

Sitting on a bench against the adobe walls, I looked into Tata's eyes as he talked to me. The stench from his decaying mouth was overwhelming, but there was something in his face that held me. It was childlike yet old and mature—old and durable.

During a lull, I looked away and saw the gifts stored in the corner in anticipation of next week's wedding. In just one week, Christine, Tata's granddaughter, would leave and could no longer call this her home, though within her, in her thoughts and by inclination, it would continue as such for a long, long time. I played with the pine needles strewn fresh on the floor. The smell brought back Christmas in Norway, but it was also peculiarly tied to this place, it bound me here as well . . . to this place, to this room, where the mood was both festive and casual, pensive and lighthearted.

A long time must have gone by, much of it in silence. Then I realized Tata was sobbing. He was talking and mumbling and cried there next to me. Without thinking I hesitated slightly and then put my arm around him. I held this frail man next to me, felt the sharp shoulder blades of this so strangely strong man against me. It wasn't pity or even sympathy, and I wasn't being patronizing, the fear of which had caused my momentary hesitation. It was . . . well, I don't quite know what it was. I touched him, that is all. I felt him there beside me.

21 APRIL 1974

After the meals and the ceremonies, the *Kuxa* was again passed around, and handing me a glass, the host, Angel's stepfather, proclaimed: "Foreigners always come and always take things away but leave nothing behind. Teach me something! What can you teach me?" I wasn't quite sure if the emphasis had been on the "you," thus making it sarcastic, or on the "what," but the statement was clear. Outsiders exploit. Could I say that I was any different? I wondered what I could teach—what it was that I could give—and then I wondered about anthropology itself.[2]

28 APRIL 1974

At get-togethers, I am frequently asked to tell jokes. Everyone likes jokes and stories (me too), which are told and retold. A great number of them make use of the double entendre, and, of course, there are the off-color jokes. Yesterday, Ernesto told me that it is we students who can screw and "get it up" all the time but that he and the other *campesinos* (peasants) who work in the fields all day are too tired to do much of anything in the evenings.

6 MAY 1974

"Drink." Francisco spoke to me above the noise of the post–wedding party gathering. "If you are here observing us, that's the price you have to pay. Drink."

I finally stumbled my way home at one thirty in the morning; up and down the *barrancas*, following the sounds of those ahead. It was only four kilometers, but they were some of the worst I had ever walked. Having slept only three hours the night before, I was "out of it" and kept wondering what all of this had to do with "medical anthropology." I also kept thinking of Francisco's demand, which put me on the defensive, made me feel guilty. I saw it as an accusation. Do I use people? I don't see myself that way, but . . . don't I try to help with the water project? (But Kris, you can leave whenever you want to.) I don't make a pretense of being like the people here. I am different. But exploitative? I don't think so. But thinking of it always makes me uneasy. There was something to it.

The beautiful face of a ten-year-old girl looks in through the window at Cristobalo and his typewriter—playing with the petals of the roses Ernesto Colaj had bought from Aguas Calientes.

There I was: doing "anthropological fieldwork." Hoping, uncertainly, that I was there for reasons other than fulfililng requirements for a Ph.D.—convincing myself that there was more to it than gathering notes to write my thesis.

There I was: expectant, hopeful, and excited but also ill at ease, confused, anxious. Was I adequately prepared? Did my knapsack contain the tools to deal with it all? Would I find a method for gathering anything worthwhile? Finally, could I properly evaluate, focus, and verbalize my observations in a dissertation that might contribute to a better understanding of the concept of health programs in rural, peasant communities, particularly in Third World countries?

There I was: in Guatemala; in the highlands; in the Cakchiquel village of Simajuleu. Simajuleu literally means "The Edge of the World." I had come to the edge of the world to perform my rite of passage into anthropology. The classic mode of entry for all fledgling anthropologists,

I was coincidentally at the edge of the world at once, both literally and figuratively. I had come to the edge of my world to look at it from the Guatemalan mountains: to see, to learn, to try to understand that edge and through it, also to look from there at the center of my own world and at myself.

Of course, there were specifics to guide me. There was a health program. How did it work? Why did it work? How could others learn from it? Were there conflicts between "cosmopolitan" and "traditional" concepts of medicine? Was the health worker experiencing an identity crisis? These were the questions to be answered. There were notes to be taken about religion, social structue, and all of the socio-anthropological aspects one is supposed to examine during fieldwork. The goal was to put bits and pieces together in an ordered whole, to say something new, to say something possibly beneficial.

I was at "the edge of the world" then, to understand and make sense of the totality of this new reality. Francisco, Ernesto, Inez, and Nana . . . a whole group of unknown people. The fields. The sheep and the pigs. The handshakes. The eating and talking. The poverty. The working, walking, and incessant *mandados* (errands). The greetings, which seemed at first so repetitive. This culture in its entirety was my discrete anthropological province. My challenge was to comprehend this culture in order properly to evaluate the health program within its context.

By being there and by beginning to understand all of this I was in the process of becoming an anthropologist (I hesitate in using the term). But that did not answer all of it. Simply writing about a subject from a perspective not written about before—in my case an innovative health care program in a Guatemalan Indian peasant village—did not, somehow, satisfy the claim that one cannot become an anthropologist just in the classroom and the library.

What was so important about fieldwork? Was it really a rite of passage? If so, in addition to the intellectual observation, analysis, and recording, what was supposed to happen?

And that was it. Much later I realized it with my head also: *It was what happened. The anthropologist's feeling must lead his thoughts into the experience, if he is to fully comprehend the experience.* In short, his head must follow his heart if fieldwork is to be a rite of passage into anthropology. What happened was not just that I very slowly began to understand a new reality—a new culture. It wasn't just a study and an understanding of people different from myself, seeing their beliefs, ordering, and systems up close. I also had to go sensuously to the edge of the world. Without having been there, felt it, smelled it, touched it and been touched by it, I was not doing anthropology.

What a realization for a staid Norwegian: head and heart.

What fieldwork was really all about was being touched by a different reality. That is what I had to "learn." It included what happened to me as much as anything else—not just what I read and saw and "understood" but what I ate, smelled, and felt. What I heard and saw—what I experienced.

The pigs waking me at three, four, five in the morning . . . the hundred pounds of wheat on my back . . . the *Kuxa* . . . the mud . . . the wind, the hailstorm, and being soaked to the bone . . . the smoke in my eyes while eating beans with my fingers, the tortillas . . . the charcoal dust and no water to wash. Esteban playing his cracked guitar, smiling with eyes that had been blind three years, suddenly crying "Why? why?" The marriages, wakes, funerals, malnutrition, amputation of a finger . . . the pride, the humility, the persistence, the weakness. Tata's laugh and rotting teeth, his patched clothes, and his thin body walking every day stooped and rhythmical, as if dancing a half-walking, half-running gait, with dignity to hoe his fields.

I am not suggesting that I saw with their eyes or felt what they felt, but their world touched mine (and mine touched theirs). I felt it. It was the feeling of it all. That is how I suddenly saw the flesh and blood on Malinowski's skeleton (1961:17). All of this was important, important not so much because I began to make sense of it, ordering it, understanding it, but because it touched me profoundly—made me feel strong, happy, sad, frustrated, angry, tired, drunk, bored, overwhelmed. All of those things.

Realization of this extrarational dimension of fieldwork did not minimize my sense that it was a luxury, a holiday of sorts. Neither did it quell the uneasy thoughts that I was exploiting people.

The realization led, however, to an important conviction, tied to the dual nature of humans as thinking and feeling beings, that both elements are necessary and significant to the anthropological perspective, and in terms of which the "anthropological dialectic" might be understood. It seemed simplistically obvious that whatever an anthropologist had to offer, whatever was special about his or her contribution—as an "anthropologist"—had to be rooted *in feeling as well as thinking.*

Influenced by this duality, and joined through it with people quite different from me, I realized that the *rationale for anthropology made sense only in terms of justice and human rights.* This makes the anthropologist automatically responsible for action and subject to *an implicit mandate to convert theory into practice.* Understanding, derived from thought, and feeling, is the answer to "why anthropology?" and the effective communication of this understanding into practice is the essential rationale for the discipline of anthropology. The purpose is to give meaning to the kinds of changes that should take place in me, in the society where I live and, if possible, to make me understand how best to assist with changes among those with whom I did fieldwork. In other words, I identify with those anthropologists who see their task as one which ultimately, and consistently, returns to an analysis of "the salient structures of exploitation."

Camus's *Myth of Sisyphus* and Hemingway's *The Old Man and the Sea* powerfully present the persistence of human struggle which, prodded by hope and perceptions of Utopia,[3] strives for change and progress no matter how overwhelming the odds. "Man is destroyed but never defeated," states Hemingway, implying that the admission of defeat heralds the destruction of man: when he stops struggling, he is no longer man. Erich Fromm concurs by saying that "when we speak of man we speak of him not as a thing but as a process" (1971:viii).

Anthropology, together with other social sciences, must be in the forefront of this struggle—in the forefront of shaping this process. It must give direction to change away from exploitation. It must show us how to improve and how to progress. It must be employed to combat self-righteous proselytizing and conversion steeped in ethnocentrism, as well as the mindless and destructive "progress" of Icarus. It must fight actively against exploitation based on a greed that causes us to rob others while unwittingly bankrupting ourselves. Based on its special attempt to understand "the human condition" in all of its different facets, anthropology must actively help us understand change and progress in terms of the realistic, contemporary needs of human beings.

I counter those who argue that anthropology is basically a theoretical discipline—belonging within the realm of the academy and museum—by identifying myself with the arguments of Richard Volpe who (using Kant [1974] in his support) claims that "nothing is as practical as good theory and that the very soundness of any theory lies in its applicability. . . . The test of any theory is in its capacity to guide action" (1975:495).

Based on my reflections during fieldwork, I feel that thoughts and emotions that result from participation in the lives of fellow human beings during a "process of creation that moves back and forth between abstract concepts and concrete experiences" (Volpe 1975:495) are the only ultimate justification for what anthropologists do.

NOTES

1. This essay is a result of Ph.D. fieldwork experiences in Chimaltenango, Guatemala, where the author was associated with the Behrhorst Health Program and living in the Cakchiquel Indian village of Simajuleu. The paper constitutes the preface of the author's Ph.D. dissertation: "Health Care for the 'Edge of the World'" (Committee on Anthropology, New School for Social Research, submitted April, 1976). The views presented in this essay are those of the author and do not necessarily represent those of the institutions with which he is affiliated.

2. This is a dilemma no doubt shared by numerous anthropologists. Consider, for example, Robert Jay's comment: "Toward the end of my fieldwork in a Malay village in 1963, I was approached by a small delegation of villagers,

who said to me, 'You are a professor in an American university who has studied our village for a whole year. You must have learned a lot about us in that time and could you help us with our problems here. Will you please tell us some of what you know?" (Jay 1974).

3. ". . . life is impossible without something for which one can hope. Recognising ourselves as members of an emerging world community, we cannot escape assumptions, open or hidden, as to that for which they hope and as to what can be hoped for them. The general problem, then, is not simply empirical . . . it is also a moral problem, a problem of one's commitments in, and to, the world. Anthropologists have indeed commonly thought of themselves as belonging to the 'party of humanity' . . . and the world view of Gay ascribed to the Enlightenment as passionate rationalism and a tragic humanism, is not alien to anthropologists. It is, I would urge, the view best suited to them. . . . The tradition intended here requires a conception of the future, indeed a 'Utopian' conception (taking 'Utopian' in a positive sense of a projected ideal, not the negative sense of an unrealisable dream) and a theory of progress as well" (Hymes 1974).

REFERENCES

DIAMOND, S.

1974   In Search of the Primitive—a Critique of Civilisation. New Brunswick, NJ: Transaction Books.

FROMM, E.

1971   Introduction. *In* Celebration of Awareness, Ivan Illich, ed. Garden City, NY: Anchor Books.

HYMES, D.

1974   The Use of Anthropology. *In* Reinventing Anthropology. Dell Hymes, ed. New York: Vintage.

JAY, R.

1974   Personal and Extrapersonal Vision in Anthropology. *In* Reinventing Anthropology. Dell Hymes, ed. New York: Vintage Books.

KANT, I.

1974   On the Old Saw: That May Be Right in Theory But It Won't Work in Practice. Philadelphia: University of Pennsylvania Press.

MALINOWSKI, B.

1961   Argonauts of the Western Pacific. New York: Dutton.

VOLPE, R.

1975   Behavioral Science Theory in Medical Education. Social Science and Medicine 9:493–499.

TWENTY-SEVEN

Some Consequences of a Fieldworker's Gender for Cross-Cultural Research

SUSAN DWYER-SHICK
Pacific Lutheran University

When an anthropologist enters a community, he or she comes most likely as a stranger. And as a stranger, the anthropologist will be expected to occupy the status, displaying its associated behaviors, of similar individuals already known to community members. Initially, if not overtly cast as a potential enemy, the fieldworker might be identified as a missionary, teacher, tourist, or even "hippie," depending on the recalled earlier encounters between locals and foreigners (see e.g., Berreman 1962; Goldstein 1964). Social scientists, particularly anthropologists, have observed that people universally tend to interpret and misinterpret in light of their own experience, to cope with "unknowns" in light of apparently similar "knowns" (see e.g., Bohannan 1966). Obviously, the newly arrived fieldworker has an advantage if he or she comes equipped with knowledge of who the previous strangers were, even had they been other anthropologists. More importantly, as the anthropologist gradually moves from "outsider" to "insider" there must be corresponding insight into what will now be expected as appropriate behavior accompanying the insider or "friend" status.

This essay focuses on one such subjective attribute of the ethnographic enterprise: the gender identity and gender role of a woman conducting fieldwork within a largely sexually segregated society. Why gender identity and role? How come the experiences of a woman? What about sexual identification? Aren't women still only a minority of those in the field?

In the anthropological literature there has been a lack of consistent agreement on or treatment of sex and gender with respect to cross-cultural research. We need, however, to first distinguish between the two terms: while sex is designated as "male" or "female," gender, partly based on distinguishable characteristics such as sex, may have its source in culture and not biology.

But *is* sexual identity highly visible, even if it is unusual (e.g., the only woman faculty member at a departmental meeting)? And if visible (i.e., unequivocal recognition and accuracy), is sex a significant variable? In response to the first question, I don't think so. To be a man or a woman, a boy or a girl, is as much a function of dress, gesture, occupation, social network, and personality as it is of possessing a particular set of genitals, as at least one individual in an unfamiliar culture context learned with some humor.

In the early 1970s Wyn Sargent traveled in the highland area of Papua, New Guinea, dressing her lanky six-foot frame in safari hat, shirt, pants, and boots. Sargent, self-described journalist and media-dubbed anthropologist, wrote about what happened when she greeted the women of the compound as they were leaving for the fields one morning:

> The Dani women are full-hipped, big-bellied creatures. When they get together they are a robust, boisterous, rowdy bunch. Their energy is volcanic. . . .
>
> Aem [a Dani male] told the women in the courtyard that I was a woman, too. They viewed this idea with curiosity. Some of them shoved in a little closer to get a better look. One old woman with a runny nose knocked my hat off my head and ran her fingers through my hair. My blouse was opened and the women took turns peeking inside at my underclothing. Another woman squeezed my bosom. Then she turned to convince the others that I really was a woman. The announcement created a pandemonium so grand that even some of the men stepped outside of the *pilaito* to watch it.
>
> "Mamma Wyn! Mamma Wyn!" they screamed. And then they smacked the daylights out of me. I was jostled and hustled around in the dirt. They slapped me with big loving punches. The punches were repeated and improved upon with such elaboration that the breath was finally knocked out of me.
>
> The Dani women do not love men as much as they love one another. . . . The women are compulsively devoted to one another because they work, eat and sleep together. They spend what other time they have in drawing attention to themselves to acquire the love and admiration from one another which they need to be happy. (1974:49–50)

The second question addresses the significance of sex as a variable when biology is not in dispute. Again, the importance of sexual identity may be more apparent than real. For example, Kenneth Goldstein and others in the audience thoroughly enjoyed this anecdote about Sargent's sojourn among the Dani women when I included it in my paper at a session on methodology during the 1977 Annual Meeting of the American Folklore Society. Interestingly, Goldstein's hearing of this story prompted recall of a related incident from his own fieldwork in north-eastern Scotland.

In the early 1960s he was collecting items of folklore and their traditional contexts, paying close attention to variations in both. On one occasion he was collecting obscene riddles and stories from several members of a women's group. The group met weekly, but it was typically Goldstein's wife, Rochelle, who was the "collector" present, having been dispatched by her husband with instructions to "remember everything." When he inquired as to the possible reluctance of the women to share such things with a man (remember, Goldstein was interested in the potential alteration of an item as well as its natural context), one woman laughed heartily before responding: "We forget what is in your pants when you are here with us!" The meeting audience enjoyed this story, too.

Finally, in an experiment to investigate the expectancy effect in anthropological research, Gary Alan Fine and Beverly J. Crane concluded that "although the sex of the interviewers by itself did not have any significant effect on the collection of riddles, the interaction of interviewer's sex and expectancy proved to be highly significant" (1977:18). In other words, sex may be a significant variable, but then again, it may not. Moreover, Fine and Crane suggest that there are considerations beyond the visible biology of the interviewer which must be evaluated. For example, were the female interviewers particularly influenced by the presence of an expectancy (i.e., a bias that operates to produce results that conform to the expectations of the person in authority) because "women have been more culturally conditioned to respond to others' expectations since women have traditionally been dependent upon pleasing others as a means of deriving a positive self-image" (1977:18–19)? Might women be more "susceptible than men to any special attention by the experimenter to the task (i.e., the Hawthorne Effect), and could this have produced increased effort by the female interviewers in the experimental expectancy situations" (1977:19)?

Nonetheless, much of the preceding represents hindsight. It is an attempt to gain perspective from a field situation wherein I was frequently the only woman present, within a study community that tolerated—even encouraged—my crossing boundaries between same-sex groups and which included the collection of data not usually available to female members of the study culture. Clearly, I remain anxious about my acceptance (or even toleration) by women and men who are participants in a cultural tradition that recognizes social segregation based on sex. This apprehension was most acute when I perceived my presence to be in conflict with any usual status role in the community, that is, when certain areas of social life, or particular segments of the community, would have been expected to be closed to me because of my femaleness.

Upon reflection, however, I am convinced that the particular status I have been able to occupy at any given point in field research has had

a significant influence on my access to, and the kinds of, data available
for collection. More importantly, I now understand that my sexual identity as perceived by the community members is a variable which must
be a conscious part of my own understanding for enactment of the appropriate behavior in the appropriate context. Of course, such role playing is often a prerequisite for acceptance within the community and
for reducing the chances of making a culturally wrong move (see e.g.,
Goldstein 1964). It is also a valuable insight into the cultural definition
of appropriate behavior of individuals within a specific social context
(e.g., the approved behavior for adult women visitors in a private home).
Quite aside from the admittedly emotional need for acceptance and the
desire to be able to recount stories of a rewarding field experience, there
is a very practical matter: acquisition of a public image which will encourage a flow of information that is frequent, in sufficient quantity,
and scientifically valid for analysis and interpretation.

What are some of the possible consequences of sexual and gender
identity when an anthropologist is in the field? There are at least three
separate, yet intimately related, points: the personal and subjective; the
ethonographic; and the theoretical and methodological (see Golde 1970).
Undoubtedly, such reflective presentations provide the first-time fieldworker with a measure of comfort in undertaking that initial trip to the
field. For the professional and experienced fieldworker, the subjective
discussion of another's fieldwork provides a comparative framework
in which to weigh his or her own experiences. Finally, anthropology
as a social scientific discipline can profit from serious attempts "to
understand the field experience in contexts consonant with current
theories of human social behavior" (Hatfield 1973:15).

For illustrations and examples, I shall use the framework and events
from my own life and fieldwork. During the summer of 1975 I traveled
to Istanbul, Turkey, accompanied by my husband (Stephen) and our then
not quite two-year-old daughter (Sarah). I had been invited to participate
in the First International Turkish Folklore Congress, and I anticipated
time for some preliminary fieldwork. However, the summer was planned
primarily as a visit with Turkish family members and friends, most of
whom I had not seen in more than ten years and none of whom had
yet met my husband or daughter. I met able and helpful colleagues at
the congress, I collected some interesting items of political folklore, and
we three thrived within the warm hospitality of the Turkish extended
family. The stay ended for all of us much, much too soon.

The following summer I returned to Turkey, but this time as a folklorist, and alone. In addition to the required preparations to leave for
the field, I had spent considerable time during the intervening year
preparing Sarah for my departure and absence. Since she had been
jointly raised by her father and me sharing her care from birth—each of

us remaining at home while the other assumed employment or research responsibilities outside on a mutually agreed to basis of approximately equal time—Sarah did not need to be prepared for change in caretakers. Of course, changes in the amount of time with one caretaker, and possible scheduling difficulties (e.g., we "rescheduled" her third birthday party for an afternoon before I left), were openly talked over, especially since Sarah appeared to enjoy such conversations. In fact, my departure and absence from Philadelphia were in many ways made easier for Sarah by her own travel to Istanbul the previous summer. She asked us often about the things she did and the people she met.

In fact, such conversations about Turkey very soon took on the feel of a storytelling session. "Tell me again, Mommy, about the time I wouldn't go to bed without the slippers Grammy [the term she used for the grandmother in the Turkish family] bought for me at the covered bazaar." "Do you remember when we took the ferry to the islands and we all rode donkeys?" "Did I really get to eat cookies for breakfast!" "Can't Togay and Anne come to visit us? I'd let them sleep in my room." "How come Dede [Grandfather] gave me sugar cubes and kissed my arm? Did I really give him my other arm to kiss, too?" During our shopping trips to purchase the several small items that I would take along as gifts for the children, Sarah was most insistent that we make the right choice: "But, Mommy, I would really like to have a Mickey Mouse puzzle. Remember how much Leyla [a three-year-old girl] wanted to meet Mickey Mouse? I know she'd like this!"

In anticipating fieldwork, a primary concern was how I as a single woman (i.e., being unaccompanied by, or absent from, my husband) would be evaluated within a cultural context having a strong emphasis on identification of a woman through some male relative—father, brother, husband, son. Furthermore, I was concerned about how a woman's separation from her young child would be judged, since Turkish women are the primary caretakers of children, particularly children as young as my own daughter. Among those Turkish friends who had met my husband and our daughter the previous summer, I encountered few, if any, problems. For these very cosmopolitan friends the reaction was most often amusement, as though my explanations of unaccompanied presence and father-caretaking were yet another strange American custom. There was neither a diminution in their welcome of me nor in their insistence that I spend more time than I was able with them. But, then, these were family and friends, not "informants," as both they and I unconsciously assumed. Unfortunately, their lack of reaction did not prepare me for what was to happen when I left Instanbul to live and work within areas of the country I had never been before and where I was largely unknown.

Many fieldworkers have learned that informants are likely to have as many, and sometimes a good deal more, inquiries of the fieldworker as he or she had posed during the formal or informal interview. Predictably, such questions related to the researcher's background. And although there is curiosity and genuine interest on the part of the inquiring informant, that individual is also securing needed information to assist in determining just where this "stranger" should be placed to "fit" within the community thereby allowing "predictability" of his or her behavior.

Inevitably, the first questions I was asked by women of all ages were about my age, marital status, and children. "How many children do you have?" These were quickly followed by inquiries about my family: "How sad your father is dead." "No brother? Too bad." Next, there were a few questions to learn my citizenship and nationality. "You come all the way from America?" "No Turkish relatives?! But you can speak Turkish; surely you must have some relatives who come from Turkey?" And, finally, the question asked of all fieldworkers: "What did you say you're doing here?" I answered each of their questions with the "truth." Self-righteous, I was not going to hide anything or distort my answers. I have never felt anything but a conscious respect for the reciprocal nature of any social interaction in the field. Unfortunately, it was only after a series of painful starts and stops that I finally understood my predicament: A basic contradiction existed between my own definition of self and that of those individuals who I hoped would become my informants. By answering questions about myself and my family "truthfully," I was hindering rapport establishment with all of the women and some of the men. Once I grasped that, I was able to determine the behavior appropriate for a Turkish woman and, therefore, by extension what the informants were expecting of me as a woman.

Interestingly, while I had been concerned with the "having left" part of the summer's arrangement, my potential women informants focused on the "with whom." When responding to inquiries about who was taking care of my daughter, I answered in Turkish (the language of the question) that the caretaker was my husband, Sarah's father. My explanation evoked puzzled expressions, muffled laughter, then a small grin on the face of the original questioner as the question was repeated, although this time more slowly and carefully so that I would not misunderstand the Turkish. In other words, my "inappropriate" response had been understood as a function of my unfamiliarity with the Turkish language.

Until I caught on to what was happening, we would go over the question again, first in Turkish, then in English (on one occasion, enlisting a young schoolboy who had an elementary knowledge of English), now back to Turkish. Finally, I realized that my reputation as a trustworthy person—a person to be trusted with information, tasks, confidences, and friendships—depended on my answering "correctly." So, I took a deep breath and lied. Ever after in response to the caretaking question, I answered that it was my mother who was looking after Sarah and, by implication, Stephen, too. Eventually, I confirmed that a Turkish woman quite often does travel in the accompaniment of some of her children, or with other women, or even alone. However, she has always made the appropriate arrangements before such a departure. These arrangements include the trusting of her children—and quite likely her husband as well—to an individual approved by the community. Such an appropriate person is most often the woman's mother; perhaps in her place it is the husband's mother, or frequently sisters or aunts if her own mother is not available. Under no circumstances, however, would a Turkish woman leave her child(ren) in the care of her husband, the(ir) father.

And there was the rub. I had answered each time carefully and truthfully, but I had only succeeded in making matters worse. While I had been concerned about the reaction of the community to my separation from my young daughter and to my temporary singleness, the community concern was directed at the arrangements that I had made for my absence. I even intercepted knowing glances from the older, married women, later confirmed in casual conversations as translating: "How nice to be without a husband. Husbands are a lot of work." When I returned to the United States, it was small gifts for my mother—and not for my husband—which some of these women entrusted to me as a token of their friendship with me and their appreciation of my mother's responsibility.

Admittedly, there were some raised eyebrows in my own family and community as I prepared to leave my husband and daughter to spend the summer doing fieldwork in Turkey, a thing and a place inadequately understood by many of them. But such misunderstandings, while at times unpleasant and uncomfortable when voiced by members of my own family or neighbors, could not be as important or as persuasive as they would be if they came from members of the study community. In Turkey I was not known, at times my work would appear abstract, and all I would have would be my explanation as to who I was, strengthened by some helpful introductions and written letters from Turkish and American colleagues.

The next examples come from time spent collecting folklore in northeastern Turkey. I was very interested in recording actual performances of traditional storytellers and singers which are still common in the coffee houses in that part of the country. The coffeehouse in traditional Turkish life is a male domain, that public area where men of all ages gather for congenial and animated conversation, enjoy music and story sessions by favorite performers, and drink cold liquids or hot tea, but rarely coffee. Whereas male community members dominate the public spaces of the community, females congregate in those which are private—behind the walls of the compound and inside the home, within special areas of the house that are defined as "female" and into which male family members do not go uninvited. In fact, when several women are visiting, particularly women outside the immediate family, men do not enter at all. In small villages where there is not a conveniently located coffeehouse, or for some other reason, a special room in the house itself may be set aside for strictly male use. Here, men entertain male family members and friends in the late afternoon and evening hours, serving refreshments, sponsoring a performance, welcoming the special guest.

In Kars, the largest city in northeastern Turkey, I was accompanied by a Turkish folklorist who had worked previously with several of the city's traditional folk musicians, or *ashiklar* (wandering or strolling minstrels). During the evening's performance in the coffeehouse owned by one of the minstrels, I felt most conspicuous. Assurances aside, I was extremely self-conscious being the only woman member of an audience that by eight o'clock had swelled to more than two hundred. However, to the three minstrels my presence was apparently without difficulty: I was a folklorist and a *hodja* (literally a religious teacher, but commonly used an an honorific). In fact, my introduction to the audience was in this formal capacity; I was consistently addressed by the performers and members of the audience as "hodja." On no occasion that evening, or during later visits to the coffeehouse, was I addressed using the common respectful greeting for women of my age (i.e., personal name plus *hanIm*). I was not perceived of as a woman, but consistently as a professional folklorist—a folklorist engaged in important folkloric research recording on tape and film the famous minstrels of Kars.

Did my presence alter the performance in any way? What about the material selected? Could audience participation have been muted? According to my informants, there had been no alterations in the performance because a woman was present. Nevertheless, they did not rule out the possibility that they had altered or modified their material, or their behavior as members of the audience, to reflect their "best" for the folklorist to record and photograph. A straightforward assessment, and one with which I essentially agree. Certainly, a trade-off. Had I not been recognized as a folklorist, I would not have been admitted as a woman.

And my own perception of this? I came to think of myself as an "honorary man." For the duration of my stay in Kars, and particularly in my work at the coffeehouse, I was "passing" as a man. Imagine my amusement when I read almost three years later a small *Newsweek* piece about Queen Elizabeth II being made an "honorary man" to permit her attendance at a banquet given in her honor by the government of Saudi Arabia during her state visit to that country.

Later, in the course of my fieldwork I stayed in a remote village a difficult day's journey by jeep from Kars, perhaps no more than five kilometers from Turkey's northeastern border with the Soviet Union. While in this village, I was received in turn by adult males who told me stories of the well-known minstrels their village had produced and by adult women and small children of both sexes who allowed me to participate in their round of daily activities (e.g., baking bread, washing clothes, preparing food for the men, caring for small children). No member of either group expressed curiosity about my time spent with the other; on no occasion was the Turkish folklorist (a man) asked to join me in the women's quarters, not even when it was obvious to everyone that I desperately needed his help in comprehending the village women's speech, and they mine!

To be sure, a "foreign" male fieldworker might have been permitted access to the folklore that I collected from the women in this secluded community, but I seriously doubt it. Instead, I think that it was perfectly clear to all members of the household, male and female, why I was there. However, the reasons each group recognized and, therefore, the data able to be collected, would depend on which of my ascribed statuses I was perceived to be occupying at any particular time.

Consequently, it is the social situation that defines gender, for gender is visible as a sum of qualities, including mannerism, way of speaking, dress, choice of topics in conversation, and so on. Gender is a visible fact most of the time; sex is not. We do not expect to see vagina or penis, breasts or hairy chest, before we react to an individual as male or female. Precisely because gender roles are very visible and most people feel competent to judge how others fill them, sanctions are likely to emanate from many sources (Oakley 1972:187–189).

During the summer of 1977 my mother traveled to Turkey to visit a Turkish family I had known for almost fifteen years. My mother had become very fond of the family's eldest daughter when, as a teenager, Zafer had been an exchange student in the local high school and had lived with our family for several months. While in Istanbul my mother met one of my Turkish colleagues, a professor who, sharing many of my own interests in folklore, had been most gracious in his encouragement and assistance while I was in the field. This is how my mother remembered that meeting with Ali Bey: "Professor Ali engaged me in a conversation, a long one, when Zafer introduced us. He told me he could understand how very worried I must have been when you traveled alone to Turkey, but that there was no reason for my worry. 'We could see Susan was from a good family. She was always polite to everyone, and she knew, understood, and showed respect for our customs. To Turkish people, these things are important. I watched out for her as I would for my own daughter, and I sent her to people who could help in her work. Susan was safe here with us.'"

So, I had passed after all; I had learned to act appropriately. And in turn this was rewarded, not only by a stimulating field experience in good company but also with the opportunity to observe traditional Turkish musicians and raconteurs and to participate in the daily social life of some Turkish men and women.

REFERENCES

BERREMAN, GERALD
1962   Behind Many Masks: Ethnography and Impression Management in a
       Himalayan Village. Society for Applied Anthropology Monographs 4:1–24.

BOHANNAN, LAURA
1966   Shakespeare in the Bush. Natural History 75 (7): 28–33.

FINE, GARY ALAN, AND BEVERLY J. CRANE
1977   The Expectancy Effect in Anthropological Research: An Experimental
       Study of Riddle Collection. American Ethnologist 3:517–524.

GOLDE, PEGGY, ED.
1970   Women in the Field. Chicago: Aldine.

GOLDSTEIN, KENNETH S.
1964   A Guide for Field Workers in Folklore. Memoirs of The American Folklore
       Society, vol. 52. Hatboro, PA: Folklore Associates.

HATFIELD, COLBY
1973   Fieldwork: Toward a Model of Mutual Exploitation. Anthropological
       Quarterly 46 (1): 15–29.

OAKLEY, ANN
1972   Sex, Gender and Society. New York: Harper & Row.

SARGENT, WYN
1974   People of the Valley: Life with a Cannibal Tribe in New Guinea. New
       York: Random House.

SUGGESTED READINGS

BOVEN, METTE
1966   The Significance of the Sex of the Fieldworker for Insights into the Male
       and Female Worlds. Ethnos 31:24–27 (supplement).

BOWEN, ELENORE (LAURA BOHANNAN)
1954   Return to Laughter. New York: Harper.

BUTLER, BARBARA, AND DIANE MICHALSKI TURNER, EDS.
1987   Children and Anthropological Research. New York: Plenum Press.

CASSELL, JOAN, ED.
1987   Children in the Field: Anthropological Experiences. Philadelphia: Temple
       University Press.

CESARA, MANDA
1982   Reflections of a Woman Anthropologist: No Hiding Place. New York:
       Academic Press.

FREILICH, MORRIS, ED.
1970   Marginal Natives: Anthropologists at Work. New York: Harper & Row.
1972   Sex and Culture. *In* The Meaning of Culture. M. Freilich, ed. Lexington, MA: Xerox College Publications.
1983   The Pleasures of Anthropology. New York: New American Library.

FRISBIE, CHARLOTTE
1975a   Fieldwork as a "Single Parent": To Be or Not to Be Accompanied by a Child. Theodore R. Frisbie, ed. Pp. 98–119. Collected Papers in Honor of Florence Hawley Ellis. Papers of the Archaeological Society of New Mexico, No. 2. Norman, OK: Hooper.
1975b   Observations on a Preschooler's First Experience with Cross-Cultural Living. Journal of Man 7 (1): 91–112.

GOLDE, PEGGY, ED.
1986   Women in the Field: Anthropological Experiences. 2d ed., expanded and updated. Berkeley: University of California Press.

KIMBALL, SOLON, AND JAMES WATSON, EDS.
1972   Crossing Cultural Boundaries: The Anthropological Experience. San Francisco: Chandler.

LAWLESS, ROBERT, VINSON H. SUTLIVE, JR., AND MARIO D. ZAMORA, EDS.
1983   Fieldwork: The Human Experience. New York: Gordon and Breach Science Publishers.

NUMEZ, THERON A.
1972   On Objectivity and Field Work. *In* Crossing Cultural Boundaries: The Anthropological Experience. Solon Kimball and James Watson, eds. Pp. 164–171. San Francisco: Chandler.

POWDERMAKER, HORTENSE
1966   Stranger and Friend: The Way of the Anthropologist. New York: Norton.

WAX, ROSALIE
1971   Doing Fieldwork: Warnings and Advice. Chicago: University of Chicago Press.

WHITEHEAD, TONY LARRY, AND MARY ELLEN CONAWAY, EDS.
1986   Self, Sex, and Gender in Cross-Cultural Fieldwork. Urbana: University of Illinois Press.